NGOS AND THE STRUGGLE FOR HUMAN RIGHTS IN EUROPE

This publication provides a fresh perspective on the litigation of the European Court of Human Rights by focusing upon the role that non-governmental organisations play in it. The inspiration for this work was the growing literature that points to human rights as the outcome of political and social struggles. The role that NGOs play in these struggles is well documented in the context of other international and regional human rights tribunals, but has been less widely written about in the context of the European Court of Human Rights. The Court is typically subject to legalistic, as opposed to socio-political, scrutiny. In this book the Court's litigation is re-cast as a site where politically motivated actors attempt to impact upon the meaning that is given to the language of the European Convention on Human Rights and to use the Convention as a mechanism that can contribute to social change.

For the purposes of this research a mixture of quantitative and qualitative research techniques are adopted. These methods facilitate the author's desire to obtain both a de-centred perspective of the Court's functions and a systematic picture of the scale of NGO involvement in the Court's litigation. The core of this work is primarily based on data obtained from a sample of cases in which the Court had delivered judgment, and a plethora of associated materials, including extensive interviews with NGOs that were involved in those cases. Ultimately, this book challenges the idea that the litigation of the Court is bound to the idea of achieving individual justice and highlights the meaningful impact that NGOs have on certain important sections of the Court's litigation.

NGOs and the Struggle for Human Rights in Europe

Loveday Hodson

·HART·
PUBLISHING

OXFORD AND PORTLAND, OREGON
2011

Published in the United Kingdom by Hart Publishing Ltd
16C Worcester Place, Oxford, OX1 2JW
Telephone: +44 (0)1865 517530
Fax: +44 (0)1865 510710
E-mail: mail@hartpub.co.uk
Website: http://www.hartpub.co.uk

Published in North America (US and Canada) by
Hart Publishing
c/o International Specialized Book Services
920 NE 58th Avenue, Suite 300
Portland, OR 97213–3786
USA
Tel: +1 503 287 3093 or toll-free: (1) 800 944 6190
Fax: +1 503 280 8832
E-mail: orders@isbs.com
Website: http://www.isbs.com

© Loveday Hodson 2011

British Library Cataloguing in Publication Data
Data Available

ISBN: 978-1-84113-961-6

Typeset by Columns Design Ltd, Reading
Printed and bound in Great Britain by
TJ International Ltd, Padstow, Cornwall

Acknowledgements

Although the research journey can at times feel long and lonely, on my own path towards the completion of this book I have met numerous talented, inspiring and energetic people who influenced my thinking beyond recognition. Although I must, of course, take the blame for any weaknesses and errors in this research, there are many who deserve credit for its strengths. I would first like to thank the people who gave so generously of their time in assisting with this research. Although too numerous to name individually, my requests for interviews and information were met with unfailing generosity and enthusiasm. Particular thanks must be given to Marie-Andrée Calame of the European Court of Human Rights who responded to my increasingly outrageous demands for access to case-files without complaint. I am particularly indebted to Istvan Pogany at the University of Warwick. He deserves credit for bringing me down to earth on numerous occasions. Lee Bridges provided me with invaluable assistance with untangling methodological conundrums. Bill Bowring, Kevin Boyle and two anonymous reviewers provided valuable comments on an earlier draft of this text. Jane St Keverne was a dedicated and eagle-eyed proof-reader. The fieldwork undertaken was made possible by funding from the Legal Research Institute and the Research and Teaching Development Fund at Warwick University. On a more personal note, there are so many ways in which Kim and Tegan made the completion of this book possible that I do not know how to even begin to thank them.

Contents

Tables and Illustrations

Abbreviations

AIRE Centre	Advice on Individual Rights in Europe Centre
BHC	Bulgarian Helsinki Committee
CEJIL	Center for Justice and International Law
ECHR	European Convention on Human Rights
ECmHR	European Commission on Human Rights
ECtHR	European Court of Human Rights
ECOSOC	Economic and Social Council (UN)
EHRAC	European Human Rights Advocacy Centre
ERRC	European Roma Rights Centre
HRA	Human Rights Association of Turkey
HRP	Human Rights Project of Sofia
IGO	Inter-Governmental Organisation
JCWI	Joint Council for the Welfare of Immigrants
KHRP	Kurdish Human Rights Project
LGBT	Lesbian, Gay, Bi-sexual and Transgender
MIA	Montgomery Improvement Association
MIND	National Association for Mental Health
NAACP	National Association for the Advancement of Colored People
NCCL	National Council for Civil Liberties
NGO	Non-Governmental Organisation
OS	'One Shotters'
PESUE	Association for Family Rights in Finland
PKK	Kurdistan Workers' Party
RP	'Repeat Players'

Table of Cases

Table of Legislation

Introductory Note

As the whole work relates to the European Convention for the Protection of Human Rights and Fundamental Freedoms, only references to specific provisions have been included in this Table.

International

National

Austria

Bulgaria

Finland

Switzerland

United Kingdom

1

Introduction

'For certain causes, we are one – for others, we are not. We must learn to work together. No one can effectively fight for justice alone'.[1]

I. The Struggle for Rights

ON 1 DECEMBER 1955 one of the most symbolically important events in the history of the American civil rights movement took place. On that day Rosa Parks, a woman travelling on a public bus in Montgomery, Alabama, refused to abide by the state law which provided that as a black person she must give up her seat for a standing white passenger.[2] She was arrested and subsequently convicted for her actions. Parks's arrest was the catalyst for a year-long boycott of the Montgomery bus service that ended only when, on 13 November 1956, the law permitting racial segregation on public buses was held to be unconstitutional by the United States Supreme Court.[3] This, now infamous, story has passed into popular consciousness as the tale of one woman's brave stand against injustice. In Michael Moore's best-selling book *Stupid White Men* it is described as 'an important reminder that the great changes in society occur when one or two people of conscience act'.[4]

It is less widely known that many African Americans had previously been arrested for carrying out the same action as Parks and that a similar bus boycott

---

[1] Rosa Parks (with Gregory J Reed), *Quiet Strength: The Faith, the Hope and the Heart of a Woman who Changed a Nation* (Grand Rapid, Zondervan Publishing House, 1994) 39.

[2] For a history of the Montgomery bus boycott, see Stewart Burns (ed), *Daybreak of Freedom: The Montgomery Bus Boycott* (Chapel Hill, University of North Carolina Press, 1997) and David J Garrow, *Bearing the Cross: Martin Luther King, Jr. and the Southern Christian Leadership Conference* (New York, William Morrow and Co, 1986).

[3] *Gayle v Browder* 352 US 903 (1956).

[4] Michael Moore, *Stupid White Men: . . . and Other Sorry Excuses for the State of the Nation!* (London, Penguin Books, 2001) xv.

had taken place the year before in Baton Rouge, Louisiana.[5] What distinguished Rosa Parks's story, however, was the network of activists who transformed that individual woman's act of bravery into an event of national political significance. In later life, Parks was careful to acknowledge this: 'Four decades later I am still uncomfortable with the credit given to me for starting the bus boycott ... I would like [people] to know I was not the only person involved. I was just one of many who fought for freedom'.[6]

In his detailed study of the history of the American civil rights movement Sean Dennis Cashman concludes that the events that took place in Montgomery were the result of a highly organised political movement. 'In fact', he writes, 'the refusal of Rosa Parks to leave her seat was anything but spontaneous, just as the swift organization of a boycott was not conjured up on the spur of the moment'.[7] A boycott of the buses had been discussed for some time amongst various groups in Montgomery prior to the arrest of Parks: her timely stand and subsequent arrest simply, yet crucially, provided the ideal opportunity to act. The boycott that took place was the result of a well-organised campaign planned by the Montgomery Improvement Association (MIA), a loosely structured – but very popular – organisation headed by Martin Luther King, Jr. This organisation was able to generate and sustain the widespread popular support that was critical to the campaign's success.

But political campaigning alone was not enough to end segregation. The success of the Montgomery bus boycott depended upon a combination of political and legal activism. The National Association for the Advancement of Colored People (NAACP) worked alongside the MIA to challenge the legality of bus segregation through selected test cases.[8] For the NAACP, a highly active national civil rights organisation founded in 1909, there was nothing new in such a strategy. They had mounted a sustained campaign of legal challenge to the 'Jim Crow' laws upon which racial segregation in the southern states based its legitimacy. In 1954, for example, they won a crucial Supreme Court victory in *Brown v Board of Education of Topeka*, which declared racial segregation in public education to be unconstitutional.[9] This judgment overturned earlier case law in which the Supreme Court had upheld the legality of the 'separate but equal

---

[5] William T Martin Riches, *The Civil Rights Movement: Struggle and Resistance* (London, Macmillan Press Ltd, 1997) 41–2.

[6] Parks, *Quiet Strength* (1994) 27.
Parks was, however, somewhat inconsistent in this, and elsewhere she downplayed the importance of the NAACP. See Rosa Parks, '"Tired of Giving In": The Launching of the Montgomery Bus Boycott' in B Collier-Thomas and VP Franklin (eds), *Sisters in the Struggle: African American Women in the Civil Rights/Black Power Movement* (New York, New York University Press, 2001).

[7] Sean Dennis Cashman, *African-Americans and the Quest for Civil Rights: 1900–1990* (New York, New York University Press, 1991) 125.

[8] *ibid*, 50. See also Burns, *Daybreak of Freedom* (1997) 19 and Garrow, *Bearing the Cross* (1986) 59.

[9] *Brown v Board of Education of Topeka* 374 US 483 (1954).

doctrine'.[10] Those active in the Montgomery NAACP and civil rights movement quickly recognised that Parks's arrest provided an ideal test-case opportunity.[11] Parks had for most of the previous decade been secretary to the local chapter of the NAACP and on her arrest she was immediately assisted by an NAACP lawyer. Ultimately, it was victory in the Supreme Court – although not in Parks's case – that was decisive in ending segregation on the buses.[12]

Whilst the personal costs to Rosa Parks of her actions were undoubtedly considerable, to describe this important period in the civil rights movement as the result of the happy accident of a brave individual acting alone does not provide a complete picture. Rather, the impact that these events had is best understood as emanating from a deliberate and organised political movement that used Rosa Parks's personal experience to press for reform through political and legal processes: it is the story of their struggle for rights.

II. The Struggle for Rights and the European Convention on Human Rights

Although it is set in America rather than Europe, this re-telling of the celebrated story of Rosa Parks is instructive in introducing the central concerns of this book, in which I examine the role that non-governmental organisations (NGOs) play in litigation before the European Court of Human Rights (ECtHR). The ECtHR is based in Strasbourg and is the regional mechanism through which the rights recognised in the Council of Europe's 1950 European Convention for the Protection of Human Rights and Fundamental Freedoms (ECHR)[13] are realised. It is well documented, particularly by scholars of international relations and politics, that NGOs play an important role in setting human rights standards and promoting human rights norms.[14] However, although the ECtHR is perhaps the most intensively scrutinised of the international and regional human rights tribunals,[15] little has been written about the role of NGOs in cases before it. This book, then, adds a new dimension to the (admittedly vast) literature that has been written on the ECtHR.

---

[10] *Plessy v Ferguson*, 163 US 537 (1896).

[11] Cashman, *African-Americans* (1991) 124–5. See also Martin Riches, *The Civil Rights Movement* (1997) 42–3.

[12] *Gayle v Browder*, 352 US 903 (1956).

[13] European Convention for the Protection of Human Rights and Fundamental Freedoms (1965 Cmnd 2643) 87 UNTS 103; ETS 5; UKTS 38.

[14] This literature is discussed in full in chapter two.

[15] On the ECtHR and ECHR in general see, for example, Pieter van Dijk, Fried van Hoof, Arjen van Rijn and Leo Zwaak (eds), *Theory and Practice of the European Convention on Human Rights*, 4th edn (Antwerp, Intersentia, 2006), which has an extensive bibliography. One might also refer to, for example: Clare Ovey and Robin CA White, *Jacobs and White, the European Convention on Human*

One explanation for this gap in the current literature is that few authors have stepped beyond consideration of the paradigm of liberal individualism that has had such an important influence on the development of European human rights law and which tends to strip the Court's litigation of political significance. As I discuss further in chapter two, cases before the Court are usually presented as a bi-partisan battle between an individual claiming to be a victim of a violation of the Convention's rights and a State party responding to those allegations. Focusing on the role of NGOs in the Court's litigation, therefore, necessitates taking a de-centred approach to the study of that process. In this book I suggest that behind the veil of individualism, the organised – and, by implication, more overtly political – nature of human rights litigation can be concealed. During the Montgomery campaign, for example, both Parks and Martin Luther King, Jr[16] downplayed the role played by NGOs and preferred to present the struggle as the spontaneous uprising of an oppressed people (Parks's politically 'naïve' nature was repeatedly highlighted[17]), rather than the result of organised political and legal activity. Belden Fields eloquently expresses the idea at the heart of this book in the following manner:

> The theory that I am trying to present roots human rights in the concrete historical experiences of people who have struggled, and who continue to struggle, against domination. It is not just an abstraction that I come up with from philosophical reasoning. It is rooted in the active social processes that we refer to when we use that expression, 'human rights'.[18]

In particular, this book examines the implications of that statement for our understanding of the body of law developed by the ECtHR.

When NGOs participate in ECtHR litigation, they usually do so outside of the formal parameters of the legal proceedings, and their role is often not identified in the Court's judgment. This research therefore provides a new perspective on the Court by opening up its litigation process to 'extra-legal' scrutiny: it is re-cast as an arena in which the struggle for rights takes place. There is a tendency in the current literature to ignore the social and political context of the applications that

---

Rights, 4th edn (Oxford, Oxford University Press, 2006); Mark Janis, Richard Kay and Anthony Bradley, *European Human Rights Law: Text and Materials*, 3rd edn (Oxford, Oxford University Press, 2008); AH Robertson and JG Merrills, *Human Rights in Europe: A Study of the European Convention on Human Rights*, 4th edn (Manchester, Manchester University Press, 2001); DJ Harris, M O'Boyle, Colin Warbrick, Ed Bates and Carla Buckley, *Law of the European Convention on Human Rights*, 2nd edn (Oxford, Oxford University Press, 2009).

[16] Martin Luther King, Jr, *Stride Towards Freedom: The Montgomery Story* (New York, Ballentine Books, 1958).

[17] Marisa Chappell, Jenny Hutchinson and Brian Ward, '"Dress modestly, neatly ... as if you were going to church": Respectability, Class and Gender in the Montgomery Bus Boycott and the Early Civil Rights Movement' in Peter J Ling and Sharon Monteith (eds), *Gender in the Civil Rights Movement* (New York, Garland Publishing, 1999).

[18] A Belden Fields, 'Underlying Propositions for Grounding a Holistic Conception of Human Rights' in Andrew Chitty et al, *Papers in Social Theory: Rights, Movements, Recognition*, vol 6 (Brighton, Warwick Social Theory Centre and Sussex Centre for Critical Social Theory, 2001) 44–5.

are presented to the Court and eventually distilled into a set of rules that are declared to be The Law. This research is located on the nexus between political science and socio-legal studies: it takes as its starting point the premise that the study of legal texts is insufficient to understand the origin and impact of human rights laws and human rights institutions, and it treats the litigation before the Court as a process rather than merely as the application of a set of rules. As Harlow and Rawlings note, the latter approach is typically legalistic:

> Generations of belief in the apolitical tradition of law have necessarily conditioned the legal profession. Lawyers are quick to divest their case law of its political and social significance, reducing it to a boxed set of sanitised legal precedents.[19]

Mark Janis et al suggest this scholarly inflexibility may be down to 'the division between lawyers and political scientists'.[20] While the focus of this book is on a law-making body (the ECtHR), it makes some attempt to bridge this gap. One reason why this is particularly important is that, although it is commonplace to be reminded of the myth of law's neutrality in domestic legal theory, it is seldom noted in relation to the ECtHR that the meaning of the Convention's rights does not emerge through reference to the legal text alone. If we recognise that courts will inevitably at times take centre stage in the struggle for rights, there seems no cogent reason to exclude the ECtHR from this observation. As Cashman notes in relation to the civil rights movement in the USA: 'If segregation were ever to be overturned by peaceful means, then a battle must be fought in the courts where segregation had been legally identified, authorized, and protected'.[21]

A further issue raised by this research is the nature of the relationship between the organisations leading the struggle for rights and the individuals they profess to represent. It is interesting to note, for example, that one of the NAACP lawyers challenging the Montgomery bus segregation laws was charged (somewhat spuriously) with using a Plaintiff's name without her consent.[22] Furthermore, the NAACP's role was not widely publicised during the bus boycott as many in the southern states saw it as a northern and elitist organisation;[23] it certainly did not have the wide-based support needed to publicly lead the Montgomery campaign.[24] This raises inevitable questions about the democratic credentials of the organisations being studied. These questions take on a particular sensitivity when legal challenges are mounted by NGOs, primarily because they highlight the fact that human rights litigation can involve a complex and troublesome negotiation between individual and community interests. As Burns suggests in relation to the

---

[19] Carol Harlow and Richard Rawlings, *Pressure Through Law* (Abingdon, Routledge, 1992) 6.

[20] Janis, Kay and Bradley, *European Human Rights Law* (2008) 113.

[21] Cashman, *African-Americans* (1991) 113.

[22] Garrow, *Bearing the Cross* (1986) 63–4.

[23] See note of MIA Executive Board Meeting, 30 January 1956, reproduced in Burns, *Daybreak of Freedom* (1997) 128–30 and 'Minutes of MIA-NAACP Meeting', 2 February 1956, reproduced at 151–2.

[24] Parks, '"Tired of Giving In"' (2001) 69.

American civil rights movement, however, drawing a rigid distinction between these interests could have hindered the realisation of the movement's aims:

> If in the larger American culture liberalism and communitarianism spoke different languages, the black world, exemplified by the Montgomery experience, could not afford a dichotomy between fighting for individual rights and fortifying the community bonds that made it possible to actualize human rights in everyday life.[25]

III. Vocabulary and Classification

In a quotation that is cited above, Belden Fields speaks rather abstractly of the connection between 'active social processes' and human rights. Indeed, many authors struggle to place a label on the social movements that are recognised as having a significant impact on the development of human rights discourse. In this book I employ the term 'NGO', the use of which is favoured in international relations and has been adopted by international lawyers. However, there is no general agreement about what type of groupings this term covers.[26] For the purposes of this book, which is not concerned in particular with the legal status of NGOs, I have found most pertinent the loose definition adopted by Martens:

> NGOs are formal (professionalized) independent societal organizations whose primary aim is to promote common goals at the national or the international level.[27]

The imprecision of this definition renders it particularly useful to describe the variety of different organisations, from Trades' Unions to campaigning groups that are involved in the Court's litigation. Martens's definition also alerts us to the fact that most of the organisations discussed in this book, while differing vastly from one another in a number of ways, are, of necessity, quite formally structured. In short, Martens's definition captures something of the strategic shift that NGOs negotiate between the structural formality that enables them to engage effectively as national and international actors and the fluidity of form that is the hallmark of social movements. Although it emerged in the field of international relations, the term NGO is used in this book to include national, international and transnational organisations.

Other associated terms are referred to in this book that merit explanation. In domestic political science the terms 'interest group' or 'pressure group' are commonly used to describe campaigning organisations. Although these terms have partisan and political overtones that many human rights organisations

---

[25] Burns, *Daybreak of Freedom* (1997) 5.

[26] For a full discussion see Kerstin Martens, 'Mission Impossible? Defining Nongovernmental Organizations' (2002) 13 *Voluntas: International Journal of Voluntary and Nonprofit Organizations* 271, and Anna-Karin Lindblom, *Non-Governmental Organisations in International Law* (Cambridge, Cambridge University Press, 2005), see especially 36–52.

[27] Martens, 'Mission Impossible?' (2002) 28.

would reject, I use them in this book to describe organisations that have an overt campaigning agenda. In domestic legal terminology the loose phrase 'public interest law' (and the related 'public interest litigation') is often used to describe legal strategies that aim to achieve social reform rather than personal benefit. Although this term is useful when writing about the campaigning litigation of NGOs, in this book it is used sparingly because it appears to be insensitive to the contested nature of what reform is in the public interest and it does not convey the ideological diversity of litigating groups.

The terms 'global civil society' and 'global social movements'[28] are useful to convey the idea of pressure for political reform that emanates 'from below', ie from the people. These terms are attractive as they reflect the diversity and fluidity of such political movements. Otto's depiction of global (or international) civil society gives some sense of the futility of trying to pin these concepts down too precisely:

> In the postliberal view, international civil society consists of a diversity of individuals, institutions and informal peoples' networks and coalitions. It is a vast, shifting web of interconnections and alliances involving multidimensional human identities. People, rather than governments, are seen as the progressive agents of social history.[29]

Although this book examines the direct involvement of groups in legal processes, and therefore tends to focus on a specific section of civil society that is both organised and established, this serves as an important reminder that there is considerable fluidity of structure amongst the NGOs discussed in this book and that the term describes a range of informal relationships between people and organisations.

Finally, in this book I also refer to the 'third-party interventions' or 'amicus curiae briefs' of NGOs. These terms describe the procedure whereby a tribunal accepts a written or oral brief (or submission) from a party not otherwise formally involved in the proceedings before it.[30]

IV. Chapter Synopsis

The ideas discussed above, which provide the rationale for investigating the role of NGOs in the Court's litigation, are developed more fully in chapter two. In that

---

[28] See Robin Cohen and Shirin Rai (eds), *Global Social Movements* (London, The Althone Press, 2000) and Neil Stammers, 'Social Movements and the Social Construction of Human Rights' (1999) 21 *Human Rights Quarterly* 980.

[29] Dianne Otto, 'Nongovernmental Organizations in the United Nations System: The Emerging Role of International Civil Society' (1996) 18 *Human Rights Quarterly* 107, 135.

[30] On the background to amicus curiae briefs see Ernest Angell, 'The Amicus Curiae: American Development of English Institutions' (1967) 16 *International and Comparative Law Quarterly* 1017 and Samuel Krislov, 'The Amicus Curiae Brief: From Friendship to Advocacy' (1963) 72 *The Yale Law Journal* 694.

chapter I argue that, as a consequence of pressing political concerns that existed when the Council of Europe was formed, the ECHR was inspired by ideas drawn from a liberal individualistic tradition. I examine the limits of liberal individualism in that chapter and establish the grounds for examining the relationship between human rights litigation and the political struggles of organised movements. I suggest that the fact that little is known about the role of NGOs in the Court's litigation is a potentially significant oversight as there is a considerable amount of literature that identifies NGOs as central actors before the United Nations and other regional human rights bodies.[31]

Once the theoretical foundations of this book were formulated, the next challenge was to establish a methodologically sound basis from which to commence this investigation. Chapter three briefly outlines the methodology that was adopted. The questions raised in this study were largely exploratory in nature and it was determined that a preliminary stage of quantitative research would be invaluable in mapping out the research territory: I therefore decided to base the research in this book on a sample of cases in which the Court had delivered judgment. The reasons for adopting this approach and the rationale behind my case selection are explained fully in the appendix. The results of the preliminary quantitative survey of the sample cases are discussed in full in chapter three. As a consequence of this stage of the investigation, a picture was created of the frequency and nature of NGO involvement in litigation before the ECtHR and tentative ideas were generated about the motivation behind NGO involvement in these cases.

This quantitative research stage was followed by in-depth qualitative research, which is presented in the form of case studies based on NGO involvement in the sample cases. Extensive interviews with people working in NGOs that had been involved in the sample cases were undertaken and, where possible, the organisations' files on the case(s) in question were also referred to. This qualitative research was supported with reference to historical, social and political texts. As a result of both quantitative and qualitative research stages it was apparent that there were three areas of NGO activity in the Court's litigation that could be said to be of particular importance. These areas form the basis of the case-study discussions in chapters four, five and six.

My research findings show a significant amount of NGO involvement in cases that involve serious violations of the Convention that take place with impunity. This is particularly true of violations in respect of the rights of people belonging to various national and ethnic minorities, such as the Roma in post-communist States and the Kurdish population of Turkey. I suggest that in these situations NGOs use human rights litigation to entrench respect for human rights in countries in which support for liberal values is particularly precarious and a

---

[31]   Although the literature on the role of NGOs before other tribunals is indeed vast, it is sparingly referred to in this book because I did not intend to undertake research in which the role of NGOs before various international and regional human rights tribunals is compared.

commitment to the rights of the minorities in question is weak. These extreme situations of sustained human rights abuse in particular show the limits of the bi-partisan model of litigation. This phenomenon is examined in more detail in chapter four of this book. In chapter five I discuss 'pure human rights' NGOs that are based in the United Kingdom. The organisations discussed in that chapter are the most well known, from a legal perspective, of the NGOs that are considered in this book. They litigate regularly before the Court and in doing so demonstrate that the struggle for rights continues even where the Convention is well established in political and legal discourse. In chapter six I consider the role of 'pressure group' litigation, which frequently raises issues at the margins of the Court's jurisprudence and is often controversial in nature. Pressure groups perhaps present the greatest challenge to the notion of the Court's neutrality and are useful in highlighting the politically sensitive nature of many of the decisions that the Court is asked to make. I suggest that in challenging the Court's established jurisprudence these organisations play an important role in ensuring that the Convention's rights are subject to dynamic interpretation.

In chapter seven I conclude that the role of NGOs before the ECtHR has been largely overlooked and that by studying their involvement in the Court's litigation we gain a valuable insight into its functions. Although the majority of cases before the Court are brought by individuals (which is not the case with other international and regional human rights tribunals), NGOs are heavily implicated in many areas of the Court's jurisprudence. In particular, NGO litigation makes a contribution towards the entrenchment of the Convention in situations where gross human rights violations have taken place with apparent impunity. Furthermore, NGOs play a role in States that do exhibit a commitment to human rights by ensuring that a human rights discourse remains central in political discussion and does not get overlooked in favour of other discourses. Finally, in framing innovative political issues in human rights terms, NGOs are central in pushing forward the Court's jurisprudence and ensuring that the Convention is indeed a living instrument. From this study it emerges that much of the momentum in the Court's jurisprudence emerges from the 'struggle for rights', the impetus for which derives from NGO activity.

2

The Limits of Individualism: NGOs and the European Convention on Human Rights

'The use of law by pressure groups to achieve reform and to establish rights may be as old as pressure groups themselves'.[1]

I. Introduction

IT IS WELL known that individuals, NGOs and groups of individuals are given standing under the ECtHR's competence *ratione personae* to lodge applications against State parties that are alleged to have violated their rights under the Convention.[2] While the Convention also provides for the collective protection of human rights through an inter-State complaints procedure,[3] individual applications have unquestionably been the most important means through which Convention rights are enforced. Within the Convention system, considerable weight has consequently come to be given to the Court's role in providing a remedy for individual victims of human rights violations. Eric Heinze, however, has suggested that there is a tendency to over-simplify the interests at stake before the Court when litigation is played out as a battle between individual victim and respondent State:

> The interests of all actors relevant to European Convention jurisprudence, then, are pitched either at the lowest level of abstraction, as purely individual interests ... or at the highest level of abstraction, as interests of society as a whole.[4]

---

[1] Carol Harlow and Richard Rawlings, *Pressure Through Law* (London, Routledge, 1992) 12.

[2] Art 34.

[3] Art 33.

[4] Eric Heinze, 'Principles for a Meta-Discourse of Liberal Rights: the Example of the European Convention on Human Rights' (1999) 9 *Indiana International and Comparative Law Review* 319, 342.

In this chapter I contend that the Convention's bi-partisan, individual versus State, model of human rights protection arose as a response to the early political concerns of the Council of Europe. This model, however, downplays the contested and contentious nature of human rights and serves to distract attention from the wider interests at play in litigation.

In this chapter I turn to the work of those who suggest that human rights have their roots in political struggles. In particular, a rich seam of literature is discussed which, while somewhat thin on law, highlights the fact that NGOs have been at the centre of the international human rights movement. This literature, which is discussed in greater detail below, takes the emphasis away from human rights as a means of achieving individual justice and recasts it as an arena in which social norms are debated and formulated. Thus, human rights emerge from a continuous process of analysis, assessment and decision-making, rather than the simple application of rules. If this vision has some validity – and I believe it does – then it offers justification for looking beyond the bi-partisan account of the Court's litigation and it opens up a space for considering the role of overtly political actors, such as NGOs, in it.

II. Individualism and the European Convention on Human Rights

A. Creating the Council of Europe: May 1948 to May 1949

It goes without saying that the story of the Council of Europe's human rights convention begins with the ending of the 1939–45 war, a period which saw a shell-shocked Europe attempt to heal some of the devastating wounds caused by years of vicious conflict.[5] The form that post-war Europe took was partly conditioned by an awareness of the appalling human rights abuses that had taken place during the war years. In Europe, 'where the fundamental rights of freedom were thought to be secured to man, those rights were first undermined and then brutally trampled down'.[6] The spectre of the Holocaust undoubtedly inspired much of the personal and passionate commitment to individual rights that was exhibited during that period.[7] But of greater urgency still for Western European

---

[5] For a detailed history of the drafting of the Convention, see AW Brian Simpson, *Human Rights and the End of Empire: Britain and the Genesis of the European Convention* (New York, Oxford University Press, 2001). See also AH Robertson and JG Merrills, *Human Rights in Europe: A Study of the European Convention on Human Rights*, 4th edn (Manchester, Manchester University Press, 2001), especially ch 1.

[6] Council of Europe, *Collected Edition of the 'Travaux Préparatoires' of the European Convention on Human Rights* (Dordrecht/Boston/Lancaster, Martinus Nijhoff, 1985) vol I, 66 (Mr Kraft, Denmark).

[7] Simpson, *Human Rights* (2001) 680–82.

States was the perceived threat of Communist expansion after the war.[8] Mark Mazower argues that the war had been 'a struggle for the social and political future of the continent itself'.[9] If that was the case, the philosophical war was far from over. New power blocs in the form of the USA and the USSR were emerging outside of the Allied States' influence and European colonies were fast disintegrating; the imperative of co-operation among Western European States was becoming increasingly pressing.[10]

As part of the process of re-building the region, the Council of Europe, emerging from the discussions of a meeting of the Hague Congress in May 1948, was formed to promote peace and security. The Statute of the Council of Europe, signed on 5 May 1949 by 10 European States, created two main bodies: the Consultative Assembly (renamed the Parliamentary Assembly in 1994), made up of democratically elected Members of Parliament who have the power to make Recommendations only; and the Committee of Ministers, which is the decision-making body composed of Ministers of Foreign Affairs.[11] However, if the creation of this organisation reflected an acceptance of the fact that inter-governmental unity was probably vital, it also conflicted with a deep-rooted attachment to the concept of State sovereignty. Writing 50 years after its creation, Mazower contends that the consequence of this conflict was the establishment of a 'bureaucratic drone' that was 'a far cry from the idealistic visions of 1943'.[12] While this assessment of the Council of Europe may be unduly negative, it is clear that pragmatism was the principal driving force behind the new organisation rather than a deep-rooted commitment to a new regionalism. The immediate challenge for the fledgling Council of Europe was to identify a philosophical rationale that could provide at least a loose intellectual coherence to this new fellowship without leading to any significant surrender of national sovereignty.

At a time that was otherwise marked by political turmoil and division, for the Council of Europe States to express their 'profound belief' in a limited range of fundamental freedoms and human rights must have appeared to be a reassuringly non-programmatic and convincing antidote to the extremes of totalitarian

[8] In October 1947 the Communist Information Bureau had been formed to coordinate the communist parties of Eastern Europe and February 1948 the Communist coup in Prague took place. See Elizabeth Wicks, 'The United Kingdom Government's Perceptions of the European Convention on Human Rights at the Time of Entry' [2000] *Public Law* 438. See also, generally, Norman Davies, *Europe: A History* (London, Pimlico, 1997) ch 12 and Mark Mazower, *Dark Continent: Europe's Twentieth Century* (London, Penguin Books, 1998).

[9] Mazower, *Dark Continent* (1998) 143.

[10] FA Hayek, *The Road to Serfdom* (London, Routledge & Kegan Paul, 1944) 175. See also Karl Popper, *The Open Society and its Enemies* (London, Routledge, 1945–47) and Richard Coudenhove-Kalegri, *The Totalitarian State against Man* (London, Paneuropa, 1938).

[11] Treaty of the Council of Europe, ETS No 1. This Statute was signed by the Governments of Belgium, Denmark, France, Ireland, Italy, Luxembourg, The Netherlands, Norway, Sweden and the United Kingdom.

[12] Mazower, *Dark Continent* (1998) 213.

power.[13] While Member States' interest in the protection of human rights may have been more pragmatic than a purely philosophical discussion would allow, the early political aims of the Council of Europe nonetheless certainly drew from a distinctly liberal tradition that – despite being decidedly unfashionable at the national level – was able to provide the organisation with a degree of intellectual coherence.

If seeking refuge under the broad umbrella of the liberal tradition was primarily a pragmatic move for Member States of the Council of Europe, its consequence was nevertheless inevitably to orientate the organisation towards a particular theoretical and philosophical perspective. Members began to stress that the coherence of the organisation – and, indeed, the superiority of the Allied States – was derived from the historic Western European attachment to liberalism and individual rights. One delegate during the drafting of the Convention introduced the crude philosophical dichotomy between totalitarianism and liberal democracy in the following way: 'We believe that the State exists for the individual, while they believe that the individual exists for the State'.[14] If the domestic political landscape of European States presented a complex picture in which there was only limited commitment to the idea of human rights, at least within the Council of Europe there were few strongly-voiced objections to dusting off ideas drawn from the liberal tradition and espousing a commitment to freedom and tolerance.[15] The protection of human rights therefore became a rallying point of the new organisation and gave it a 'moral basis'.[16] Consequently, one of the central aims identified in Article 1 of the Statute of the Council of Europe is 'the maintenance and further realisation of human rights and fundamental freedoms'. Article 8 further provides that serious violation of that provision can lead to suspension or expulsion of a Member State from the organisation. Liberalism, in the form of the protection of a limited range of individual rights and fundamental freedoms, had become synonymous with the Allied States and, consequently, with the new Council of Europe.

---

[13]   The Preamble to the ECHR states that the 'aim of the Council of Europe is the achievement of greater unity between its members', and reaffirms 'their profound belief in those fundamental freedoms which are the foundation of justice and peace in the world and are best maintained on the one hand by an effective political democracy and on the other by a common understanding and observance of the human rights upon which they depend'.

[14]   *Collected Edition of the 'Travaux Préparatoires'* vol II, 90 (Mr Sweetman, Ireland).

[15]   Simpson writes of the British interest in human rights during this period: 'If it [the Council of Europe] needed, as Bevin [the Foreign Secretary] thought, to be given something harmless to do, what better than a statement of western ideological values?' See Simpson, *Human Rights* (2001) 639.

[16]   *Collected Edition of the 'Travaux Préparatoires'* vol I, 16 (Mr Mollet, France).

B.   The Drafting of the Convention: August 1949 to November 1950

In order to signify Europe's recovery and to display their unity and purpose, members of the Council of Europe were anxious to translate their professed commitment to individual rights into binding obligations. On 8 September 1949 the Consultative Assembly adopted a Recommendation that sought the drafting of a treaty to ensure the effective enjoyment of human rights.[17] This Recommendation contained a draft convention that listed 12 basic freedoms that were inspired by – although considerably more limited than – the Universal Declaration of Human Rights, which had been adopted by the General Assembly of the United Nations on 10 December 1948.[18] The draft convention also envisaged the establishment of a human rights commission that would be competent to hear complaints both from individuals and Member States, as well as a court of justice that would hear inter-State cases only. The Assembly's convention therefore appeared to give priority to the idea of a European *ordre public*, for which States took on collective responsibility, while at the same time recognising a need to provide individual redress for victims of human rights violations.

Although the idea that individuals should be given standing before an international tribunal was not entirely without precedent,[19] it was undoubtedly a progressive development of international law. In 1905 Lassa Oppenheim had stated the classic position of international law as follows: 'Since the Law of Nations is a law between States only and exclusively, States only and exclusively are subjects of the Law of Nations'.[20] However, during the post-war period a challenge to the State-centric nature of international law was emerging amongst prominent international lawyers who were inspired by the stark evidence of the damage that is caused when law does not stand in the way of grossly misused

---

[17]   Recommendation 38 (1949).

[18]   UN Res 217 A (III) of 10 December 1948.

[19]   Article II of the Convention for the Establishment of a Central American Court of Justice adopted by the Central American Peace Conference in 1907 (and in force until March 1918) provided for an individual application procedure: five such applications were submitted but all were declared inadmissible. The text of this treaty is available at (1908) 2 *American Journal of International Law* (Supp) 231. For a discussion of this treaty see Manley Hudson, 'The Central American Court of Justice' (1932) 26 *American Journal of International Law* 759.

The Council of the League of Nations also developed procedures for dealing with individual petitions. Some of its treaties that aimed to protect minorities, such as the German-Polish Convention on Upper Silesia of May 15 1922, provided for the right of group or individual petition. The relevant section of this treaty is available at (1923) 118 *British and Foreign State Papers* 365, 412.

On the individual in international law generally, see: Carl Aage Nørgaard, *The Position of the Individual in International Law* (Copenhagen, Munksgaard, 1962); Donald Parson, 'The Individual Right of Petition: A Study of Methods used by International Organizations to Utilize the Individual as a Source of Information on the Violations of Human Rights' (1967) 13 *Wayne Law Review* 678; Rosalyn Higgins, 'Conceptual Thinking about the Individual in International Law' (1978) 4 *British Journal of International Studies* 1.

[20]   Lassa Oppenheim, *International Law: A Treatise* (London, Longmans & Green, 1905) 341.

State power. For some jurists, notably Hersch Lauterpacht, this challenge drew from central strands of the liberal tradition:

> When in the following decade [after WWI] pagan absolutism as perfected in the German State threatened to engulf man, in countries opposed to that ideology the tradition of the law of nature became once more a vital element in the affirmation of the sanctity of the individual and in the craving to find a basis of the law more enduring than the enforceable will of the sovereign.[21]

Indeed, in the post-war period international law showed signs of responding to calls for change and individuals had already been recognised as subjects of international criminal law. The Charter of the International Military Tribunal at Nuremberg, for example, had provided for individual responsibility for war crimes, crimes against peace and crimes against humanity.[22] The judgment of the Nuremberg Tribunal asserted that 'international law imposes duties and liabilities upon individuals as well as upon states'.[23] The question raised by the Consultative Assembly's draft human rights convention was whether the emerging recognition of individuals as subjects of international law, which appeared to offer a coherent legal foundation for the protection of human rights, could be reconciled with the inevitable anxiety that States would have about ceding sovereignty in such an unprecedented fashion.

Several representatives in the Council of Europe expressed reservations about the practical implications of the right to individual petition, and many argued that it could 'rapidly degenerate into a dangerous aim that could be used against the freedoms which we seek to guarantee and against our established democratic systems'.[24] Some were satisfied that an inter-State application procedure was sufficient to guarantee that human rights in Europe would be respected. Nevertheless, the majority in the Assembly insisted that the adoption of an individual application procedure was fundamental to the convention's success. The Greek representative summed up the prevailing mood thus:

> Man is an end in himself! The City and the State are so many organs constituting the means of preserving his dignity, of ensuring the pacific development of his personality and of guaranteeing for him humane living conditions. This, it seems to me, is the

---

[21] Hersch Lauterpacht *International Law and Human Rights* (London, Stevens & Sons, 1950) 112. See also Hersch Lauterpacht, *An International Bill of the Rights of Man* (New York, Columbia University Press, 1945).

[22] Agreement for the Prosecution and Punishment of the Major War Criminals of the European Axis, 82 UNTS 279, entered into force 8 August 1945.

[23] *Trial of the Major War Criminals before the International Military Tribunal* (Nuremberg, 1947) vol 1, 223. See also Resolution 95(1) (1946) of the General Assembly, which affirmed the Charter's principles and this judgment, and Resolution 96(1) (1946) of the General Assembly, which stated that genocide was a crime under international law bearing individual responsibility. The principle of individual responsibility was also subsequently adopted in the UN's Convention on the Prevention and Punishment of the Crime of Genocide, 78 UNTS 277, entered into force 12 January 1951.

[24] *Collected Edition of the 'Travaux Préparatoires'* vol V, 64 (amendment to remove the right to individual petition proposed by Greek delegation). The UK, Netherlands, Turkey and Greece were against the proposal.

common ideology of free Europe, the ideology which, down the centuries, has been subject to many attacks but which, from the times of ancient Greece – which gave it birth – up to our own time, has shaped that European culture without which existence itself cannot be conceived.[25]

Although the outcome of the drafting process was a compromise that betrayed concerns to protect state sovereignty, it was nevertheless a remarkable legal development and a significant assertion of the importance accorded to individuals within the Convention system.

The ECHR was signed on 14 November 1948 by 13 members of the Council of Europe and came in to force on 3 September 1953, following the tenth ratification. It established a two-tier system for hearing applications in the form of a European Commission on Human Rights and a European Court of Human Rights, although the competence of these bodies to hear individual applications had been compromised during the drafting procedure. While the inter-State complaint procedure was made compulsory,[26] the Commission's competence to accept applications from individuals was subject to a declaration by the relevant State in accordance with Article 25(1) of the Convention.[27] Only Member States and the Commission could refer a case to the Court, and, in any event, the acceptance of its jurisdiction by a State was optional.[28] Despite the compromises that they had been prepared to make, the drafters of the ECHR had left a remarkable legacy: they had set the stage for individuals to play a central role in protecting human rights in Europe.

C.   The Individual Application Procedure: 1953 to Present

If there was some resistance at the time of drafting the Convention towards the idea of an individual application procedure, it has since come to be accepted as a natural and vital part of the Strasbourg regime. In contrast, the notion of an *ordre public* maintained by inter-State complaints has proven to be of very limited value in practice.[29] A clear perception has developed that the 'primary effect of the Convention has been to provide a remedy [for individuals] before an

---

[25]   *Collected Edition of the 'Travaux Préparatoires'* vol I, 56 (Mr Antonopoulos, Greece).

[26]   Former Art 24.

[27]   Sweden was the first country to recognise the Commission's competence in this respect in February 1952, followed by Ireland and Denmark a year later. By July 1955 the Commission became competent to receive individual applications.

[28]   Former Art 44.

[29]   For a full discussion of inter-State complaints under the ECHR, see Søren C Prebensen, 'Inter-State Complaints under Treaty Provisions: The Experience under the European Convention on Human Rights' (1999) 20 *Human Rights Law Journal* 446.

international court of justice when all national remedies have failed'.[30] Indeed, this perception emerged at a surprisingly early stage in the Convention's history and has strengthened over time.[31]

As early as 24 September 1953 the Consultative Assembly unanimously passed a Recommendation urging members who had not already done so to ratify the Convention and to accept its optional clauses allowing individual petitions.[32] Over the following decades, this show of commitment to human rights and slight surrender of sovereignty gradually became the norm for members of the Council of Europe. Although it remained optional in theory until 1998, David Harris et al wrote in 1995 that the 'acceptance of the right of individual petition has become a political obligation of membership of the Council of Europe'.[33]

Once it was constituted, the ECtHR immediately took informal steps to give some recognition to originating individual applicants (who, it will be recalled, lacked formal standing in cases before it).[34] Although there was a limit to the accommodation that the Court could make for individuals while the Convention retained its original form, from the outset it was clear that individuals, rather than States, were submitting the vast majority of applications under the ECHR. By 1986 the Committee of Ministers acknowledged that the situation was anomalous and decided that the question of the locus standi of individuals should be looked at in the context of reforming the procedures of the Strasbourg machinery.[35] To this end, Protocol 9 was drafted and came in to force on 1 October 1994.[36] The most important part of this (now repealed) Protocol was that it amended former Article 44 of the Convention, thereby giving individuals and non-governmental organisations standing to refer their cases directly to the Court.

An unsurprising consequence of these changes was a marked increase in the number of individual applications to the Strasbourg organs. This increase was particularly problematic because the system contained significant elements of over-lap and duplication of functions and could be accused of being unnecessarily complex. At its 89th session in November 1991, the Committee of Ministers

---

[30]   DJ Harris, Michael O'Boyle and Colin Warbrick, *Law of the European Convention on Human Rights* (London, Butterworths, 1995) 31.
[31]   For a detailed discussion of these early developments see Paul Mahoney, 'Developments in the Procedure of the European Court of Human Rights: The Revised Rules of Court' (1983) 3 *Yearbook of European Law* 127 and Jan De Meyer, 'La Situation des "personnes physiques", "organisation non-gouvernementales" et "groupes de particuliers" dans la procédure devant la Cour Européenne des Droits de l'Homme', in *Annales de droit* (Louvain, Université Catholique de Louvain, 1974) 65.
[32]   Recommendation 52 (1953).
[33]   Harris, O'Boyle and Warbrick, *Law of the European Convention* (1995) 580.
[34]   See *Lawless v Ireland (No 1)* Series A no 1 (1960) 1 EHRR 1.
[35]   *Third Medium-Term Plan (1987–1991: adopted by the Committee of Ministers on 20th November 1986* (Strasbourg, Council of Europe, 1986).
[36]   ETS No.140.

instructed that priority be given to streamlining the ECHR application procedures. Consequently, Protocol 11 came into force on 1 November 1998.[37] This Protocol established a single Court that sits full-time in Strasbourg, which replaced the former double-tiered Court and Commission system.[38] Under the current Article 34 of the Convention – which is a mandatory provision – the Court may receive applications from

> any person, non-governmental organisation or group of individuals claiming to be the victim of a violation by one of the High Contracting Parties of the rights set forth in the Convention.[39]

Each registered application is dealt with judicially either by a chamber of the Court or, in exceptional circumstances, the Grand Chamber.

These developments in the ECtHR's procedures are frequently cited as evidence of the Court's success and its superiority as a mechanism for protecting human rights. Many authors describe the individual application procedure as the principal achievement of the drafters of the ECHR.[40] Mark Janis et al, for example, state that the Convention 'establishes not only the world's most successful system of international law for the protection of human rights, but one of the most advanced forms of any kind of international legal process'.[41] Indeed, while the inter-State application procedure has been rarely utilised,[42] the number of individual applications continues to increase so rapidly that in 2004 the

---

[37] ETS No 155. See Henry Schermers, 'The Eleventh Protocol to the European Convention on Human Rights' (1994) 19 *European Law Review* 367, and Nicola Rowe and Volker Schlette, 'The Protection of Human Rights in Europe after the Eleventh Protocol to the ECHR' (1998) 23 *European Law Review* (Supp) Hrs, 3.

[38] Arts 19–51.

[39] Under Art 56(4), States are able to make a declaration that the right to individual application does not apply to the citizens of its overseas territories.

[40] See, for example: Robertson and Merrills, *Human Rights in Europe* (2001) 258; Brice Dickson, 'The Council of Europe and the European Convention' in Dickson (ed), *Human Rights and the European Convention: The effects of the Convention on the United Kingdom and Ireland* (London, Sweet & Maxwell, 1997) 8; Simpson, *Human Rights* (2001) 3; Costas Douzinas, *The End of Human Rights: Critical Legal Thought at the Turn of the Century* (Oxford, Hart Publishing, 2000) 119, fn 20; Laurence R Helfer, 'Redesigning the European Court of Human Rights: Embeddedness as a Deep Structural Principle of the European Human Rights Regime' (2008) 19(1) *European Journal of International Law* 125, 126.

[41] Mark Janis, Richard Kay and Anthony Bradley, *European Human Rights Law: Texts and Materials* 3rd edn (Oxford, Oxford University Press, 2008) 3.

[42] The Explanatory Report to Protocol 14 of the Convention states that as at 1 January 2004 only 20 inter-State applications had been made. See Council of Europe, *Protocol No 14 to the Convention for the Protection of Human Rights and Fundamental Freedoms, amending the control system of the Convention: Explanatory Report*, available at: conventions.coe.int/Treaty/EN/Reports/Html/194.htm.

More recently, Georgia has lodged an application against Russia that has recently been declared admissible. See *Georgia v Russia* (dec) (App no 13255/07) ECHR 30 June 2009.

On the dearth of ECHR inter-State applications see, for example: Robin CA White, 'Tackling Political Disputes Through Individual Applications' (1998) 1 *European Human Rights Law Review* 61, 62–4; P van Dijk and GJH van Hoof, *Theory and Practice of the European Convention on Human Rights*, 3rd edn (The Hague, Kluwer Law International, 1998) 43–4; Robertson and Merrills, *Human Rights in Europe* (2001) 273–4.

Council of Europe produced yet another Protocol (Protocol 14, which comes into force in June 2010) to streamline the Court's mechanisms for dealing with them.[43] Yet even the changes this Protocol brings will be insufficient to deal with the increased workload, and the reform discussions continue. Indeed, it is unlikely to be controversial today to suggest that the Convention is popularly perceived to be first and foremost a means of achieving individual justice. It is also noteworthy that an individual application procedure has subsequently been adopted under several other international human rights treaties. For example, individual complaints may now be received by the UN's Human Rights Committee,[44] the Committee for the Elimination of Racial Discrimination,[45] the Committee Against Torture[46] and, more recently, the Women's Committee,[47] the Committee on Economic, Social and Cultural Rights,[48] the Committee on Migrant Workers[49] and the Committee on the Rights of Persons with Disabilities.[50] They may also be received by the Inter-American Commission of Human Rights[51] as well as the African Commission on Human and Peoples' Rights[52] and the newly operational African Court of Human and Peoples' Rights.[53]

Certainly, Member States of the Council of Europe can rightfully take credit for having led the way in giving individuals standing as the subjects of international human rights law and making a reality of their original moral and

---

[43] Protocol 14 (2004) ETS No 194. See Steven Greer, 'Reforming the European Convention on Human Rights: Towards Protocol 14' [2003] *Public Law* 663, Steven Greer, 'Protocol 14 and the Future of the European Court of Human Rights' [2005] *Public Law* 83, and Marie-Aude Beernaert, 'Protocol 14 and New Strasbourg Procedures: Towards Greater Efficiency? And at What Price?' (2004) 5 *European Human Rights Law Review* 544.

[44] Art 1, (First) Optional Protocol to the International Covenant on Civil and Political Rights (1966) 999 UNTS 302, entered into force 23 March 1976.

[45] Art 14, International Convention on the Elimination of All Forms of Racial Discrimination (1966) 660 UNTS 195, entered into force 4 January 1969, which is optional.

[46] Art 22, Convention against Torture and Other Cruel, Inhuman or Degrading Treatment or Punishment (1984) 1465 UNTS 85, entered into force 26 June 1987, which is optional.

[47] Art 2, Optional Protocol to the Convention on the Elimination of All Forms of Discrimination against Women (1999) GA Res 54/4, entered into force 22 December 2000.

[48] Art 2, Optional Protocol to the International Covenant on Economic, Social and Cultural Rights (2008), UN Doc A/63/435, not yet entered into force.

[49] Art 77, International Convention on the Protection of the Rights of All Migrant Workers and Members of Their Families (1990), UN Doc A/RES/45/158, entered into force 1 July 2003, which is optional.

[50] Art 1, Optional Protocol to the Convention on the Rights of Persons with Disabilities (2006), UN Doc A/61/611, entered into force 3 May 2008.

[51] Art 44, American Convention on Human Rights (1969), OAS Treaty Series No 36, 1144 UNTS 123, entered into force 18 July 1978, which is mandatory.

[52] Art 55, African Charter on Human and Peoples' Rights (1981), adopted 27 June 1981, OAU Doc CAB/LEG/67/3 rev 5, (1982) 21 ILM 58, entered into force 21 October 1986, which is mandatory.

[53] Art 5(3), Protocol to the African Charter on Human and Peoples' Rights on the Establishment of an African Court on Human and Peoples' Rights (1998), adopted 10 June 1998, reprinted in (1997) 9 *African Journal of International and Comparative Law* 953, entered into force 15 January 2004, which is optional.
   Interestingly, the Court's recently delivered first judgment hinged on the question of whether Senegal had accepted the Court's jurisdiction to hear individual cases. See *Michelot Yogogombaye v The Republic of Senegal* (App no 001/2008), ACHPR 15 December 2009.

philosophical commitment to liberal individualism. In sum, the individual application procedure was born out of an understanding that human rights inhere in the individual and any violation thereof is consequently both personal and discrete. Even if the steps that led to the adoption and increased acceptance of this mechanism were primarily pragmatic and not explicitly philosophical, its best justification must lie in an understanding that individuals are autonomous beings who are ontologically prior to their society. This in turn, I suggest, has led to a rather particular understanding of the Court's litigation, which has come to be almost exclusively played out as an epic battle between an individual (the right-holder) and a respondent State (the duty-bearer).

With the exception of State parties to the ECHR, those making an application to the Court must claim to be the victim of a violation of the Convention's rights personally.[54] The Court held in the case of *Eckle v FRG* that the word 'victim' 'denotes the person directly affected by the act or omission which is in issue'.[55] Pursuant to this logic, the Court has held that Article 25 'does not institute for individuals a kind of *actio popularis* for the interpretation of the Convention; it does not permit individuals to complain against a law *in abstracto* simply because they feel that it contravenes the Convention'.[56] The Commission held in relation to the standing of NGOs to bring a complaint that an 'association, with a social aim, may not itself claim to be a victim of a decision which only affects those persons whose interests it decides to defend'.[57] While the Court has noted that there should be some flexibility in applying the Convention's rules of admissibility[58] – and indeed it has taken some steps towards this,[59] including relaxing its rules concerning the standing of NGOs to bring cases on behalf of members[60] – its procedures clearly envisage an isolated individual applicant, pursuing a case that is of unique importance to her.

III. The Politics of Human Rights Litigation

There is a reassuring conceptual clarity that comes from addressing violations of the Convention in isolation and treating them as discrete events. This approach helps to delineate the Court's function and allows the Court to be seen as a

---

[54] See, generally, van Dijk and van Hoof, *Theory and Practice* (1998) 46–60.

[55] *Eckle v Federal Republic of Germany* Series A no 51 (1983) 5 EHRR 1 [66].

[56] *Klass v Federal Republic of Germany* Series A no 28 (1979–80) 2 EHRR 214 [33].

[57] *Nineteen Chilean nationals and the S Association v Sweden* (App Nos 9959/82 and 10357/83), Commission decision of 14 March 1984, 37 DR 87.

[58] *Cardot v France* Series A no 200 (1991) 13 EHRR 853 [18].

[59] Van Dijk and van Hoof note, for example, that the Commission and Court have recognised a limited concept of 'indirect', 'future' and 'potential' victimhood. See van Dijk and van Hoof, *Theory and Practice* (1998) 52–8.

[60] See *Gorraiz Lizarraga and Others v Spain* ECHR 2004-III, (2007) 45 EHRR 45.

politically neutral body that applies a fixed set of rules to individual circumstances; but in adopting it we become myopic and overlook the myriad interests that intuitively we know are at stake when human rights are given form. Recent theorists have responded to criticisms of the excessive individualism of human rights by suggesting that this aspect of human rights theory has been overstated.[61] A number of authors instead present human rights as 'a space beyond the boundaries of states where individuals and groups interact and shape collective life'.[62]

In light of the seriousness with which claims about the failure of liberalism to formulate a rational morality of universal validity have been treated recently both by liberals and others, it certainly does not seem too far-fetched to suggest that human rights are at least to *some* extent dependent upon political claims for their substance. Indeed, Donnelly goes some way to acknowledging the political nature and complex authorship of human rights claims when he writes:

> Lists of human rights are based only loosely on abstract philosophical reasoning and a priori moral principles. They emerge instead from the concrete experiences, especially the sufferings, of real human beings and their political struggles to defend or realize their dignity. Internationally recognized human rights reflect a politically driven process of social learning.[63]

Otto goes further in her discussion of the politics of human rights, and suggests that we can draw from post-modern theory to understand social movements emerging as 'resistance' to concentrations of power within the international community.[64] To this end, Costas Douzinas's conception of human rights as challenges to political power resonates with Otto's vision:

> Human rights as a principle of popular politics express the indeterminacy and openness of society and politics. They undermine the attempt to police some social identities and sanction others and their indeterminacy means that the boundaries of society are always contested and never coincide fully with whatever crystallizations, power and legal entitlement impose.[65]

---

[61]   See for example: Mary Ann Glendon, *Rights Talk: The Impoverishment of Political Discourse* (New York, The Free Press, 1991); Michael Freeman, *Human Rights: an Interdisciplinary Approach* (Cambridge, Polity Press, 2002); Francesca Klug, *Values for a Godless Age: The Story of the United Kingdom's New Bill of Rights* (London, Penguin, 2000).

[62]   Julie Mertus, 'Doing Democracy "Differently": The Transformative Potential of Human Rights NGOs in Transnational Civil Society' (1998–99) *Third World Legal Studies* 205, 208. See also Upendra Baxi, *The Future of Human Rights* (New Delhi, Oxford University Press, 2002); Sally Engle Merry, Mihaela Şerban Rosen, Peggy Levitt, Diana H Yoon, 'Law from Below: Women's Human Rights and Social Movements in New York City' (2010) 44(1) *Law and Society Review* 101.

[63]   Jack Donnelly, *Universal Human Rights in Theory and Practice* (Ithaca, Cornell University Press, 2003) 58. See also Freeman, *Human Rights* (2002).

[64]   Dianne Otto, 'Nongovernmental Organizations in the United Nations System: The Emerging Role of International Civil Society' (1996) 18 *Human Rights Quarterly* 107, 135.

[65]   Douzinas, *The End of Human Rights* (2000) 375. See also Neil Stammers, *Human Rights and Social Movements* (London, Pluto Press, 2009).

The irresistible implication of this position seems to be that the foundations of human rights are located within struggles for human rights, the site of their creation.[66]

Human rights are often incarnated as formal laws. It should not be too surprising, therefore, when human rights litigation becomes a site for political communities to make their claims for recognition. In turn, such claims have the capacity to give form and meaning to human rights laws. That two supposedly fundamental rights within the ECHR, for example, can conflict with one another starkly illustrates that the mere assertion of a right is insufficient to give full meaning to the Convention. When the Court decides whether or not the right to life, protected under Article 2 of the Convention, encompasses the right to euthanasia it is, behind the veil provided by the Convention's 'neutral framework', making hard choices.[67] Michael Waltzer must surely be right when he voices the suspicion that these 'can only be political choices'.[68] That this has application in relation to the Court's function was made clear in its well-known and dynamic assertion that the Convention 'is a living instrument which … must be interpreted in the light of present day conditions'.[69]

From recognising the indeterminacy of human rights, it is a short step to allowing that human rights litigation is sometimes a battle of ideals, rather than a mere conflict between the isolated individual and her State over the correct application of rules. From this standpoint, with the political underbelly of human rights litigation laid bare, interests other than those of the individual applicant enter into our line of vision. To cite Donnelly again:

> Human rights is the language of victims and the dispossessed. Human rights claims are used principally to seek to alter legal or political practices … To assert one's human rights is to attempt to change political structures and practices so that it will no longer be necessary to claim those rights (as human rights).[70]

Although in relation to legal claims that is probably over-stating the case (ignoring, as it does, the fact that many human rights cases concern a very narrow range of interests identifiable only by the applicant), it is certainly an interesting alternative position to the excessive individualism that has dominated understanding of the ECHR. Taking the above position as a starting point, it seems perfectly coherent to question the limits of the bi-partisan approach to the Court's litigation and to open up an enquiry as to whether there is a systematic

---

[66]   The inspiration for these ideas was Baxi, *The Future of Human Rights* (2002), especially ch 6.

[67]   This was the stark issue that faced the ECtHR in *Pretty v United Kingdom* (App no 2346/02) ECHR 2002-III, (2002) 35 EHRR 1.

[68]   Michael Waltzer, 'Welfare, Membership and Need' in Michael Sandel (ed), *Liberalism and Its Critics* (Oxford, Blackwell Publishers, 1984) 202. Baxi is rather more blunt when he says that human rights norms are created by 'messy political trade offs and power calculi'. See Baxi, *The Future of Human Rights* (2002) 61.

[69]   *Tyrer v United Kingdom* Series A no 26 (1979–80) 2 EHRR 1 [31].

[70]   Jack Donnelly, *International Human Rights* (Boulder, Westview Press, 1998) 20.

approach being taken to making these 'intense demands' at the door of the Court. This book focuses on the largely unexplored role that non-governmental organisations play in this respect.

IV. NGOs and the International Human Rights Movement

At the national level, there is now a rich literature in the political sciences that focuses on the role of pressure groups (or interest groups) as agents of social movements.[71] Several studies bridging the academic divide between law and politics have examined the use that such groups make of law as a tool to bring about social change. A number of authors have followed Galanter's lead in looking at litigation 'through the wrong end of the telescope'[72] and have recognised the interaction between legal process and social struggles[73] and the role that strategic NGO litigation campaigns can play in bringing about social change.[74] Joseph Sax, an American writer, was one of the earliest academics to suggest that 'an essential format for reasserting participation in the governmental process is in the courtrooms'.[75] Litigiousness has, as Graham Wilson notes, become a 'distinctive feature of American interest groups'.[76] But the idea of linking legal strategies to political struggles is now widely recognised beyond the

---

[71]   The literature is vast but one might, for example, refer to Arthur F Bentley, *The Process of Government: A Study of Social Pressure* (Evanston, Principia Press, 1908) and Jeremy Richardson (ed), *Pressure Groups* (Oxford, Oxford University Press, 1993). Bill Coxall, *Pressure Groups in British Politics* (New York, Longman, 2001) contains a useful and comprehensive bibliography on the subject.

[72]   Marc Galanter, 'The Radiating Effects of Courts' in Keith O Boyum and Lynn Mather (eds), *Empirical Theories about Courts* (New York, Longman, 1983) 135.

[73]   Michael McCann, 'Reform Litigation on Trial' (1992) 17 *Law and Social Inquiry* 715, 734; Stuart Scheingold, *The Politics of Rights: Lawyers, Public Policy, and Political Change* (New Haven, Yale University Press, 1974); Charles R Epp, *The Rights Revolution: Lawyers, Activists, and Supreme Courts in Comparative Perspective* (Chicago, University of Chicago Press, 1998).

[74]   William Eskridge, 'Some Effects of Identity-Based Social Movements on Constitutional Law in the Twentieth Century' (2002) 100 *Michigan Law Review* 2062; Christopher Coleman, Laurence D Nee and Leonard S Rubinowitz, 'Social Movements and Social-Change Litigation: Synergy in the Montgomery Bus Protest' (2005) 30 *Law and Social Inquiry* 663.

For a more sceptical view about the capacity of litigation to bring about significant reform, see Stuart Scheingold, *The Politics of Rights: Lawyers, Public Policy, and Political Change* (New Haven, Yale University Press, 1974); N Rosenberg, *The Hollow Hope: Can Courts Bring about Social Change?* (Chicago, University of Chicago Press, 1991); Davison M Douglas, 'The Limits of Law in Accomplishing Racial Change: School Segregation in the Pre-Brown North' (1997) 44 *UCLA Law Review* 677.

[75]   Joseph Sax, *Defending the Environment: A Strategy for Citizen Action* (New York, Alfred A Knopf, 1971) xviii.

[76]   Graham Wilson, 'American Interest Groups' in Jeremy J Richardson (ed), *Pressure Groups* (Oxford, Oxford University Press, 1993) 134.

United States, and others have noted the prevalence of interest group litigation (or public interest litigation) elsewhere.[77]

That NGOs have made generous use of human rights arguments in their strategic litigation campaigns is hardly surprising given the indeterminacy of human rights and the added leverage that human rights discourse can offer advocates. Examples such as the NAACP's high-profile trail-blazing litigation in cases such as *Brown v Board of Education of Topeka* demonstrate why human rights arguments have been seized upon by NGOs[78] and, conversely, why NGOs have been credited with the capacity to infuse legal interpretation with dynamic ideology that reflects the interests of excluded and marginalised groups.[79] As Bob Clifford notes, the adoption of rights language is a tactical, political choice:

> Rights emerge in much the same way as other policy ... In this view, there are numerous human needs, grievances, and problems, the majority of which go unnoticed most of the time. Reframing these issues as rights violations is a strategic choice aimed at exerting greater pressure to solve them.[80]

At the national level, then, NGOs use human rights-based arguments to target attention and bring pressure to bear on their chosen issues; and their claims are sometimes made in formal legal arenas because of the additional pressure that this can bring to bear.

What, then, of NGOs' use of international legal leverage? At the international level there remains a marked divergence between the study of international relations and international law, although human rights in particular is beginning to narrow this gap.[81] While students of both disciplines quickly learn that States should be the principal subjects of their attention, human rights challenges this narrow and State-centric approach; in its place is introduced – albeit in a rudimentary and imperfect way – the more cosmopolitan idea of a global

---

[77] On the considerable presence of NGOs in Indian litigation, for example, see: Upendra Baxi, 'Taking Suffering Seriously' in Rajeev Dhavan, R Sudarshan and Salman Khurshid, *Judges and the Judicial Power* (London, Sweet & Maxwell, 1985); Upendra Baxi, 'Judicial Discourse: The Dialects of the Face and the Mask' (1993) 35 *Journal of the Indian Law Institute* 1; SP Sathe, *Judicial Activism in India: Transgressing Borders and Enforcing Limits* (New Delhi, Oxford University Press, 2002), especially ch 6; Modhurima Dasgupta, 'Social Action for Women? Public Interest Litigation in India's Supreme Court' (2002) *Law, Social Justice & Global Development Journal* (LGD) 1, at: www2.warwick.ac.uk/fac/soc/law/elj/lgd/2002_1/dasgupta.

[78] *Brown v Board of Education of Topeka* 374 US 483 (1954). In a seminal study on pressure groups and the law, Clement Vose highlighted the remarkable role that the NAACP's litigation strategy played in the civil rights movement. See Clement Vose, *Caucasians Only: The Supreme Court, the NAACP and the Restrictive Covenant Cases* (Berkeley, University of California Press, 1959).

[79] See, for example, Eskridge, 'Some Effects of Identity-Based Social Movements' (2002).

[80] Clifford Bob, 'Introduction: Fighting for New Rights' in Clifford Bob (ed), *The International Struggle for New Human Rights* (Philadelphia, University of Pennsylvania Press, 2009) 8.

[81] See, for example, Donnelly, *International Human Rights* (1998); Donnelly, *Universal Human Rights* (2003); Tim Dunne and Nicholas Wheeler (eds), *Human Rights in Global Politics* (Cambridge, Cambridge University Press, 1999); Freeman, *Human Rights* (2002); Thomas G Weiss and Leon Gordenker (eds), *NGOs, the UN and Global Governance* (London, Lynne Rienner Publishers, 1996); Anna-Karin Lindblom, *Non-Governmental Organisations in International Law* (Cambridge, Cambridge University Press, 2005).

'human rights culture', the creation, maintenance and development of which involves a myriad of actors, including individuals and NGOs. As Upendra Baxi notes, 'the authorship of contemporary human rights is multitudinous'.[82] NGOs, in particular, are now coming to be recognised as significant – although relatively weak and compromised – actors in the field of international human rights.[83] High-profile organisations such as Amnesty International, Human Rights Watch, the International League for Human Rights and the International Federation for Human Rights have raised the profile of international NGO activities greatly. But the momentum for reform is not generated by such 'big hitters' acting alone. A number of authors have commented upon the capacity of transnational networks of organisations to mobilise pressure and communicate the concerns of the oppressed and marginalised to the institutional world of international law.[84] Mary Kaldor comments in relation to the wider – but closely related – concept of civil society that it adds to 'human rights discourse the notion of individual

---

[82]   Baxi, *The Future of Human Rights* (2002) 31. For a similar point, see also Mary Kaldor, 'Transnational Civil Society' in Dunne and Wheeler (eds), *Human Rights in Global Politics* (1999) 210; Andrew Hurrell, 'Power, Principles and Prudence: Protecting Human Rights in a Deeply Divided World' in Dunne and Wheeler (eds), *Human Rights in Global Politics* (1999).

[83]   See, for example: Peter Willetts (ed), *Pressure Groups in the Global System: The Transnational Relations of Issue-Orientated Non-Governmental Organizations* (London, Frances Pinter, 1982); Peter Willetts (ed), *'The Conscience of the World': The Influence of Non-Governmental Organisation in the U.N. System* (London, Hurst & Co, 1996); William Korey, *NGOs and the Universal Declaration of Human Rights: 'A Curious Grapevine'* (New York, St Martin's Press, 1998); Henry Steiner, *Diverse Partners: Non-Governmental Organizations in the Human Rights Movement* (Cambridge MA, Harvard Law School Human Rights Program, 1991); James Green, 'NGOs' in Abdul Aziz Said (ed), *Human Rights and World Order* (New York, Praeger, 1978); Nigel Rodley, 'Monitoring Human Rights Violations in the 1980s' in Jorge Dominguez et al (eds), *Enhancing Global Human Rights* (New York, McGraw-Hill, 1979); David Weissbrodt, 'The Role of International Nongovernmental Organizations in the Implementation of Human Rights' (1977) 12 *Texas International Law Journal* 293; Antonio Cassese, 'How Could Nongovernmental Organizations Use U.N. Bodies More Effectively?' (1979) 1(4) *Universal Human Rights* 73; Jackie Smith, Ron Pagnucco and George A Lopez, 'Globalizing Human Rights: The Work of Transnational Human Rights NGOs in the 1990s' (1998) 20 *Human Rights Quarterly* 379; Claude E Welch, *NGOs and Human Rights: Promise and Performance* (Philadelphia PA, University of Pennsylvania Press, 2000); Holly Cullen and Karen Morrow, 'International Civil Society in International Law: The Growth of NGO Participation' (2001) 1 *Non-State Actors and International Law* 7; Ann Marie Clark, *Diplomacy of Conscience: Amnesty International and Changing Human Rights Norms* (Princeton NJ, Princeton University Press, 2001); Tullio Treves (ed), *Civil Society, International Courts and Compliance Bodies* (The Hague, TMC Asser Press, 2005); Jonathan Graubart, 'NGOs and the Security Council: authority all around but for whose benefit?' in Bruce Cronin and Ian Hurd (eds), *The UN Security Council and the Politics of International Authority* (London, Routledge, 2008); Steve Charnovitz, 'Nongovernmental Organizations and International Law' (2006) 100 *American Journal of International Law* 348; Zoe Pearson, 'Non-Governmental Organizations and the International Criminal Court: Changing Landscapes of International Law' (2006) 39 *Cornell International Law Journal* 243; Clifford Bob (ed), *The International Struggle for New Human Rights* (Philadelphia PA, University of Pennsylvania Press, 2009).

[84]   Stammers, *Human Rights* (2009) 248. See also Margaret E Keck and Kathryn Sikkink, *Activists Beyond Borders: Advocacy Networks in International Politics* (Ithaca NY, Cornell University Press, 1998) and Jutta M Joachim, *Agenda Setting, the UN, and NGOs: Gender Violence and Reproductive Rights* (Washington DC, Georgetown University Press, 2007).

responsibility for respect of human rights through political action'.[85] Steve Charnovitz goes so far as to credit NGOs with 'helping to humanize modern international law'.[86]

NGOs have long seized upon international law's capacity to give concrete form and status to the principles that human rights discourse embodies.[87] As William Korey argues,

> [i]f the treaties and their enforcement mechanisms are perceived as the foundation of a future international human rights legal community, NGOs stood and still stand at the cutting edge of the early initiatives that would make this future possible.[88]

One of the earliest NGOs that played a crucial role in the development and promotion of international law was the International Committee of the Red Cross, which has worked tirelessly in the field of humanitarian law since it was founded in 1863.[89] Anti-Slavery International is another organisation that has contributed to the development of international law for well over a century.[90] It is also noteworthy that NGOs gained recognition under Article 147 of the German-Polish Convention Concerning Upper Silesia of 1922, which provided that minority associations could make collective complaints to the Minorities Office set up in German and Polish Upper Silesia. Simpson states that this was 'the first recognition of non-governmental organizations as having official standing to bring proceedings over violations of individual rights'.[91] However, it was the creation of the UN – and in particular the adoption by the General Assembly of the Universal Declaration of Human Rights – that provided a significant opportunity for organised political movements to participate in the development of the international law of human rights.

A.   NGOs and the United Nations' Human Rights Bodies

As soon as the drafting of the UN Charter was underway, NGOs were active in ensuring that it contained provisions for protecting human rights. In particular, they were responsible for the reference to the creation of a Human Rights

---

[85]   Kaldor, 'Transnational Civil Society' (1999) 211.

[86]   Charnovitz, 'Nongovernmental Organizations and International Law' (2006) 361.

[87]   Felix Ermacora, 'Non-Governmental Organizations as Promoters of Human Rights' in Franz Matscher and Herbert Petzold (eds), *Protecting Human Rights: The European Dimension* (Koln, Carl Heymanns Verlag KG, 1988).

[88]   Korey, *NGOs and the Universal Declaration of Human Rights* (1998) 5.

[89]   See, for example, Thomas St G Bissell, 'The International Committee of the Red Cross and the Protection of Human Rights' (1968) 1 *Revue des Droits de l'Homme* 255. On the ICRC's increasing use of human rights frameworks, see David P Forsythe, 'Human Rights and the International Committee of the Red Cross' (1990) 12 *Human Rights Quarterly* 265 and Sergey Sayapin, 'The International Committee of the Red Cross and International Human Rights Law' (2009) 9 *Human Rights Law Review* 95.

[90]   See Claude E Welch, 'Defining Contemporary Forms of Slavery: Updating a Venerable NGO' (2009) 31 *Human Rights Quarterly* 70.

[91]   Simpson, *Human Rights* (2001) 136.

Commission in Article 68, and for the Charter's provision in Article 71 for formal consultation between NGOs and the UN's Economic and Social Council (ECOSOC).[92] As Clark notes in his study of the International League for Human Rights' activities in relation to South West Africa, these provisions helped carve out for NGOs 'a role in the process of creating and enforcing the norms of a corpus of international human rights law'.[93] The UN's latest figures list 3,289 NGOs with Consultative Status before ECOSOC.[94] Diane Otto enthusiastically credits this groundswell of NGO participation with introducing 'a new dynamic of embryonic participatory democracy to the global community and to the shaping of international law'.[95]

Indeed, for many commentators, the emergence of NGOs as key actors within the UN has been a welcome development. Antonio Cassese identifies three main levels upon which NGOs can play a role in ensuring respect for human rights within the UN:

> The first level might be termed the *level of imagination*, that is, the plane of elaboration of proposals concerning new avenues for the promotion of human rights, or new areas of concern. Second, NGOs might contribute to the *standard-setting activity* of the U.N. as well as to translating U.N. standards into national patterns of behaviour. Third, they can spur U.N. efforts for the *implementation* of human rights and in addition contribute directly to such implementation by taking action within the national domain.[96]

For some, what distinguishes NGOs from State actors in particular is their greater freedom from political and diplomatic constraints, which enhances their capacity to energise the UN system. In the words of Theo Van Boven, this is particularly 'important as a counterweight to immobility and lethargy, which are characteristics for quite a few national and international bureaucracies'.[97] Although NGOs,

---

[92] Art 71 of the UN Charter reads: 'The Economic and Social Council may make suitable arrangements for consultation with non-governmental organizations which are concerned with matters within its competence. Such arrangements may be made with international organizations and, where appropriate, with national organizations after consultation with the Member of the United Nations concerned'. Consultation arrangements are now governed by ECOSOC Res 1996/31, 25 July 1996. See Bill Seary, 'The Early History: From the Congress of Vienna to the San Francisco Conference' in Willetts (ed), *'The Conscience of the World'* (1996), and Korey, *NGOs and the Universal Declaration of Human Rights* (1998).

On the early days of the consultative arrangements, see Michael M Gunter, 'Towards a Consultative Relationship Between the United Nations and Non-Governmental Organizations' (1977) 10 *Vanderbilt Journal of Transnational Law* 557.

[93] Roger Clark, 'The International League for Human Rights and South West Africa 1947–1957: The Human Rights NGO as Catalyst in the International Legal Process' (1981) 3(4) *Human Rights Quarterly* 101, 105.

[94] This figure has risen from 40 in 1948. For further details, see: www.un.org/esa/coordination/ngo.

[95] Otto, 'Nongovernmental Organizations in the United Nations System' (1996) 120.

[96] Cassese, 'How Could Nongovernmental Organizations' (1979) 76.

[97] Theo van Boven, 'The Role of Non-Governmental Organizations in International Human Rights Standard-Setting: A Prerequisite for Democracy' (1990) 20 *Californian Western International Law Journal* 207, 217. See also Virginia Leary, 'A New Role for Non-Governmental Organizations in

who still operate largely at the parameters of international institutions, may not always be able to live up to such great expectations – and while some critical voices have begun to emerge questioning the legitimacy of their influence[98] – they have certainly become impossible to ignore.

In practice, NGOs have used various means to promote and ensure respect for human rights at the United Nations. Van Boven notes that, primarily as a result of their legal expertise, 'NGOs often act as full participants and sometimes as principal actors' during the drafting of UN human rights conventions.[99] NGO involvement in the drafting of the Convention on the Rights of the Child, for example, ensured they were given a role in monitoring its implementation.[100] Amnesty International has been credited with ensuring that measures were taken at the UN level to combat torture,[101] and they were also the force behind the creation of the role of UN Human Rights Commissioner.[102]

Carol Harlow and Richard Rawlings note that seeking the enforcement of human rights 'goes hand in hand' with a 'more aggressive and more legalistic' campaigning style.[103] Laurie Wiseberg and Harry Scoble argued as long ago as 1977 that the need in international human rights law was for improved implementation, not for more legislation.[104] It is therefore unsurprising that NGOs have emerged as significant actors in the quasi-judicial individual communications human rights procedures of the United Nations, although the data available

Human Rights: A Case Study of Non-Governmental Participation in the Development of International Norms on Torture' in Antonio Cassese (ed), *UN Law/Fundamental Rights* (Alphen aan den Rijn, Sijthoff & Noordhoof, 1979) 198, and Charnovitz, 'Nongovernmental Organizations and International Law' (2006).

[98]   Kenneth Anderson, 'The Ottawa Convention Banning Landmines, the Role of International Non-governmental Organizations and the Idea of International Civil Society' (2000) 11(1) *European Journal of International Law* 91 and David Kennedy, 'The International Human Rights Movement: Part of the Problem?' (2002) 15 *Harvard Human Rights Journal* 101. See also Carol Harlow, 'Public Law and Popular Justice' (2002) 65 *Modern Law Review* 1.
For an interesting discussion of how groups might increase their legitimacy, see Eric Heinze, 'Even-handedness and the Politics of Human Rights' (2008) 21 *Harvard Human Rights Journal* 7.

[99]   van Boven, 'The Role of Non-Governmental Organizations' (1990) 218.

[100]   Art 45, Convention on the Rights of the Child. See Michael Longford, 'NGOs and the Rights of the Child' in Willetts (ed), '*The Conscience of the World*' (1996) and Cynthia Price Cohen, 'The Role of Nongovernmental Organizations in the Drafting of the Convention on the Rights of the Child' (1990) 12(1) *Human Rights Quarterly* 137. See also Claire Breen, 'The Role of NGOs in the Formulation of and Compliance with the Optional Protocol to the Convention on the Rights of the Child on Involvement of Children in Armed Conflict' (2003) 25(2) *Human Rights Quarterly* 453. An NGO group for the Convention on the Rights of the Child was formed in 1983. For details, see: www.crin.org/NGOGroupforCRC.

[101]   Leary, 'A New Role for Non-Governmental Organizations' (1979). See also Helena Cook, 'Amnesty International at the United Nations' in P Willetts (ed), '*The Conscience of the World*' (1996) and Dean Zagorac, 'International Courts and Compliance Bodies: The Experience of Amnesty International' in T Treves (ed), *Civil Society, International Courts* (2005).

[102]   Andrew Clapham, 'Creating the High Commissioner for Human Rights: The Outside Story' (1994) 5 *European Journal of International Law* 556.

[103]   Carol Harlow and Richard Rawlings, *Pressure Through Law* (London, Routledge, 1992) 246.

[104]   Laurie Wiseberg and Harry Scoble, 'The International League for Human Rights: The Strategy of a Human Rights NGO' (1977) 7 *Georgia Journal of International and Comparative Law* 289, 297.

about this is rather limited.[105] NGOs have, for example, been prominent in channeling individual complaints to the Human Rights Council.[106] Felix Ermacora, writing in 1988, noted that 'nearly all' of the situations that the (now replaced) Human Rights Commission had dealt with under its 1503 procedure for individual communications had been brought to that body's attention by NGOs.[107] He makes the startling point that a sole individual had never been able to utilise the 1503 procedure successfully, and concludes that 'through this procedure NGOs have gained the function of an international ombudsman for human rights'.[108] In relation to the special procedures, Korey wrote in 1998: 'Virtually every report by a Special Rapporteur, whether on a theme or on a country, has carried references to the contributions of NGOs'.[109] The Office of the High Commissioner for Human Rights continues to view civil society as essential to the operation of the special procedures.[110] With the establishment of the Human Rights Council, NGO involvement continues to flourish. The OHCHR recently reported that at the seventh regular session of the Human Rights Council, '180 NGOs were represented by a total of 1116 individuals. At this same session, NGOs submitted 98 written statements, made 224 oral statements and hosted 69 parallel events'.[111]

By the time that the Vienna Declaration and Programme of Action was adopted at the 1993 World Conference on Human Rights, the centrality of NGOs to the UN's human rights regime was confirmed by the multiple references to NGOs contained in that document.[112] In September 1994, former UN Secretary-General, Boutros Boutros-Ghali, stated that NGOs 'are now considered full participants in international life'.[113] Willetts embraces this view, referring enthusiastically to NGOs as 'partners' in the international law-making process.[114]

---

[105]   See, for example: David Weissbrodt, 'The Contribution of International Nongovernmental Organizations to the Protection of Human Rights' in Theodor Meron (ed), *Human Rights in International Law: Legal and Policy Issues* (Oxford, Clarendon Press, 1984); Wendy Schoener, 'Non-Governmental Organizations and Global Activism: Legal and Informal Approaches' (1997) 4 *Indiana Journal of Global Legal Studies* 537.
   The International League for Human Rights, for example, responded to the increasing number of individual complaints they received by setting up the Lawyer's Committee on International Human Rights. See Wiseberg and Scoble, 'The International League for Human Rights' (1977) 308.
[106]   Office of the High Commissioner for Human Rights, *Working with the United Nations Human Rights Programme: A Handbook for Civil Society* (New York, OHCHR, 2008) 159.
[107]   Ermacora, 'Non-Governmental Organizations' (1998) 176.
[108]   *ibid*, 177.
[109]   Korey, *NGOs and the Universal Declaration of Human Rights* (1998) 263.
[110]   Office of the High Commissioner for Human Rights, *Working with the United Nations Human Rights Programme* (2008) 119.
[111]   *ibid*, 97. See also Lucia Nader, 'The Role of NGOs in the Human Rights Council' (2007) 7 *Sur: International Journal on Human Rights* 7.
[112]   See, in particular, para 38.
[113]   'Statement at the UN Department of Public Information Forty-Seventh Annual Conference of Non-Governmental Organizations: New York, 20 September 1994', reproduced in Willetts, '*The Conscience of the World*' (1996) 311.
[114]   Peter Willetts, 'From "Consultative Arrangements" to "Partnership": The Changing Status of NGOs in Diplomacy at the UN' (2000) 6 *Global Governance* 191.

While this may be something of an overstatement – Article 71 of the UN Charter clearly does not provide for the equal formal status of NGOs in the international community – it is obvious, in practice, that NGOs are key players in the UN human rights regime.

B. NGOs and Other Regional Human Rights Treaty Bodies

The importance of NGOs can also be readily identified in respect of regional human rights bodies other than the ECtHR. Dinah Shelton, in a study that incorporates several international legal tribunals, identifies a high level of third-party intervention by NGOs in litigation before the Inter-American Court of Human Rights. Perhaps unsurprisingly, given the popularity of the amicus curiae brief in North America, she found that that body had 'the most extensive amicus practice' of the tribunals that she studied.[115] The Rules of Court, both in their present and previous form, are drafted sufficiently broadly so that amicus can be received in both contentious and advisory cases.[116] Shelton reports that 'the Inter-American Court appears never to have rejected an amicus filing', which has naturally served as encouragement for numerous human rights groups to submit briefs to it.[117] Antonio Trindade, for example, notes that the Inter-American Court, in delivering its first 14 advisory opinions, accepted 41 interventions.[118] A quick review of all the Court's judgments on the merits in contentious cases in 2009 reveals only three cases in which no amicus curiae brief was submitted. Shelton applauds this high level of NGO participation because, thereby, 'the public interest is broadly served and the work of the Inter-American Commission supplemented to ensure a full and fair hearing for all issues presented by cases before the Court'.[119]

---

[115] Dinah Shelton, 'The Participation of Non-governmental Organisations in International Judicial Proceedings' (1994) 88 *American Journal of International Law* 611, 638.

For an interesting case-study of an NGO's use of the Inter-American human rights system, see Todd Howland, 'How El Rescate, a Small Nongovernmental Organization, Contributed to the Transformation of the Human Rights System in El Salvador' (2008) 30 *Human Rights Quarterly* 703.

[116] Under Article 44 of the Rules of Procedure of the Inter-American Court of Human Rights, 24 November 2009, any person or institution may submit an amicus brief to the Court.

[117] Shelton, 'The Participation of Non-governmental Organisations' (1994) 638.

[118] Antonio Trindade, 'The Operation of the Inter-American Court of Human Rights' in David Harris and Stephen Livingstone (eds), *The Inter-American System of Human Rights* (Oxford, Clarendon Press, 1998) 142. See also Charles Moyer, 'The Role of Amicus Curiae in the Inter-American Court of Human Rights' in *La Corte Interamericana de Derechos Humanos: Estudios y Documentos* (San Jose, Instituto Interamericano de Derechos Humanos, 1985) and Jose Miguel Vivanco and Lisa Bhansali, 'Procedural Shortcomings in the Defense of Human Rights: An Inequality of Arms' in Harris and Livingstone (eds), *The Inter-American System of Human Rights* (1998) 436.

For an example of a brief submitted to the Inter-American Court, see Patrick Macklem and Ed Morgan, 'Indigenous Rights in the Inter-American System: The Amicus Brief of the Assembly of First Nations in *Awas Tingni v Republic of Nicaragua*' (2000) 22(2) *Human Rights Quarterly* 569.

[119] Shelton, 'The Participation of Non-governmental Organisations' (1994) 640.

Furthermore, the Inter-American Commission has relaxed rules of standing which provide that NGOs may petition it in relation to human rights violations on behalf of others; it does not have the victim-hood requirement that operates to prevent this happening in applications to the ECtHR.[120] Strikingly, the Center for Justice and International Law (CEJIL), an NGO based in Washington DC, claim that their docket consists of over 200 cases in the Inter-American system. They further claim to act 'as representatives of the victims and as legal advisers to the Commission, in practically all the cases pending before the Court'.[121] This, needless to say, indicates a remarkable level of NGO activity within the Inter-American human rights system.

Kwado Appiagyei-Atua notes that Article 10 of the African Charter, which provides for freedom of association for everyone 'provided he abides by the law', is 'antithetical to NGO flourishing'.[122] Nonetheless, NGOs have been at the heart of the African Charter system from its conception.[123] The African Charter on Human and Peoples' Rights appears not to restrict its Commission's competence *ratione personae*,[124] and perusal of a collection of the Commission's decisions (dated between 1994 and 1999) reveals that the vast majority of communications under that treaty originate from NGOs, both national and international.[125] The recently operational African Court on Human and Peoples' Rights is empowered to receive cases referred by individuals and by NGOs with observer status before the African Commission on Human and Peoples' Rights, provided the State concerned has made a declaration accepting this procedure.[126] Furthermore,

> the Court may receive written and oral evidence including expert testimony and it shall make its decision on the basis of such evidence,

---

[120]   Art 44, American Convention on Human Rights (1969).

[121]   Information obtained for www.cejil.org.
On the role of NGOs in the landmark disappearance cases before the Commission and Court, see Juan E Mendez and Jose Miguel Vivanco, 'Disappearances and the Inter-American Court: Reflections on a Litigation Experience' (1990) 13 *Hamline Law Review* 507.

[122]   Kwadi Appiagyei-Atua, 'Human Rights NGOs and their Role in the Promotion and Protection of Rights in Africa' (2002) 9 *International Journal on Minority and Group Rights* 265, 278.

[123]   Chidi Anselm Odinkalu and Camilla Christensen, 'The African Commission on Human and Peoples' Rights: the Development of its Non-State Communication Procedures' (1998) 20 *Human Rights Quarterly* 235.

[124]   Art 55, African Charter on Human and Peoples' Rights (1981). Art 56, however, provides for some requirements as to the admissibility of applications that have not been introduced by State parties.

[125]   Institute for Human Rights and Development, *Compilation of Decisions on Communications of the African Commission on Human and Peoples' Rights Extracted from the Commission's Activity Reports 1994–1999* (Banjul, Institute for Human Rights and Development, 1999).

[126]   The Protocol to the African Charter on Human and Peoples' Rights on the Establishment of an African Court on Human and Peoples' Rights (1988) entered into force on 15 January 2004 having received the necessary fifteen ratifications.

which at least opens up the possibility of admitting NGOs as third-party interveners.[127] Abdelsam Mohamed, doubtless influenced by the significant contribution that NGOs have made to the promotion of international human rights law, sees these provisions as 'a welcome innovation'.[128] He concludes his powerful analysis of the importance of NGOs to African human rights litigation by noting that if the Court 'does not open up to … NGO participation, it might be guilty of clinging to an outmoded view of human rights adjudication'.[129]

V.   Beyond Individualism: A Fresh Approach to the European Convention on Human Rights

NGOs are now widely acknowledged to be the life-blood of international human rights, acting to highlight human rights abuses, pressing for new human rights norms to be recognised, and applying considerable pressure to bring about political and legal reform. Yet, the divide between the study of human rights in the fields of international relations and international law, which has now been traversed by many authors writing about the human rights mechanisms of the United Nations, retains considerable importance in scholarly understanding of the ECHR. The vast literature on the ECHR – almost wholly written by legal academics – is remarkable for its continued focus on 'lawyer's law', which, as Upendra Baxi argues, 'can scarcely exhaust sources of meaning and movement in human rights'.[130] The Court's individual application procedure is usually subjected to legal, as opposed to social or political, analysis: in the academic separation of law and politics, the Court's litigation falls readily into the former category. As a result of the discussion in this chapter, however, it is suggested that there is scope to subject the ECHR mechanisms to analysis in which the role of social movements in shaping and realising the Convention's rights is brought into light.

Lawyerly analysis of the ECHR provides little room for consideration of the role of politically-motivated actors such as NGOs, within the Court's procedures. Felix Ermacora's linkage of the individual petition procedure to the dearth of NGO activity is typical:

---

[127]   Art 26(2).

[128]   Abdelsam Mohamed, 'Individual and NGO Participation in Human Rights Litigation before the African Court of Human and Peoples' Rights: Lessons from the European and Inter-American Courts of Human Rights' (1999) 43 *Journal of African Law* 201, 201.

[129]   *ibid*, 212–13. For a more cautious view of the role of NGOs in the African context see Chidi Odinkalu, 'Back to the Future: The Imperative of Prioritizing for the Protection of Human Rights in Africa' (2003) 47 *Journal of African Law* 1.

[130]   Baxi, *The Future of Human Rights* (2002) v.

From the very outset it must be stated that the influence of NGOs is diminishing with the increased use made of the individual petition system and the closed meetings within that system. When individual cases are dealt with and when the individual has a right to participate in proceedings before international bodies, the fact that a concrete case and not a situation is at issue diminishes the influence of NGOs … Since the real petition proceedings are adversarial and since the international body may not be able to base its opinion on all available sources, the material of NGOs has only a limited value in this type of procedure.[131]

Similarly, in an article on the contribution of NGOs to international human rights procedures, Weissbrodt deals with their role in relation to the ECHR with the following sentence: 'Nongovernmental organizations have not been particularly active in fostering individual applications to the European Commission of Human Rights'.[132] However, a study of the (albeit limited) existing literature on NGOs and the ECtHR, which is discussed in detail in the following chapter, gives some indication that NGOs are in fact active in litigation before the ECtHR.

Understanding the socio-political dimensions of the Court's function is imperative because the Court, as a number of commentators have noted, appears to be increasingly taking on a role akin to that of a constitutional court.[133] The earliest identification of the wider role that the ECtHR might play was in an inter-State case (for which there is no victim-hood requirement). The collective enforcement of the inter-State proceedings was said by the Court to serve 'the public order of Europe'.[134] In the case of *Ireland v United Kingdom*, the Court held:

---

[131] Ermacora, 'Non-Governmental Organizations' (1998) 174. Di Rattalma makes a similar point, arguing that as the rights in the ECHR are individualistic, increased NGO involvement would represent an interference with the essential nature of the Convention. See Marco Frigessi di Rattalma, 'NGOs before the European Court of Human Rights: Beyond *Amicus Curiae* Participation?' in Treves (ed), *Civil Society, International Courts* (2005).

[132] Weissbrodt, 'The Contribution of International Nongovernmental Organizations' (1984) 425. This statement was expressly reaffirmed in a 1996 study by Marek Nowicki, 'NGOs before the European Commission and Court of Human Rights' (1996) 14(3) *Netherlands Quarterly of Human Rights* 289, 301.
Charnovitz in his studies of the NGOs and international law passes over the ECHR with only a brief reference to NGOs as victims. See Charnovitz, 'Nongovernmental Organizations and International Law' (2006) 354.

[133] See: Rudolf Berhardt, 'Human Rights and Judicial Review: The European Court of Human Rights' in David M Beatty (ed), *Human Rights and Judicial Review: A Comparative Perspective* (Dordrecht, Kluwer, 1994); Rolv Ryssdal, 'On the Road to a European Constitutional Court' (1992) 12 *Collected Courses of the Academy of European Law* 1; Colin Warbrick, '"Federal" Aspects of the European Convention on Human Rights' (1989) 10 *Michigan Journal of International Law* 698; Steven Greer, The European Convention on Human Rights: Achievements, Problems and Prospects (Cambridge, Cambridge University Press, 2006); Steven Greer, 'What's Wrong with the European Convention on Human Rights?' (2008) 30 *Human Rights Quarterly* 680.
The Court itself has referred to the Convention as a constitutional 'instrument of European public order' on several occasions. See, for example, *Loizidou v Turkey* (preliminary objections) Series A no 310 (1995) 20 EHRR 99 [75] and *Cyprus v Turkey* ECHR 2001-IV, (2002) 35 EHRR 30 [78].

[134] *Austria v Italy* (dec) (1961) 4 *Yearbook of the European Convention on Human Rights* 116, 140.

The Court's judgments in fact serve not only to decide those cases brought before the Court but, more generally, to elucidate, safeguard and develop the rules instituted by the Convention, thereby contributing to the observance by the States of the engagements undertaken by them as Contracting Parties.[135]

That there might be an interest beyond that of an individual applicant in pursuing a case was also acknowledged in the case of *Tyrer v United Kingdom*, in which the applicant's request to withdraw his claim was refused by the Commission (a decision upheld by the Court) on the grounds that the case 'raised questions of a general character affecting the observance of the Convention which necessitated a further examination of the issues involved'.[136] Furthermore, the concept of 'indirect victim-hood' has been recognised by the Court in so far as family members are entitled to pursue cases on behalf of victims who are unable to do so themselves because of death or incapacity.[137] This concept was extended more recently in the 2003 case of *Karner v Austria*,[138] in which the applicant had died whilst his case was advancing through the Strasbourg procedures and left no heirs wishing to pursue his claim. The Court, clearly desirous to deliver judgment in a case that it considered to be of general importance, held that the victim-hood criterion should not be applied 'in a rigid, mechanical and inflexible way throughout the whole proceedings'.[139] Its judgment appears to favour a wider understanding of the Court's function than the mere resolution of individual violations of the Convention:

> Although the primary purpose of the Convention system is to provide individual relief, its mission is also to determine issues on public-policy grounds in the common interest, thereby raising the general standards of protection of human rights and extending human-rights jurisprudence throughout the community of Convention States.[140]

These cases suggest that the Court is increasing gaining confidence in dealing with complex issues of general importance and is beginning to take a less restrictive view of the interests involved in litigation before it. As this (controversial) role gains in prominence, it will doubtless be more readily accepted that the Court has an important role, beyond that of delivering individual justice, in shaping European society.

Furthermore, the centrality of NGOs to the UN system gives some indication that there might be a practical imperative for facilitating the role of NGOs in the ECtHR system if we are to take the protection of human rights in Europe

---

[135]   *Ireland v United Kingdom* Series A no 25 (1979–80) 2 EHRR 25 [154].

[136]   *Tyrer v United Kingdom* Series A no 26 (1979–80) 2 EHRR 1 [24]–[25].

[137]   See, for example, *Deweer v Belgium* Series A no 35 (1979–80) 2 EHRR 439 [37]–[38]; *X v UK* Series A no 46 (1982) 4 EHRR 188 [32]; *Vocaturo v Italy* (App no 11891/85) ECHR 24 May 1991, Series A no 206-C [2]; and for a decision refusing to continue a hearing on an applicant's death see *Scherer v Switzerland* (App no 17116/90) ECHR 25 March 1994, Series A no 287 [31]–[32].

[138]   *Karner v Austria* (App no 40016/98) ECHR 24 July 2003 (2004) 38 EHRR 24.

[139]   *ibid*, para 1.

[140]   *ibid*, para 26. See also *Malhous v Czech Republic* (dec) (App no 33071/96) ECHR 2001-XII.

seriously. In recognising the significance of NGO participation in human rights litigation, we might begin to question whether such participation is sufficiently facilitated in the current practice of the Court. It is often commented that liberalism is not programmatic; that it is an ideology without a method. Indeed, it is rather counter-intuitive for States to provide the means for their citizens to achieve liberty. Even if one fully respects human rights norms/laws (as they are currently understood), one still needs to address the question of how those rights can best be realised. Although the Convention's mechanisms have been much lauded, it is possible that there has been confusion between expressing ends (the protection of human rights) and the best means by which to achieve these ends (the individual). Certainly, experience suggests there are very good practical reasons for not isolating victims of rights violations if one is seeking to ensure effective compliance with human rights standards.

VI. Conclusion

In this chapter I have suggested that liberal individualism dominated the Council of Europe's vision in the post-World Wars period and continues to inform much of our understanding of the Convention's mechanisms. However, it has been argued in this chapter that an individualistic account of the Court's litigation may well have too many limitations. It is widely-recognised that social actors such as NGOs play a vital role in activating the law's cumbersome apparatus, and it seems perfectly coherent to question whether, given the multi-faceted and pluralistic nature of many questions dealt with by the ECtHR, NGOs play a central role in activating the Court's machinery and shaping its litigation. In the following chapters I turn to socio-legal enquiry to explore whether envisaging the Court's litigation as a site of 'epic battle' between individual and State has impeded full understanding of the Convention. In particular, I examine the role that 'communities of resistance'[141] – in the form of NGOs – play in the Court's litigation. The theories discussed in this chapter have at least provided a key to open the door through which this exploration begins.

---

[141] Baxi, *The Future of Human Rights* (2002) vi.

3

The Role of NGOs in ECHR Litigation

'It is possible to take a Supreme Court decision, in which nothing appears on the surface but finespun points of law, and cut through all the dialectic till we get down to the actual groups of men underlying the decisions and producing the decisions through the differentiated activity of the justices'.[1]

I. Introduction

THIS RESEARCH INITIALLY raised basic questions about the nature and incidence of NGO involvement in ECtHR cases. The first part of this chapter examines the current literature on the role of NGOs before the ECtHR. The insights and gaps therein proved an invaluable guide to the formulation of this research project. The aim of the second part of this chapter, which presents a statistical overview of NGO participation in a sample of ECHR cases, is to reveal the number of NGOs that were involved in those cases and the form that their involvement in litigation took. Setting out this information is important because the quantitative data that is currently available, in particular concerning 'informal' NGO participation in ECHR litigation, is sparse. Having identified the NGOs that participated in the sample cases, I go on to consider whether patterns can be discerned relating to the types of NGOs involved in the sample cases, and the types of cases in which they were involved.

A further aim of this chapter is to begin to develop a satisfactory explanation for the patterns of NGO involvement that emerge from the sample cases. Quantitative analysis has a role to play in testing, and perhaps modifying, the theoretical approach underpinning this research project; in particular, it is a useful means of determining if the prevalence of NGO involvement in ECtHR cases is significant enough to support the non-individualistic model of human

---

[1] Arthur F Bentley, *The Process of Government: A Study of Social Pressures* (Evanston, Principia, 1908) 205.

rights litigation that was outlined in chapter two. It can also serve to guide the researcher as to where subsequent case studies can be usefully focused. In short, with the statistical data presented in this chapter it is possible to begin to sketch the outlines of the research findings; the results of the qualitative analysis, which are set out in subsequent chapters, add depth, colour and perspective to this picture.

II. The Current Literature on NGOs and the ECHR

Upendra Baxi notes that the 'communities of resistance' discussed in the previous chapter are demoted 'to a lowly status' by standard scholarship.[2] While we have seen that this is now less true of international human rights scholarship in general, it is certainly still true of ECHR scholarship, which remains almost exclusively the preserve of lawyers who pay little attention to the social and political contexts in which cases arise. The contrast between our knowledge of NGO activity under the ECHR and other international human rights mechanisms is striking. Nevertheless, while comparatively little attention has been paid to NGO activity in cases brought under the ECHR, there is a small body of literature written on this subject that can operate as a useful starting point to understand the ways in which NGOs are participating in ECHR litigation and suggest gaps in current knowledge that might usefully be filled.[3] It is to this literature that I now turn.

A. Legal Studies

Legal academics have begun to shed light on the type of NGO participation in litigation that is formally recognised within the Court's procedures. In particular, their work has pointed to the importance of NGOs as third party interveners. By virtue of Article 36(2) of the Convention, the Court may, 'in the interests of the proper administration of justice', invite written or oral comments from 'any person concerned'.[4] This can, of course, include NGOs. Although interveners are

---

[2] Upendra Baxi, *The Future of Human Rights* (New Delhi, Oxford University Press, 2002) vi.

[3] With regard to NGOs and the Council of Europe, see Andrew Drzemczewski, 'The Role of NGOs in Human Rights Matters in the Council of Europe' (1987) 8 *Human Rights Law Journal* 273. The Council of Europe provides International NGOs with the opportunity of acquiring participatory status, the rules of which are governed by Committee of Ministers' Resolution (2003) 8. There are currently over 400 organisations that have taken advantage of this, which collectively make up the Conference of International Non-Governmental Organisations of the Council of Europe.

[4] Article 36(2) reads: 'The President of the Court may, in the interests of the proper administration of justice, invite any High Contracting Party which is not a party to the proceedings or any person concerned who is not the applicant to submit written comments or take part in hearings'.

not formal parties to the proceedings and their influence over proceedings is minimal, a number of organisations have taken on this role in an effort to shape the Court's case law.

The possibility of the Court accepting such interventions was first formally recognised under the revised Rules of Court adopted on 24 November 1982, although in practice interventions were accepted before this.[5] Writing on this development in 1990, Anthony Lester noted that it provided 'new and important opportunities for third parties' to participate in the Court's litigation.[6] Although he does not comment upon it directly, Lester's study reveals that each of the five successful requests to intervene under the new Rules of Court at that time had come from NGOs.[7]

Dinah Shelton highlighted a similar pattern some four years later in her study of NGO participation in international judicial proceedings. Shelton's data reveals that of the 25 applications to intervene before the ECtHR up to that time, all but three had come from NGOs.[8] Amongst those she identifies as making a request to the Court were Amnesty International (twice, successfully); 'Article 19' (four times, successfully); and Interights (three times; each jointly and each successfully). Shelton's statistics on interventions suggest that in the years since Lester's study, high-profile human rights NGOs had begun to recognise the potential that intervening in ECHR litigation offered. From the emerging patterns, Shelton is able to draw some conclusions about the significance of NGO involvement in ECtHR litigation:

> Because nongovernmental organizations intervene in the more important cases before the plenary Court, where there is no clear precedent and where the Court may be divided, they fulfil a role of assisting the Court in new areas of law where the impact is particularly broad. They provide comparative law analysis and practical information that the parties may be unable to marshal and the Court would otherwise be unable to acquire, thus facilitating the decision-making process.[9]

---

[5] For more information, see Paul Mahoney, 'Developments in the Procedure of the European Court of Human Rights: The Revised Rules of Court' (1983) 3 *Yearbook of European Law* 127.
On third party interventions in particular, see Anthony Lester, 'Amici Curiae: Third-Party Interventions Before the European Court of Human Rights' in Franz Matscher and Herbert Petzold (eds), *Protecting Human Rights: The European Dimension* (Koln, Carl Heymanns Verlag KG, 1990) 341–50 and Olivier De Schutter, 'Sur l'émergence de la société civile en droit international: le role des associations devant la Cour européenne des droits de l'homme' (1996) 7 *European Journal of International Law* 372.

[6] Lester, 'Amici Curiae' (1990) 341.

[7] The NGOs in question were the Post Office Engineering Union, MIND, the International Press Institute (in association with Interights), JUSTICE and the Rome Bar Association.

[8] Dinah Shelton, 'The Participation of Non-governmental Organizations in International Judicial Proceedings' (1994) 88 *American Journal of International Law* 611.

[9] Shelton, 'The Participation of Non-Governmental Organizations' (1994) 638. See also Abdelslam Mohamed, 'Individual and NGO Participation in Human Rights Litigation before the African Court of Human and Peoples' Rights: Lessons from the European and Inter-American Courts of Human Rights' (1999) 43 *Journal of African Law* 201.

The data in Lester and Shelton's studies has subsequently been up-dated by information provided by the Court itself. In 1998 the Court provided statistics for third party interventions during its first 40 years of activity (information which it had not previously provided and which it has not subsequently made available on a consistent basis).[10] From these comprehensive statistics it can be established that by the end of 1998 there had been at least 80[11] requests to intervene made in 58 cases (which included three requests made before the Court's rules were adapted to formally allow interventions).[12] Of these, 67 were made by NGOs. In sum, while the practice is not extensive, the vast majority of interventions before the ECtHR have come from NGOs.

More recently, Anna-Karin Lindblom's excellent and extremely detailed legal analysis of NGOs in international law offers valuable data on formal participation (but pays little attention to informal participation).[13] She names 36 cases before the 'old' court in which NGOs submitted third party interventions (the most active interveners were Amnesty International, Article 19, Interights, Liberty and Rights International). Again, this is not a substantial number given that the total number of judgments delivered by the old court was 1009. From November 1998 to September 2004, she found, NGOs intervened in 31 cases. Hinting at a possible reason for such a relatively modest number of interventions, Lindblom reveals that the contents of the amicus briefs were not referred to in the final judgment in 29 of those cases.[14] She also suggests that the Court's current approach to interventions is rather formulaic; their contents are outlined in a discrete section of the judgment, but no mention of them is made in the evaluative sections.[15] She also contends that briefs submitted by well-established NGOs 'seem to be more seriously considered by the Court'.[16] Although the evidence for this assertion seems somewhat scant, Lindblom nonetheless raises here an interesting question about the nature and effectiveness of interventions before the Court. Lindblom's focus on formal participation also enables her to look at NGOs as victims of ECHR violations. She reveals that of all cases in which the Court delivered judgment up to 2003, 'at least' 29 were brought by NGOs in

---

[10] Council of Europe, *Survey: Forty Years of Activity 1959–1998* (Strasbourg, Council of Europe, 1998) 134–7. The more recent survey, *50 Years of Activity: The European Court of Human Rights, Some Facts and Figures* (available from the Court's website at: www.echr.coe.int) does not contain this information. The annual section activity reports from 2002–07 contain some limited information about third party interventions, but these are no longer produced.

[11] This figure is reached if joint applications to intervene are treated as a single application. It is not always clear from the Court's statistics if applications have been made jointly or individually; where this is the case I have treated it as a joint-application to avoid inflating the figures.

[12] This figure is reached if joined cases are treated as one case.

[13] Anna-Karin Lindblom, *Non-Governmental Organisations in International Law* (Cambridge, Cambridge University Press, 2005).

[14] *ibid*, 328–45.

[15] *ibid*, 343.

[16] *ibid*, 345.

their own name, most of which related to interferences with freedom of association, assembly and expression.[17] This rather low figure stands testimony to the
impact of the ECHR's restrictive approach to the Convention's victim-hood
requirement.

Alongside the collection of statistical data, the process of reflecting on the role
and impact of NGOs has tentatively begun. A collection of essays published in
2005, *Civil Society, International Courts and Compliance Bodies*, offers some
assessment of NGO involvement before the ECtHR, primarily from the perspective of lawyers. However, Marco Frigessi di Rattalma's contribution suggests there
is a continued attachment to liberal individualism that still prevents legal
academics concerned with the ECHR from taking NGOs very seriously as an
object of study:

> The strong individual nature of the rights enshrined in the European Convention
> entails the consequence that as a rule, only the victim of the violation of the rights
> should have the procedural right to bring action.[18]

Thus, to extend genuine interest to the role of NGOs in litigation is to challenge
the individualism that lies at the heart of much ECHR scholarship. While this
collection of essays does make some attempts to break from the traditional
mould of ECHR scholarship, ultimately the dominant view expressed therein is
that NGOs' legitimacy is only ensured if they recognise and accept the constraints
under which they operate in the legal sphere. NGOs can potentially be useful,
these essays suggest, provided they act as *servants* of the law and its institutions.
Judge Vajic, for example, noting the growth of NGO involvement in ECHR
litigation, writes:

> In the current situation where the ECHR is faced with an enormous volume of clearly
> inadmissible cases, it is particularly important that NGOs do act responsibly and do not
> create unjustified expectations for applicants whose hopes will inevitably be frus-
> trated.[19]

This vision of a 'tamed' and compliant civil society is very different from that
presented by political scientists and sociologists, and raises interesting questions
for this study about the nature of the relationship between NGOs and the
institutions with which they interact and the nature of the ECtHR as a human
rights institution.

---

[17] *ibid*, 253–4.

[18] Marco Frigessi di Rattalma, 'NGOs Before the European Court of Human Rights: Beyond
Amicus Curiae Participation?' in Tullio Treves et al (eds), *Civil Society, International Courts and
Compliance Bodies* (Asser Press, The Hague, 2005) 63.

[19] Nina Vajic, 'Some Concluding Remarks on NGOs and the European Court of Human Rights' in
Treves et al (eds), *Civil Society* (2005).

B. Inter-disciplinary and Non-legal Studies

Inter-disciplinary and non-legal studies show how NGO activity criss-crosses between legal and non-legal strategies, without much care or concern for the boundaries cherished by lawyers. Thus, they highlight the importance of focusing research on NGO involvement beyond 'formal participation' in the Court's litigation, and they can also help us to understand what motivates the NGOs that participate in cases brought under the Convention. To this end, studies of individual NGOs are enlightening, as the following examples illustrate. Ann Marie Clark's study of Amnesty International's role in changing human rights norms reveals that the process of NGO engagement in ECHR litigation began almost immediately, with the Scandinavian countries relying on information provided to them by Amnesty International in their submissions in *The Greek Case*.[20] Dean Zagorac's study reveals that Amnesty had considerable involvement in the Court's work over a number of years, choosing to act as amicus in 10 cases between 1989–2003 in which the ECtHR 'was expected to rule on important legal principles'.[21]

One of the first NGOs to develop a litigation strategy that incorporated the ECHR was the National Association for Mental Health (MIND). The instigator of that strategy was Larry Gostin, an American who was MIND's legal director from 1975 to 1982.[22] In order to try to improve the situation of mental health patients in the United Kingdom, MIND filed several briefs before the European Commission on Human Rights. It is clear that MIND's aim in doing so was in part to impact upon the parliamentary process, and its litigation was central to the important law reforms introduced under the Mental Health (Amendment) Act 1982. The Joint Council for the Welfare of Immigrants (JCWI) was also quick to recognise the potential of ECtHR litigation to further its aims. Ian Martin wrote in a 1986 study of that organisation that, while it 'would be an exaggeration to say that a coherent test-case strategy has been developed', the JCWI was active in steering clients towards lawyers who could take their case to Strasbourg, thereby

---

[20] *The Greek Case* (1969) 12 YB 1. Ann Marie Clark, *Diplomacy of Conscience: Amnesty International and Changing Human Rights Norms* (Princeton, Princeton University Press, 2001) 40.

[21] Dean Zagorac, 'International Courts and Compliance Bodies: The Experience of Amnesty International' in Treves et al (eds), *Civil Society* (2005) 25.
Amnesty International did not intervene in any of the sample cases in this study. Zagorac suggests that this is because in 2000 the organisation's attention was focussed on the Pinochet litigation. However, it seems that Amnesty's formal involvement in cases before the Court has waned anyway in recent years. I have found only two cases since 2003 in which it intervened as a third party, and even then its name was simply joined to the intervention of another organisation. See *Ramzy v Netherlands* (dec) (App no 25424/05) 27 May 2008 and *A v Netherlands* (dec) (App no 4900/06) 17 November 2009.

[22] See Larry Gostin, *A Human Condition: The Law Relating to Mentally Abnormal Offenders: Observations, Analysis and Proposals for Reform* (London, MIND, 1977) and Larry Gostin, 'Contemporary Social Historical Perspectives on Mental Health Reform' (1983) 10 *Journal of Law and Society* 47.

allowing 'legal and campaigning strategies to be co-ordinated'.[23] Much has also been written about Liberty (formerly known as the National Council of Civil Liberties), from which it emerges that that organisation has taken numerous cases under the ECHR. I return to discuss this literature and Liberty's litigation strategy in greater depth in chapter five.

Stephen Grosz and Susan Hulton, in research published in 1986 on the use that the JCWI, Liberty and MIND made of the ECHR, shed further light on NGO litigation that aimed to challenge specific legislative provisions.[24] Their study is particularly useful in pointing to some of the drawbacks of test-case strategies from the perspective of NGOs themselves, and it highlights the rather mixed success that NGOs had in their early engagement with cases before the ECtHR. In the light of their findings, Grosz and Hulton argue that NGOs should not see ECtHR litigation as a panacea: it is time-consuming, costly and unpredictable because many of the factors that determine a case's 'success' are largely out of the organisation's control. Ultimately, however, they conclude that 'the Convention's cutting edge could be sharpened by procedural and institutional reforms, but for all its inadequacies it is, for a variety of reasons, an important weapon in the hands of legal reformers'.[25]

Although the studies discussed above are illuminating, they show that it would have been disadvantageous to adopt a purely qualitative approach for the purposes of this research. In particular, in terms of providing statistical information about the incidence of NGO involvement in litigation before the Court, a case study approach adopted in isolation is clearly unhelpful. The literature on individual NGOs is vast and primarily focused on larger NGOs: furthermore, it tends to pay only very limited attention to the question of law's transformative potential. Nevertheless, the studies discussed in this section offer an important reminder that in examining the meeting point of law and political movements the role of law should not be exaggerated. They also point to the value of examining the wider context to NGOs' litigation activities and the rich potential of taking an inter-disciplinary and qualitative approach to this research.

A small number of inter-disciplinary studies have attempted to use quantitative methods to provide a comprehensive picture of the scale of NGO involvement in ECHR litigation. Carol Harlow and Richard Rawlings, whose research interest is in the meeting-point of law and political science, dedicate a few pages of their study on the role of pressure groups in the British legal system to cases

---

[23] Ian Martin, 'Combining Casework and Strategy: The Joint Council for the Welfare of Immigrants' in Jeremy Cooper and Rajeev Dhavan (eds), *Public Interest Law* (Oxford, Basil Blackwell, 1986) 266.

[24] The particular examples these authors explore are MIND, the NCCL and The Joint Council for the Welfare of Immigrants.

[25] Stephen Grosz and Susan Hulton, 'Using the European Convention on Human Rights' in Cooper and Dhavan (eds), *Public Interest Law* (1986) 155.

brought under the ECHR.[26] Their study was of particular assistance in developing the methodology for this project because its authors do not confine themselves to consideration of formal participation by 'pressure groups' in the Commission and Court's proceedings. The authors compile a list of 13 organisations that were involved or sought to be involved – either formally or otherwise – in 16 cases heard by the Court between 1970 and 1984 (their methodology is not fully explained).[27] Only four of these cases involved a formal request to intervene. Harlow and Rawlings's findings show that taking a wide approach to NGO participation is useful because pressure groups 'sponsor cases' (which the authors define as 'active support including representation and not merely help with funding'[28]) with much greater frequency than they formally intervene in cases.[29] This highlights the importance of considering 'informal' NGO involvement in litigation in this research. Harlow and Rawlings found, however, that 'no accurate statistical profile of [informal] group involvement … is possible', not least because the 'Commission is not always aware of group involvement and the official reports do not usually record it'.[30] Nevertheless, their study concludes with an observation that is extremely encouraging for this research project:

> It is on the European scene that the authors confidently expect the main developments. As we started to write, the focus of attention was the European Convention on Human Rights, a document grounded in legal rights whose institutions provided the obvious forum for an American-style litigation strategy.[31]

Also influential in developing this research was a 1996 article by Marek Nowicki, in which the author develops a coherent justification for encouraging the participation of NGOs in ECHR proceedings.[32] Nowicki's study provides an in-depth analysis of the role of NGOs as victims of a violation of the Convention themselves, and points to a set of precedents that suggest the Commission was reluctant to allow NGOs to take cases on behalf of members.[33] Although he

---

[26]   Carol Harlow and Richard Rawlings, *Pressure Through Law* (London, Routledge, 1992) 254–68.

[27]   *ibid*, 257.

[28]   *ibid*.

[29]   See also the Public Law Project's secondary findings in relation to 'informal interventions' by public interest organisations in judicial review proceedings in England and Wales in *Third Party Interventions in Judicial Review: An Action Research Study* (London, Public Law Project, 2001) 21–2.

[30]   Harlow and Rawlings, *Pressure Through Law* (1992) 255.

[31]   *ibid*, 321.

[32]   Marek Nowicki, 'NGOs before the European Commission and the Court of Human Rights' (1996) 14(3) *Netherlands Quarterly of Human Rights* 289.

[33]   For case-law on this point see: *Union of Air Hostesses & Others v Greece* (App no 19634/92), Commission decision of 20 February 1995 (unreported); *X Union v France* (App no 9900/82), Commission decision of 4 May 1983, 32 DR 261; *Association X and 165 liquidators and court appointed administrators v France* (App no 9939/82), Commission decision of 4 July 1983, 34 DR 213; *G Hodgson, D Woolf Productions Ltd, National Union of Journalists, Channel Four Television Co Ltd v UK* (App no 11553/85), Commission decision of 9 March 1987, 51 DR 136.
Reluctance to allow NGOs to litigate on behalf of their members extends to human rights organisations. See *Nineteen Chilean nationals and the S Association v Sweden* (App nos 9959/82 and 10357/83), Commission decision of 14 March 1984, 37 DR 87.

mentions the role that NGOs can play as third parties to proceedings, he does not explore this in any detail. Nowicki's study also shows the important 'behind the scenes' role NGOs play representing victims before the Court, finding representatives to pursue cases, providing support and advising applicants, and compiling reports that the Court relies upon for information.[34] In relation to this last point, he argues that it is the experience that NGOs bring to litigation that is important, not least because it 'helps to *reduce the inequality of parties to proceedings*'.[35] Nowicki suggests that NGOs can fill in gaps where lawyers lack knowledge about the Convention,[36] and he further suggests that they can increase efficiency by deterring people who come to them for assistance from pursuing cases that are manifestly inadmissible.[37] He concludes that NGOs are 'among the basic conditions of existence and sources of power of all systems of human rights protection, both within the individual States and at the international level' and he describes them as 'advocates of truth and honesty in relations between the State and its agencies on the one hand and the individual'.[38] It was Nowicki's tentative insights that indicated most clearly to me the scope for more detailed investigation of these issues.

Despite the limited role that the Convention envisages for NGOs within the context of its bi-partisan model of litigation, the literature that is currently available suggests that NGOs have nevertheless began to forge a role for themselves in the Court's procedures. However, the scholarly response to this development has been oddly muted: there has been little systematic analysis to see if patterns of NGO participation can be identified, and few conclusions have been drawn about the role that NGOs play in ECHR litigation. Furthermore, there is sparse qualitative research in the area. Finally, much of the data that is available is now somewhat out-dated. The studies discussed above offered the enticing suggestion that there was NGO activity taking place before the Court that warranted further, and more intense, analysis.

---

[34] Nowicki, 'NGOs before the European Commission' (1996) 293–4. He cites the example of the Association Francaise des Hémophiles, the Association de Défence des Transfusés, and the Association des Polytransfusés who supported numerous cases lodged against the French authorities by persons infected with HIV during a blood transfusion. See, for example, *X v France* Series A no 234-C (1992) 14 EHRR 483.

[35] *ibid*, 296.

[36] *ibid*, 300.

[37] *ibid*, 296.

[38] *ibid*, 291–2. See also Council of Europe, *Digest of Strasbourg Case-Law Relating to the European Convention on Human Rights*, vol 4 (Koln, Carl Heymanns Verlag KG, 1985) 355–6.

III. A Brief Outline of the Adopted Methodology

For the purposes of this research, the involvement of NGOs in ECHR litigation was explored using a two-stage process. The full methodology adopted is outlined in the appendix to this book for those who are interested in the detail. For the purposes of this chapter, a brief summary of the adopted methodology is provided.

During the first research stage, a sample of ECtHR cases was selected and analysed for incidence and type of NGO involvement (the quantitative stage). The aim was to obtain a systematic picture of the nature and frequency of NGO involvement in ECHR cases. Ultimately, the core of the research was based on data obtained from an analysis of cases in which the Court delivered judgment in 2000.[39] NGO involvement in a case – both formal and informal – was established though a variety of sources. Primarily, these were: the relevant judgments; the Court's case files; internet searches; direct requests to NGOs for information about their involvement in a case where this seemed likely. Importantly, this research stage can only be said to have identified a *minimum* level of NGO involvement and inevitably some NGO involvement in the sample cases was missed.

The initial quantitative research stage was followed by intense qualitative research based on case studies of those NGOs whose involvement in the sample cases had been identified. This took the form of semi-structured interviews conducted with key personnel from the relevant NGOs.[40] Given that the working languages of the Court are English and French, it was unsurprising that the NGOs contacted for the purposes of this research were able to communicate well in one of those languages and more often than not in English. Interviews were semi-structured in order not to impose any pre-conceptions on the interviewees about the significance of the organisation's participation in ECtHR litigation.[41] NGO employees tend to change jobs frequently, and occasionally there was nobody working within an organisation who had been involved in the sample case(s) in question. In such situations, the interview unavoidably was based on more generalised questions about the organisation's litigation strategy. In some

---

[39] Although this may appear to be a considerable restriction on the number of cases considered, the Court's statistics show that the number of judgments delivered in 2000 had risen dramatically from previous years and in fact represent 40% of the total number of judgments delivered by the Court up to that date. A full explanation can be found in the appendix.

[40] For a discussion of the value of using mixed-method research techniques and, in particular, following quantitative with qualitative methods, see Jane Ritchie, 'The Application of Qualitative Methods to Social Research' in Jane Ritchie and Jane Lewis (eds), *Qualitative Research Practice: A Guide for Social Science Students and Researchers* (London, Sage, 2003) 42–3.

[41] Interviews for the initial research project referred to in this chapter were undertaken with the ERRC's Executive Director, a Senior Staff Attorney and a Staff Attorney in September 2002. Interviews were undertaken with the KHRP's Executive Director, Legal Director and Translator in October and November 2002.

cases former employees of the relevant organisations were contacted in order to discuss their involvement in the sample cases.

Consulting the relevant organisations' documentation was a useful means of understanding the meaning that their litigation has to them. I sought access to their files on the relevant ECtHR case(s) in which their involvement had been identified. The reason for this request was to fill in gaps in memory that the passage of time would inevitably have created. While most NGOs were happy to agree to this request, a small number did not give me permission to access their files, citing reasons of client confidentiality. The organisations' publications were also a useful source of information, and these were scrutinised both for references to the particular sample cases in question and for more general references to their involvement in litigation. In general, the NGOs approached for the purpose of this study were open, helpful and keen to assist. The only reservations expressed were based on their limited time and the issue of client confidentiality.

IV. The Incidence of NGO Involvement in the Sample Cases

Ultimately, a sample of 149 cases in which the Court delivered judgment in 2000 was selected for the purposes of this research. That sample forms the basis of the statistical survey that follows. At this stage it is pertinent to note that the number of cases analysed below may not appear great when viewed from a quantitative perspective alone. However, this was inevitable because of the time-consuming nature of the research that was needed to discover the extent and forms of informal participation by NGOs, coupled with my desire to conduct a subsequent stage of in-depth qualitative research based on case studies drawn from the research sample.

A. The Total Number of Cases with NGO Involvement

Carol Harlow asserts that NGOs occupy a privileged position in international human rights litigation:

> The place of NGOs in international courts represents a halfway house between the inter-state legal proceedings of international law and the legal systems of nation states, invariably open to individuals. Their privileged role in the legal process derives from the inevitable problems of enforcing international law. The law enforcement function of NGOs has escalated with the introduction of human rights conventions and their attendant courts … The more proactive groups have developed sophisticated test case strategies and several are experienced 'repeat players'.[42]

---

[42] Carol Harlow, 'Public Law and Popular Justice' (2002) 65 *Modern Law Review* 1, 12.

However, my findings suggest that the role of NGOs should not be over-stated in relation to the proceedings of the ECtHR. Of the 149 sample cases, direct involvement by an NGO – whether formal or informal – could be clearly identified in 32 cases (that is, 21.5 per cent). The total number of NGOs involved in the sample cases was 17, and no more than two NGOs participated in any one case. This information is displayed in the table in Figure 1 below. In a further 19 cases there was some evidence that pointed to NGO involvement, but this could not be confirmed due to language difficulties and other practical considerations. It can therefore be established that although NGOs litigate in a significant number of ECtHR cases, a clear majority of cases do not attract NGO involvement. Consequently, certain preconceptions that I might have had at the commencement of this project about NGOs dominating the Court's litigation stand in need of modification.

B.   NGOs as Applicants

It was noted earlier that the Convention's victim-hood requirement has been interpreted in a way that limits the ability of organisations to submit applications on behalf of their members. It was therefore unsurprising that only two of the sample cases were brought directly by NGOs in their own names. One of these cases was a complaint under Article 6 (right to a fair trial), which related to the process by which the Hungarian authorities decided to refuse to allow an organisation to register itself under a particular (defamatory) name.[43] Another case, which was brought by a Jewish liturgical association claiming a violation of Articles 9 and 14 of the Convention, concerned the French authorities' refusal to grant approval to that organisation to carry out ritual slaughters in accordance with the religious prescriptions of its members.[44] Given that NGOs litigating before the Court in their own names can only do so in such limited circumstances, this aspect of the research findings does little to shed light on the broader theoretical concerns that are at the heart of this book.

C.   NGOs as Third-Party Interveners

Article 36(1) of the Convention gives a Contracting Party whose national is an applicant the *right* to submit written comments and to take part in hearings before the ECtHR. Article 36(2) further provides, it will be recalled, that the Court *may*, invite written comments or oral interventions from 'any High Contracting Party which is not a party to the proceedings or any person

---

[43]   *APEH Üldözötteinek Szövetsége and Others v Hungary* ECHR 2000-X, (2002) 34 EHRR 34.
[44]   *Cha'are Shalom Ve Tsedek v France* (App no 27417/95) ECHR 2000-VIII.

Figure 1: NGO involvement in the sample cases

Name of NGO	Nature of NGO's work	State NGO is based in	Respondent to NGOs litigation	No of Cases NGO was applicant in	No Of Cases NGO intervened in	No Of Cases NGO involved informally in	Total No of cases NGO involved in[1]
Advice on Individual Rights in Europe Centre	European Human Rights	UK	Austria; Romania	0	1	1	2
Association Consistoriale Israélite de Paris	Jewish Liturgical Association	France	France	0	1	0	1
APEH Üldözötteinek Szövetsége	Protestors Against Tax Authority	Hungary	Hungary	1	0	0	1
Bulgarian Helsinki Committee	Human Rights	Bulgaria	Bulgaria	0	0	3	3
Center for Justice in International Law	Human Rights in the Americas	USA	Turkey	0	1	0	1
Cha'are Shalom Ve Tsedek	Jewish Liturgical Association	France	France	1	0	0	1
European Roma Rights Centre	Roma Rights in Europe	Hungary	Bulgaria	.0	0	1	1
Iranian Refugee Alliance	Iranian Refugee Rights	USA	Turkey	0	0	1	1

[1] In many cases more than one NGO was involved in a case. Therefore this column, of course, does not add up to 32, the total number of cases in which there was direct NGO involvement.

Name of NGO	Nature of NGO's work	State NGO is based in	Respondent to NGOs litigation	No of Cases NGO was applicant in	No Of Cases NGO intervened in	No Of Cases NGO involved informally in	Total No of cases NGO involved in
JUSTICE	Civil Liberties	UK	UK	0	1	3	4
Kurdish Human Rights Project	Human Rights in Kurdish regions	UK	Turkey	0	0	11	11
Liberty	Human Rights	UK	UK	0	2	6	8
Perheen Suojelun Keskusliitto PESUEry	Family Rights	Finland	Finland	0	0	2	2
Prisoners' Advice Service	Prisoners' Rights	UK	UK	0	0	1	1
Reunite	Abducted Children	UK	Romania	0	1	0	1
Rights International	Human Rights	USA	Turkey	0	0	1	1
Stonewall	Gay and Lesbian Rights	UK	UK	0	0	1	1

concerned who is not the applicant'.[45] In practice, it is almost invariably the party seeking to intervene, rather than the Court itself, who initiates an intervention under Article 36(2). In total there were eight third-party interventions in the sample cases. Four of those interventions were made by NGOs that had a general interest in the issues raised by the litigation in question, which has consistently proven to be the most important type of intervention before the ECtHR.[46] Such submissions, which others have labelled 'public interest interventions',[47] can be distinguished from interventions submitted by individuals or NGOs who are perceived to be directly and personally affected by issues raised in the litigation. The latter form of intervention best describes two interventions that were made within the sample, one of which came from an NGO and another from an individual.[48] Interventions from High Contracting Parties were submitted in two of the sample cases.[49]

Statistics provided by the Court show that it received a similar number of interventions in 2000 as it did between 1996 and 1998, during which period there was an average of 9.67 interventions each year.[50] Therefore, there has not been a continuous growth in the practice of intervening before the ECtHR. Indeed, if the number of interventions received by the Court is expressed as a percentage of the number of judgments delivered in the same years, it can be said that the practice of intervening was actually in decline by 2000. For example, in 1996 the Court received 14 interventions and delivered 72 judgments. In that year, therefore, interventions were made in 19.4 per cent of cases in which the Court delivered a judgment. In 1997 this figure was 4.72 per cent, in 1998 it was 9.5 per cent, and in 2000 it was 1.1 per cent. This suggests that the number of 'important' cases of the sort that is likely to attract third-party interventions is relatively stable and unaffected by the rapid overall increase in the Court's caseload.

No more than one intervention from NGOs was submitted in any sample case, although on two occasions interventions were submitted by two organisations acting jointly. In total, six NGOs intervened in the sample cases. Cases in which the Court receives multiple requests from NGOs seeking leave to intervene – such as *McCann & Others v UK*,[51] in which five NGOs intervened, and *John Murray v*

---

[45]   Rule 9.2 of the Rules of the Committee of Ministers for the Supervision of the Execution of Judgments and of the Term of Friendly Settlements adopted on 10 May 2006 also enables the Committee of Ministers to receive any communication from NGOs regarding the execution of judgments.

[46]   For a list of interveners before the Court, see Council of Europe, *Survey: Forty Years* (1998) 134–7.

[47]   See Sarah Hannett, 'Third Party Intervention: In the Public Interest?' [2004] *Public Law* 128.

[48]   The Association Consistoriale Israélite de Paris and the Chief Rabbi of France both intervened on the side of the Government on a matter that arose out of disagreements within the French Jewish community over the correct interpretation of the requirements laid down in the Torah for the preparation of meat. See *Cha'are Shalom Ve Tsedek v France* (App no 27417/95) ECHR 2000-VIII.

[49]   Interventions were submitted by the Belgian and Turkish Governments.

[50]   Information obtained from Council of Europe, *Survey: Forty Years* (1998) 134–7.

[51]   *McCann and Others v United Kingdom*, Series A no 324 (1996) 21 EHRR 97.

UK,[52] in which six organisations intervened (neither of which fell within the sample) – appear to be exceptional. There is little data, therefore, to suggest that the 'affected group' hypothesis of third-party interventions, which argues that 'amicus briefs are efficacious because they signal to the Court that a wide variety of outsiders to the suit will be affected by the Court's decision',[53] has had much impact on ECtHR litigation. NGOs do provide joint submissions, but this appears to be based on the more limited rationale that this can add credibility to the information provided (because it emanates from a coalition of experts), rather than any notion that by being responsive to public opinion the Court's judgments gain a greater degree of legitimacy.[54] As a point of contrast, it is interesting to note that Kearney and Merrill report growing numbers of US Supreme Court cases attracting high numbers of interventions (a case with 78 interventions submitted by a collection of over 400 organisations is cited by those authors as the 'record-setter').[55]

Interventions before the ECtHR tend to be drawn from a surprisingly narrow pool of NGOs. The sample shows that British NGOs are by far the most prolific 'public interest interveners', a finding that is consistent with the information available for interventions in previous years. Four of the six NGOs that intervened in the sample were based in the United Kingdom. The Center for Justice and International Law (CEJIL), whose main offices are in Washington DC, intervened at the request of the Kurdish Human Rights Project (KHRP), which is based in London and was funding the litigation in question. Three of the four British organisations that intervened in the sample cases have a particular orientation towards human rights *laws* – the Advice on Individual Rights in Europe Centre (AIRE Centre), Liberty and JUSTICE – and have intervened before the Court on several other occasions.

The sample cases suggest that Lester's hope, expressed in 1990, that 'the practice [of intervening before the ECtHR] will become more widespread and that the Court will actively encourage the use of the new procedure'[56] has not been fully realised. This is somewhat surprising, given the various reasons that can be put forward for organisations to adopt this means of participating in litigation. In particular, third party interventions can influence the outcome of a case by strengthening the legal and policy arguments in an unsatisfactory party brief, providing technical information and new material to the Court, presenting

---

[52] *John Murray v United Kingdom*, Judgments and Decisions 1996-I (1996) 22 EHRR 29.

[53] Paul M Collins Jr, 'Friends of the Court: Examining the Influence of Amicus Curiae Participation in U.S. Supreme Court Litigation' (2004) 38 *Law and Society Review* 807, 808.

[54] This was the rationale, for example, behind the joint-submission in the sample case of *Ignaccolo-Zenide v Romania* ECHR 2000-I, (2001) 31 EHRR 7. The AIRE Centre asked Reunite to jointly submit an intervention in that case on the basis of their expertise in child abduction, but Reunite was not actually involved in its drafting (telephone interview, Denise Carter, Director of Reunite, 9 May 2003).

[55] Joseph D Kearney and Thomas W Merrill, 'The Influence of Amicus Curiae Briefs on the Supreme Court' (1999–2000) 148 *University of Pennsylvania Law Review* 743, 755.

[56] Lester, 'Amici Curiae' (1990) 350.

'risky' arguments that a party may not want to raise, and providing evidence of popular support for a particular position.[57] It is worth adding that while the primary reason for an NGO to intervene will undoubtedly be to influence the outcome of litigation, interventions can also be motivated by an organisation's 'secondary goals'. Collins notes that interventions can be a means of publicly demonstrating a group's industriousness on issues, they can build credibility and status, and consequently funding potential, and joint interventions can help organisations to build relationships with one another.[58]

Returning to the particularities of intervening before the ECtHR, it would seem to be an attractive option available to NGOs because it is a relatively cheap way to participate in litigation. The Registry does not charge third party interveners a fee, and costs are not awarded against them if their arguments are unsuccessful. Furthermore, the Court does not appear to discourage interventions: indeed, within the sample cases no request from an NGO seeking leave to intervene was refused.[59] During interview, one of the Section Registrars described the Court as having 'a healthy practice' of interventions that 'we're doing our best to promote'.[60] Although he admitted that judges and Member States had previously been somewhat uncertain about the value of interventions, he noted that the old court had nevertheless 'built-up' a practice of accepting interventions that was being maintained by the new Chambers.[61] Given the nature of this research, which focuses on those organisations that have actually been involved in the Court's litigation, it is not possible to conclusively explain why for all but a handful of NGOs intervening in ECHR litigation is a course that is rarely pursued. Nevertheless, this question merits some consideration, however speculative.

In the context of judicial review applications in England and Wales, the Public Law Project has identified a lack of knowledge about the procedure as one cause of the low numbers of interventions.[62] This argument would appear to be equally

---

[57] The vast literature on third party interventions in the US is enlightening. See, for example: Collins, 'Friends of the Court' (2004); Paul M Collins Jr, 'Lobbyists Before the U.S. Supreme Court: Investigating the Influence of Amicus Curiae Briefs' (2007) 60(1) *Political Research Quarterly* 55; Kearney and Merrill, 'The Influence of Amicus Curiae Briefs' (1999–2000); Gregory A Caldeira and John R Wright, 'Amici Curiae before the Supreme Court: Who Participates, When, and How Much?' (1990) 52 *The Journal of Politics* 782; Lucius J Barker, 'Third Parties in Litigation: A Systematic View of the Judicial Function' (1967) 29 *The Journal of Politics* 41; Karen O'Connor, *Women's Organizations' Use of the Courts* (Lexington, Lexington Books, 1980).

[58] Collins, 'Friends of the Court' (2004) 807.

[59] The only request to intervene in a sample case that was not wholly successful was made in *Ignaccolo-Zenide v Romania* ECHR 2000-I, (2001) 31 EHRR 7, which concerned the non-return of abducted children. In that case the children that were the subject of the application sent their unsolicited thoughts about the case in a letter to the Court. Although their observations were out of time, they were left on file.

[60] Interview, Michael O'Boyle, Section Registrar, 4 September 2002, Strasbourg. See also Vajic, 'Some Concluding Remarks' (2005) 100–102.

[61] ibid.

[62] Public Law Project, *Third Party Interventions in Judicial Review* (2001).

applicable to interventions in Strasbourg. It has already been noted that interventions before the ECtHR have been the subject of little academic attention, and the studies that are available have almost invariably been conducted by lawyers. Furthermore, the Court has not issued clear guidelines outlining the circumstances in which it will accept interventions and the limitations that it is likely to impose upon them. It therefore seems logical to conclude that those organisations with legal expertise, and in particular those with a specialist knowledge of the ECHR, are best placed to take advantage of the intervention procedure. Other organisations, even those with a particular interest in and knowledge of the subject-matter of a case to be heard by the Court, are less likely to be aware of the possibilities that intervening offers.

NGOs obviously need to be aware of pending cases before they can establish if there are any in which they would wish to intervene. However, at the time that the sample cases were before the Court no system had been established by the Court's registry for providing publicly-available and comprehensive information about applications that are in the early stages of proceedings.[63] Consequently, by the time the Court had publicised information about an imminent judgment, there was little time for organisations to undertake the detailed work that effective intervention requires.[64] The Public Law Project noted that its findings tended 'to support the hypothesis that such information [about pending cases] is mainly obtained through informal networks that favour larger and better-resourced groups'.[65] This mundane reality, that it is important 'who you know' when it comes to intervening, is reflected in my research findings, which show that intervening is a practice that relies heavily upon informal channels of communication.

I have already referred to the fact that in one sample case CEJIL, an American human rights NGO, was invited to intervene by the organisation sponsoring the application.[66] Examining the background to the intervention in another of the sample cases, *Ignaccolo-Zenide v Romania*,[67] further highlights the significance of NGO networks. The AIRE Centre, a UK-based NGO that has been involved in several cases before the Court, was (informally) being sent information about certain pending cases by the Registry. When the AIRE Centre identified that a case concerning child-abduction was to be heard by the Court – which was an issue that it had a particular interest in – it arranged a joint intervention with Reunite, a British organisation that specialises in combating child-abduction.[68] The Court's registry has itself also been known to approach an NGO if they

---

[63] Recently, the Registry has begun to provide information about communicated cases at a much earlier stage of the process on the Court's website.

[64] This point was made by Eric Metcalfe, Director of Human Rights Policy of JUSTICE (interview, 10 April 2003, London).

[65] Public Law Project, *Third Party Interventions in Judicial Review* (2001) 24.

[66] *Timurtas v Turkey* ECHR 2000-VI, (2001) 33 EHRR 6.

[67] *Ignaccolo-Zenide v Romania* ECHR 2000-I, (2001) 31 EHRR 7.

[68] Interview, Nuala Mole, Director of AIRE Centre, 8 April 2003, London.

believe that an intervention from them would be useful. A notable example – although not one of the sample cases – was the case of *Christine Goodwin v UK*,[69] in which a refusal to alter the passport of a transsexual woman in order to reflect her new gender was held to be a violation of Article 8 (the right to respect for private and family life). Liberty was informally approached by the Court about the impending judgment and asked whether it would be seeking to intervene.[70] This request resulted from Liberty's earlier intervention in *Sheffield & Horsham v UK*,[71] in which it had provided the Court with a comparative survey relating to the legal position of transsexual people throughout the Member States. While establishing contacts and networks is clearly a crucial means for NGOs to hear about ECtHR cases that are suitable for intervening, this does mean that interventions tend to arise in a rather ad hoc way and tend to be drawn from a small pool of NGOs.

Other practical considerations might also have a bearing on whether NGOs choose to intervene. Although it is exceptional for the Court to hear oral arguments from the parties before delivering a judgment on the merits in cases submitted under the individual application procedure, oral hearings were in fact held in each of the sample cases in which a third-party intervened. Nevertheless, none of the NGOs that were granted leave to intervene in these cases was allowed to present its arguments orally, although both Liberty and the AIRE Centre sought leave to do so. Indeed, rule 44(2)(a) of the Court's current rules of procedure provides that permission to present oral arguments will be granted only 'in exceptional cases' to those parties that are invited to intervene by virtue of Article 36(2). Given that oral argument is an important tool of the advocate, this clearly has the potential to reduce the impact of the intervener's submissions. In addition, with one exception, the length of each of the interventions received from NGOs was subjected to a limit (usually of 10 pages). Whilst the purpose of this restriction is clear, it operates as a considerable restriction on those seeking to contribute to the development of the Court's jurisprudence through written comments. Finally, and consistently with the finding of Lindblom, the arguments of two of the interveners in the sample cases were not referred to at all in the subsequent judgments. In such circumstances NGOs can have little idea how persuasive their arguments have been, and consequently may feel uncertain about the utility of the procedure in furthering their aims.

Furthermore, intervening is inherently reactive and it offers organisations little control over how litigation develops. At the most fundamental level, an applicant might reach a friendly settlement after an intervention has been made, rendering the intervention pointless. Equally, an applicant may decide at any stage not to

---

[69]   *Christine Goodwin v United Kingdom* ECHR 2002-VI, (2002) 35 EHRR 18.
[70]   Interview, John Wadham, Director of Liberty, 20 January 2003, London.
[71]   *Sheffield & Horsham v United Kingdom* Reports of Judgments and Decisions 1998-V, (1999) 27 EHRR 163.

pursue an argument that an intervener considers to be of fundamental importance, or the Court may choose to simply ignore a point that an intervener has
raised. The decision to intervene is, as already noted, conditional upon identifying a suitable case in sufficient time. Although this has been made somewhat
easier since rule 44(2) of the Rules of the Court changed in November 2003 to
allow interventions from the moment a case is communicated (rather than after
it is declared admissible), in practice, the decision to intervene is still often, of
necessity, a last-minute one, which makes it inconsistent with the long-term
planning that is the hallmark of many NGO campaigns.

Finally, it is worth noting that 'public interest' interventions in cases before the
Court usually conform to what Kearney and Merrill refer to as the 'legal model',
which 'posits that Justices resolve cases in accordance with their understanding of
the requirements of the authoritative sources of law relevant to the question
presented'.[72] This model assumes that the contribution that interveners can make
to the reasoning in a case lies in their ability to present the Court with
high-quality 'legally relevant' argument, and not, for example, in their ability to
enhance the legitimacy of the Court's decision-making through increasing its
sensitivity to shifts in public opinion. Within the sample cases, NGOs presented
written comments relating to criminal law reforms in the United Kingdom, the
1980 Hague Convention on the Civil Aspects of International Child Abduction,
the jurisprudence of the Inter-American Court of Human Rights, and the
ECtHR's rules relating to the award of just satisfaction. The effectiveness of this
type of intervention is largely dependent upon the ability of the NGO to present
skillful and detailed legal research, and the limited subject-matter of interventions presumably reduces its relevance for organisations that do not have
specialist legal knowledge. In sum, a legal model has tended to inform and limit
understanding of the purpose of interventions before the ECtHR, and there is so
far little evidence that NGOs have explored the potential that might lie within
third-party interventions to significantly alter or expand the framework in which
ECHR cases are argued.[73]

D. NGOs as Informal Participants

Informal participation by an NGO was identified in 26 of the sample cases (17.45
per cent), and in five of those cases two NGOs were involved. In total, 12 NGOs
were informally involved in the sample cases. These research findings point to a
significant level of NGO activity in Strasbourg that takes place 'behind the
scenes'. Certainly, they provide support for Harlow and Rawlings's finding that a
wider and more diverse body of NGOs chose to involve themselves in ECtHR

---

[72] Kearney and Merrill, 'The Influence of Amicus Curiae Briefs' (1999–2000) 776.
[73] For a view that is critical of public interest interventions, see Hannett, 'Third Party Intervention' (2004).

litigation through informal rather than formal means.[74] The term 'informal participation' describes varying degrees of involvement in a case, which makes it particularly suited to the in-depth qualitative analysis of the subsequent three chapters. Nevertheless, while there is no 'typical' pattern to informal participation, some characteristics begin to emerge from the current analysis of the sample cases.

It is most common for an NGO involved informally in a case to represent an applicant directly. This was the situation with cases litigated by Liberty, the Prisoners' Advice Service, Rights International, the Iranian Refugee Alliance, the Bulgarian Helsinki Committee, PESUE (the Association for Family Rights in Finland) and the AIRE Centre. Both PESUE (in another sample cases in which it was involved) and Stonewall were described by the Court as the applicant's 'adviser', a designation which seems to indicate that both the 'adviser' and a separate – but co-operating – representative have communicated with the Court on the applicant's behalf.

Other NGOs adopt a 'co-ordinating' or 'intermediary' role, which is usually unacknowledged by the Court. This involves selecting and funding cases as part of a broad litigation strategy, while relying heavily upon external lawyers to represent applicants and to draft applications. Within the sample, this best describes the role played in litigation by both the KHRP and the European Roma Rights Centre (ERRC). Although NGOs that adopt this strategy often have little or no contact with the Court themselves, they obviously retain a considerable 'behind the scenes' involvement in the litigation.

Other types of informal participation were identified in the sample cases. In *Rowe & Davis v UK*,[75] *Jasper v UK*,[76] *and Fitt v UK*,[77] which were heard jointly by the Court, the then Director of JUSTICE wrote an affidavit in support of the applications, which was annexed to the applicants' memorials. In effect this can be described as a kind of 'informal intervention'. The involvement of Greenpeace Schweiz (Swiss Greenpeace) in another sample case followed a unique pattern, moving from formal to informal participation. Greenpeace itself lodged an application against Switzerland, claiming that its right to a fair trial had been violated. Although the Commission refused to recognise Greenpeace's standing to bring these complaints, sympathetic individuals who continued to work closely with Greenpeace pursued the application.[78]

---

[74]   Harlow and Rawlings, *Pressure Through Law* (1992) 257.

[75]   *Rowe and Davis v United Kingdom* ECHR 2000-II, (2000) 30 EHRR 1.

[76]   *Jasper v United Kingdom* (App no 27052/95) (2000) 30 EHRR 441.

[77]   *Fitt v UK* ECHR 2000-II, (2000) 30 EHRR 480.

[78]   E-mail correspondence, Leo Scherer, Nuclear Campaigner for Greenpeace Switzerland, 8 August 2002.

V.   The Type of NGOs Involved in Litigation

A.   'Repeat Players'

Figure 1 shows that a small number of NGOs had a considerable and repeated involvement in the sample cases. The KHRP (which was involved in 11 sample cases) and Liberty (which was involved in eight) are particularly notable in that respect. When these findings are coupled with those from earlier research by others, it can be seen that some NGOs that were involved in the sample cases have had a sustained, and often lengthy, history of participation in ECHR litigation. The majority of these are legally-orientated organisations that have no particular constituency beyond human rights laws themselves. Liberty, for example, sponsored *Golder v UK* (which was filed in 1970),[79] and has been involved in several ECHR cases in the intervening years;[80] JUSTICE assisted the intervener in *Malone v UK* (in which judgment was delivered in 1984),[81] which was the beginning of its regular involvement in a rather more modest number of ECHR cases. Alongside these 'old hands' one can also identify NGOs, such as the KHRP and the ERRC, that have come to ECHR litigation more recently, but have nonetheless taken a significant number of cases in a short number of years in order to highlight (and remedy) sustained human rights violations in specific contexts.

These findings suggest that Marc Galanter's well-known article, which speculates on the characteristics of litigants that influence the outcome of cases, has some relevance to our understanding of how NGO involvement might impact upon ECtHR litigation. Galanter describes two 'ideal types' of litigants, which represent opposite ends of a continuum: 'repeat players' (RPs), 'who are engaged in many similar litigations over time', and 'one shotters' (OSs), 'who have only occasional recourse to the courts'.[82] Galanter observes that RPs enjoy considerable advantages of experience and (usually) better resources over OSs when embarking upon litigation. He consequently suggests that a co-ordinated approach to litigation can benefit less-advantaged groups in society by giving them greater 'power' as litigants, by 'upgrading capacities for managing claims'.[83] That argument, it is easy to imagine, has particular relevance for those seeking to promote human rights.

Galanter further surmises that his two types of litigants will tend to adopt different litigation strategies:

---

[79]   *Golder v United Kingdom* Series A no 18 (1979–80) 1 EHRR 524. Information obtained from Harlow and Rawlings, *Pressure Through Law* (1992) 257.
[80]   For a more detailed discussion of Liberty's work, see ch 5.
[81]   *Malone v United Kingdom* Series A no 82 (1985) 7 EHRR 14. Information obtained from Lester, 'Amici Curiae' (1990) 345.
[82]   Marc Galanter, 'Why the "Haves" Come out Ahead: Speculations on the Limits of Legal Change' (1974) 9 *Law and Society Review* 95, 97.
[83]   *ibid*, 141.

Because his stakes in the immediate outcome are high and because by definition OS is unconcerned with the outcome of similar litigation in future, OS will have little interest in that element of the outcome which might influence the disposition of the decision-maker next time around. For the RP, on the other hand, anything that will favourably influence the outcomes of future cases is a worthwhile result. The larger the stake for any player and the lower the probability of repeat play, the less likely that he will be concerned with the rules which govern future cases of some kind.[84]

This means, inter alia, that RPs 'can adopt strategies calculated to maximise gain over a long series of cases, even where this involves the risk of maximum loss' and that they can therefore 'play for the rules in litigation itself'.[85] If these speculations are correct, litigiously active NGOs are well placed to embark upon socially transformative litigation. They are, in particular, well placed to act as opponents of the representatives of States, who are, on Galanter's analysis, formidable litigants indeed.

B. 'One Shotters'

The most sustained contribution to the Court's litigation is made by a small number of NGOs. Nevertheless, reference to Figure 1 shows that a modest, but not insignificant, number of single-issues groups, not readily classifiable as RPs, were involved in the sample cases. It is particularly interesting to note the involvement in litigation of those organisations that are not specialist in human rights law. Swiss Greenpeace, a national branch of a global environmental pressure group, was involved in one sample case (which, as Figure 2 below shows, was the only 'NGO case' taken against Switzerland). Similarly, two cases against Finland were litigated by PESUE, a national campaigning organisation for family rights. It can also be seen from my findings that two single-issue groups based in the United Kingdom, Reunite and Stonewall, were also involved in one sample case each.

As Galanter himself acknowledges, the 'party factors' that impact upon litigation become more complex when one of the parties to litigation is a Government. First, the potential benefits to be gained from a success in such litigation are almost without parallel: it will lead, almost invariably, to policy or legislative changes. Secondly, outside of the normal political channels, there is little scope for negotiating with Governments. Both of these factors mean that organisations seeking to bring about social transformation may quickly turn to what might otherwise be the 'last resort' of litigation. Furthermore, the ultimate significance of the Court's judgments tends to lie more in the resolution of policy issues rather than in the distribution of goods (which was at the heart of Galanter's analysis). This means that certain actors in ECtHR litigation are likely to be

---

[84]   *ibid*, 100.
[85]   *ibid.*

driven more by broad policy aims than by a narrow analysis of the expected outcome of a case. Finally, because unsuccessful applicants do not pay costs, NGOs that are inexperienced litigators can pursue their policy objectives through an application to the ECtHR with considerable freedom. Undoubtedly these factors have contributed to small numbers of non-specialist NGOs becoming intermittently involved in the Court's litigation. Given the lack of academic attention paid to 'OSs' in the context of international human rights litigation, the involvement of single-issue groups (or pressure groups) in the sample cases is explored in greater detail in chapter six.

VI.   The Types of Cases in Which NGOs are Involved

Having put aside the notion that NGO participation is pervasive in litigation under the ECHR, it is possible to begin to appraise the nature of the cases in which NGOs become involved.

A.   By Respondent State

Figure 2 below shows the number of the sample cases in which NGOs were involved by respondent State.

It is immediately obvious that NGO involvement is more marked in litigation against some countries in the Council of Europe than others. It is particularly noteworthy that of the 26 countries that were respondents to cases that fell within the sample, NGOs were involved in litigation against only nine. In those nine countries the level of NGO involvement varied considerably. NGOs were involved, for example, in all three cases in which judgment was delivered against Bulgaria (100 per cent), in the sole case against Hungary (100 per cent), and in two of the four cases taken against Finland (50 per cent). Perhaps the most outstanding finding is that 10 of the 19 cases against the UK (52.6 per cent), and 12 of the 25 cases against Turkey (48 per cent) attracted NGO involvement. These figures demonstrate that the practice of NGO litigation before the ECtHR is, geographically speaking, extremely concentrated. Although an interesting question looms about NGO *in*activity in certain States, this falls outside of the scope of the present research.

It is particularly noteworthy that the NGOs that litigate before the ECtHR have flourished in the UK. Seven of the 17 NGOs involved in the sample cases were based in the UK. Of the 32 cases identified as attracting NGO participation, 23 involved NGOs based in the UK (72 per cent). The 'old hands' that are referred to above, such as Liberty, are responsible for a good proportion of this activity. It is quite remarkable that these 'old hands', with their lengthy and considerable involvement in ECtHR litigation, have no equivalent in other countries. The very idea of 'public interest litigation' appears to have its roots in a common-law

Figure 2: NGO involvement in the sample cases by respondent State

State	Total No of cases respondent to	No of cases with NGO involvement	Country	Total No of cases respondent to	No of cases with NGO involvement
Austria	12	1	Malta	1	0
Belgium	1	0	Netherlands	3	0
Bulgaria	3	3	Norway	1	0
Cyprus	1	0	Poland	8	0
Czech Republic	4	0	Portugal	2	0
Finland	4	2	Romania	3	1
France	15	1	San Marino	2	0
Germany	1	0	Slovakia	1	0
Greece	9	0	Slovenia	1	0
Hungary	1	1	Spain	3	0
Ireland	2	0	Switzerland	5	1
Italy	18	0	Turkey	25	12
Lithuania	4	0	United Kingdom	19	10

tradition, and while the idea has perhaps been most developed in the United States it has certainly taken root in the United Kingdom.[86] These organisations are considered in detail in chapter five.

A cross-reference to Figure 1 shows that many NGOs are transnational activists, whose involvement in litigation before the ECtHR extends to cases taken against countries other than their host State. The most prolific 'RP' in the sample, the UK-based KHRP, was involved in 11 of the 25 cases against Turkey (44 per cent). It is interesting to note in this context, as it has not emerged in previous studies in this area, the rather surprising fact that three of the organisations that were involved in the sample cases are based in the United States. Furthermore, other organisations, particularly those based in Eastern and Central European

---

[86] For an examination of the growth and development of public interest litigation in the UK, see Harlow and Rawlings, *Pressure Through Law* (1992), and Cooper and Dhavan (eds), *Public Interest Law* (1986).

countries, such as the ERRC, are primarily funded by American foundations. The work of these transnational activists is considered in greater depth in chapter four.

B.   By Article of the Convention

NGO involvement is particularly notable in cases that relate to the most serious and brutal violations of the Convention. Of the 10 sample cases in which the Court found a violation of Article 2 (the right to life), NGOs were involved in nine. Specifically, eight were cases sponsored by the KHRP against Turkey, and the other case was taken by the ERRC against Bulgaria. This 90 per cent total suggests that NGOs have an important role to play in bringing violations of the right to life to the attention of the Court. A similar, although not quite as marked, pattern can be seen in cases alleging a violation of Article 3 (freedom from torture and inhuman or degrading treatment or punishment). Of the 15 successful applications in the sample cases made under that Article, seven (that is, 46.7 per cent) were NGO cases, all of which were sponsored by the KHRP.[87]

The high level of NGO involvement in such cases shows the important role that NGOs play in allocating responsibility for, and expressing international condemnation of, the most serious, persistent and gross violations of the Convention.[88] Margaret Keck and Kathryn Sikkink's study of global human rights movements found that 'campaigns against practices involving bodily harm to populations perceived as vulnerable or innocent are most likely to be effective transnationally'.[89] Some organisations – and within the sample the KHRP and the ERRC are particularly notable in this respect – appear to be aware of the contribution that ECtHR litigation can make to focusing international attention upon human rights violations that offend the most basic and engrained principles of humanity.

The majority of successful Article 13 (the right to an effective remedy for human rights violations) claims in the sample were made in cases in which NGOs were involved. Of the 18 sample cases in which successful claims were made under this Article, 12 were 'NGO cases' (66.67 per cent). This supports the contention that NGOs are particularly important actors in cases in which

---

[87]   Although the KHRP was the only NGO to successfully argue an Art 3 claim within the sample, several other organisations unsuccessfully tried to raise a complaint under this Article.

[88]   In contrast to the findings concerning Articles 2 and 3, it is interesting to note that NGOs are not heavily involved in cases involving violations of Article 6 of the Convention, which provides for the minimum standards for all trials in order that they are considered to be fair. Even after cases concerning delay in domestic proceedings were excluded from the sample, there were still sixty-nine cases left in which the Court heard Article 6 complaints (46.3%), making it by far the most frequently litigated Article. As only six of these were 'NGO cases', it can be seen that there are proportionately far fewer NGOs concerning themselves in cases alleging violations of this Article.

[89]   Margaret Keck and Kathryn Sikkink, *Activists Beyond Borders: Advocacy Networks in International Politics* (Ithaca, Cornell University Press, 1998) 27.

domestic authorities have been reluctant to address the complaints raised therein, thereby allowing human rights violations to occur with impunity.

Further support for the suggestion that NGOs have a particular role to play in litigating against recalcitrant States is provided by the remarkable fact that, within the sample, the only cases in which a complaint was successfully made under former Article 25(1) of the Convention (which is now Article 34) were supported by NGOs. The relevant section of Article 25 provided that

> High Contracting Parties who have made such a declaration [accepting the right of individual petition] undertake not to hinder in any way the effective exercise of this right.

Three successful applications were made under this Article in KHRP cases.

Analysis of NGO participation in ECHR litigation by Article of the Convention shows the importance that NGOs have in successfully bringing to the Court's attention serious violations of the Convention's rights. NGO litigation also appears to have a role to play in bringing to light systemic inadequacies of domestic laws and procedures for dealing with human rights violations, and can also be directed towards addressing State party reluctance to answer human rights complaints that have been made against them. These findings provide compelling reasons to examine the work of these organisations in greater depth, which follows in chapter four.

C.   Cases Heard by the Grand Chamber

It is hard to establish satisfactory criteria by which one can assess the 'importance' of a case that is before the Court. Nevertheless, if a case has been heard by the Grand Chamber, this at least indicates its jurisprudential significance. Article 30 of the Convention provides:

> Where a case pending before a Chamber raises a serious question affecting the interpretation of the Convention or the protocols thereto, or where the resolution of a question before the Chamber might have a result inconsistent with a judgment previously delivered by the Court, the Chamber may, at any time before it has rendered its judgment, relinquish jurisdiction in favour of the Grand Chamber, unless one of the parties to the case objects.

Article 43(2) further provides that the Grand Chamber shall accept a referral of a case in which a Chamber has already delivered judgment if it

> raises a serious question affecting the interpretation or application of the Convention or the protocols thereto, or a serious issue of general importance.

The incidence of NGO involvement in the sample cases heard by the Grand Chamber is significantly higher than in those cases that were dealt with exclusively by one of the Court's Chambers. NGOs were involved in nine of the 18 sample cases that were heard by the Grand Chamber under Article 30. Of the four cases in the sample that were referred to the Grand Chamber under Article 43, two were 'NGO cases'. NGOs were therefore involved in half of all sample cases in which the Grand Chamber delivered a judgment. So the likelihood of an NGO participating in litigation depends, at least in part, on the case in question having a potential importance that extends beyond securing the rights of an individual applicant.

VII.   The Success-Rate of NGO Cases

Given the methodology adopted in this research, it is not possible to make significant judgements about how 'successful' the cases that NGOs are involved in actually are, because by the time a case has reached the judgment stage there is a very strong likelihood that the Court will thereafter go on to find in the applicant's favour.[90] The Court found that there was no violation of any provision of the Convention in only 14 of the sample cases (that is, 9.4 per cent); four of the 26 'NGO cases' were entirely unsuccessful (15.4 per cent). With the exception of the remarkable success rate of the KHRP (the Court found a violation of a Convention right in all KHRP-sponsored cases), the involvement of an NGO in an ECtHR case does not generally appear to increase its chances of receiving a favourable judgment. However, two significant caveats should be added to that comment. First, it has already been suggested that NGOs are particularly involved in ground-breaking litigation: in these circumstances, a favourable judgment is clearly something of an achievement, and certainly more so than in cases in which the Court's jurisprudence is established. Secondly, my findings do not show whether or not 'NGO cases' have a better chance of being declared admissible and of reaching the judgment stage.

It is, in any event, too simplistic to judge the success of 'NGO cases' on the basis of a finding of a violation alone, and a quantitative evaluation of this question is probably insufficient. Galanter makes this point concisely when he says in relation to 'RPs' that there is 'a difference in what they regard as a favourable outcome', because for them 'anything that will favourably influence the outcomes of future cases is worthwhile'.[91] An NGO might, for example, be satisfied by a negative judgment if it leads to debate and publicity, and consequently increases pressure for reform.[92] It might also be added that intervening in a high-profile case also adds to the prestige (and funding-potential) of the organisation concerned. Conversely, a positive judgment by the Court might be

---

[90]   For example, the Court found at least one violation of the Convention in 422 judgments in 2000; it found no violation of the Convention in only 20 of its judgments. See Council of Europe, *Survey of Activities, 2000* (Strasbourg, Council of Europe, 2001) 73.

[91]   Galanter, 'Why the "Haves" Come Out Ahead' (1974) 100.

[92]   The fact that any coverage is good was mentioned by, for example, the Director of Reunite (telephone interview, Denise Carter, 9 May 2003); the Communications Officer of Stonewall

unwelcome if it does not deal with an issue of central importance to the NGO or if the Government concerned responds to it by, for example, entering a reservation to the Convention.

VIII. Conclusion

This statistical survey of the sample cases suggests that the judicial process of the ECtHR remains largely unaffected by a political model of litigation: the majority of issues before the Court tend to be contained as narrow disputes between individuals and States. Quantitative analysis of the level of NGO involvement in the sample cases reveals that NGOs do not, statistically speaking, dominate the entire body of ECtHR litigation to the same extent that they appear to before other international human rights tribunals. Nevertheless, there are certain types of ECtHR cases in which NGOs play a central role. Basic analysis of the nature of cases that NGOs were involved in highlights some interesting patterns that warrant further exploration. In particular, the initial quantitative research reveals three distinct areas of NGO activity before the ECtHR that are especially marked.

First, there is a high level of NGO involvement in cases that concern extreme and persistent situations of human rights violations, particularly where the violations have taken place with impunity at a national level. Secondly, there is a small but significant group of legally-orientated 'RPs' that have a history of repeated involvement in litigation before the ECtHR. This is made up of NGOs (invariably based in the United Kingdom) that have a general interest in the protection of human rights. Thirdly and finally, there is a small number of single-issue groups (or pressure groups) that occasionally involve themselves in cases before the Court. Although these organisations are involved in litigation with less regularity, they are of particular interest because their role in ECtHR litigation has hitherto received little academic attention. The following three chapters are taken up with considering in greater detail each of these areas in order to assess the contribution that NGOs make to cases brought under the Convention.

mentioned that failed test-cases can have a 'huge impact on the media' (interview, Helen Marsh, 12 August 2003, London); John Wadham, Director of Liberty, mentioned that even failed cases can help to shape public opinion.

4

States of Impunity: The Role of NGOs in Addressing Gross and Systematic Violations of the Convention

'We'll finish terrorism but we are being held back by democracy and human rights'.[1]

I. Introduction

ASTRIKING FEATURE of the sample cases is the degree of NGO involvement in those cases in which a successful claim is made under Article 2 or 3 of the ECHR. Those Articles protect the right to life and prohibit torture respectively, and cases in which they are raised are therefore the most extreme with which the ECtHR is faced. The involvement of NGOs in litigation that addresses serious violations of the Convention is particularly marked where those violations form part of systematic patterns of abuse by government officials that take place with impunity. In these situations there is typically no effective investigation at the domestic level into the alleged violation and once the case reaches the Court in Strasbourg, the State concerned often remains unwilling to co-operate fully and openly with the proceedings.

It is upon such gross and systemic violations of human rights, including extra-judicial executions, disappearances, unexplained deaths in custody and torture, that this chapter focuses. Of the cases selected for this research, those that were sponsored by the European Roma Rights Centre (ERRC) and the Kurdish Human Rights Project (KHRP) were of particular relevance to the discussion of these issues and form the basis of the case studies that begin this chapter. After

---

[1] Turkish Deputy Chief of Staff, General Ahmet Corekci, July 1995, quoted in Amnesty International, *Turkey: No Security Without Human Rights* (London, Amnesty International Publications, 1996) 3.

detailed consideration of the involvement that these NGOs had in the sample cases, this chapter goes on to examine the reasons for the prominent part that NGOs play in bringing gross and systematic violations of the Convention to the Court's attention and explores why the bi-partisan model of litigation is of limited value in such circumstances.

II. The European Roma Rights Centre: Challenging Police Brutality Against The Roma

This case study begins with an outline of one of the most troubling of the sample cases, *Anya Velikova v Bulgaria*,[2] which concerned the untimely death of a Roma male at the hands of the Bulgarian police. This case – which is notable for the lack of anxiety shown by the Bulgarian authorities to establish the cause of death of the man concerned and to bring those responsible to justice – forms part of a wider pattern of systematic discrimination and casual violence that the Roma face, particularly in Eastern and Central European countries. Although it is not apparent from the judgment of the Court, this case was sponsored by the ERRC (who collaborated on it with the Human Rights Project and the Bulgarian Helsinki Committee), and it forms part of a strategic litigation campaign that that organisation has undertaken on behalf of the Roma. This case therefore acts as a lens through which to commence a detailed examination of the role that the ERRC has played (usually acting in co-operation with other NGOs) in highlighting before the ECtHR the significant human rights abuses that are experienced by the Roma of Europe. The wider background to these abuses is returned to and explained in greater depth in the second part of this chapter.

A.   *Anya Velikova v Bulgaria*

Although the facts presented in this case were not complex, they were, as one might expect given the subject-matter of this chapter, a source of disagreement between the parties. The case arose from the death of the applicant's partner, Mr Slavtcho Tsonchev, whilst he was held in police custody in September 1994. Mr Tsonchev, a member of the Roma minority, died after spending 12 hours in detention following his arrest for the theft of cattle. The applicant believed that prior to his arrest Mr Tsonchev had been perfectly fit and healthy and she concluded, perhaps without any great difficulty, that he had therefore died as a result of police brutality. The initial investigation in to the cause of death was, however, inconclusive. A decree issued by the regional prosecutor accepted that Mr Tsonchev death was the result of a deliberate beating, but found that 'it

---

[2]   *Anya Velikova v Bulgaria* (App no 41488/98), ECHR 2000-VI.

proved impossible to determine where [Mr Tsonchev] was beaten up, in the Pleven Police Department or outside it'.[3] In September 1996 the applicant appealed to the Chief Public Prosecutor's Office for the case to be re-opened, which was granted on the basis that the investigation was not 'thorough and complete'. Nevertheless, although the case was not formally suspended and pressure from the lawyers involved was unremitting, the investigation continued to be characterised by stalling and inactivity and there were no further significant steps taken towards bringing those responsible for Mr Tsonchev's death to justice at the national level.

The applicant's complaint under Articles 2, 6(1),[4] 13[5] and 14[6] of the Convention was introduced to the EcmHR ('the Commission') on 12 February 1998. The position taken by the respondent State when faced with those allegations suggested that resolving the issues surrounding the death of Mr Tsonchev would continue to be an uphill struggle. The Bulgarian Government made various wide-ranging challenges to the admissibility of the application before the Commission, none of which was successful. For example, they challenged the standing of the applicant to bring the complaint because, despite the fact that she had lived with Mr Tsonchev for over 12 years and had three children with him, she had not been married to him. They also argued that the applicant had not exhausted domestic remedies, because she could have pursued damages in a civil case.[7] Before the Court a further unsuccessful objection was raised concerning the authenticity of the applicant's signature on the power of attorney. The latter argument, in particular, had little hope of being taken seriously, given that the applicant attended the hearing in Strasbourg in person and was able to confirm that it was in fact her signature.

Despite the grave and troubling nature of the allegations that were made by the applicant, resolving the merits of her case was not difficult from a jurisprudential perspective. It had already been established in the case law of the Court that where an allegation is made that injuries obtained whilst in custody result from ill-treatment, the burden of proof falls on the respondent Government to establish an alternative plausible cause of death.[8] In its judgment, delivered on 18 May 2000, the Court held that it was not, due to the paucity of supporting evidence and the lack of effective investigation in to the surrounding events, persuaded by the Government's speculative explanations for Mr Tsonchev's

---

[3] Part of this Decree is reproduced in *Velikova v Bulgaria* (dec) (App no 41488/98), ECHR 1999-V.

[4] The right to a fair trial within a reasonable time.

[5] The right to an effective remedy.

[6] The prohibition of discrimination. This parasitic Article was pleaded in conjunction with Articles 2 and 13.

[7] Pursuant to *Assenov v Bulgaria* ECHR 1998-VIII, (1999) 28 EHRR 652, the Court in *Velikova* reiterated that civil damages do not constitute an adequate remedy for violations of Art 2.

[8] *Selmouni v France* ECHR 1999-V (2000) 29 EHRR 403, [87].

injuries.[9] The Court consequently found a violation of Article 2, resulting from the deliberate ill treatment of Mr Tsonchev by the Bulgarian police and a violation of Articles 2 and 13 resulting from the inadequate investigation.[10] The judges did not, however, find that there had been a violation of Article 14 (the prohibition of discrimination) in conjunction with those Articles, as they were, on the evidence before them, unable 'to conclude beyond reasonable doubt that Mr Tsonchev's killing and the lack of a meaningful investigation into it were motivated by racial prejudice'.[11] The Government sought a referral of the case to the Grand Chamber, which was refused. Therefore, some six years after the killing of Mr Tsonchev, the ECtHR's judgment provided some attribution of responsibility and some sense of justice in respect of what appears to have been, in the eyes of the Bulgarian authorities, the inconsequential death of a Roma male.

B.   NGO Involvement in the *Velikova* Case

The ERRC is a public interest law organisation founded in 1996 and based in Budapest, Hungary. As its names suggests, it is concerned with the protection of the rights of Roma people throughout Europe. Understandably, given that this is where the majority of Europe's Roma live, the organisation's primary focus has been on Central and Eastern European countries. The aims of this organisation are:

> Firstly to facilitate access of Roma to rights. Secondly, to participate in the construction of public interest law in Central and Eastern Europe. Not just for Roma, but to bring about legal reform.[12]

The ERRC is a comparatively large and well-funded organisation that receives financial support from several sources, including private foundations, governments and inter-governmental organisations.[13] The establishment of that organisation was the brainchild of the Open Society Institute, a private foundation that remains one of its principal sponsors.[14] At the time of my research visit to the

---

[9]   *Anya Velikova v Bulgaria* (App no 41488/98) ECHR 2000-VI [72–3].

[10]   The Court did not consider the Art 6(1) complaint, finding that Art 13 was the appropriate provision to consider the lack of effective investigation into Mr Tsonchev's death.

[11]   *Anya Velikova v Bulgaria* (App no 41488/98) ECHR 2000-VI [94]. For a dissenting voice on this approach to the standard of proof under Article 14 and the Court's general reluctance to find a violation under this Article, see the separate opinion of Judge Bonello in *Anguelova v Bulgaria* ECHR 2002-IV, (2004) 38 EHRR 31.

Partly thanks to written comments received by the ERRC, the Court has subsequently revised its approach to this issue. See *Nachova & Ors v Bulgaria* (App nos 43577/98 and 43579/98) (2004) 39 EHRR 37 [152]–[175].

[12]   Interview with Dimitrina Petrova, founder and then Executive Director of ERRC, 20 September 2002, Budapest.

[13]   For details of the ERRC's principal donors, see the ERRC's website at: www.errc.org.

[14]   Interview, Dimitrina Petrova, 20 September 2002.

For more information on the Open Society Institute, see: www.soros.org/about.

ERRC it had about 24 permanent members of staff,[15] which included six in-house lawyers. While the number of staff working at the ERRC has changed little since, the number of legal staff has been slightly reduced. In additional to its permanent staff, the ERRC also has a number of interns, externs and local monitors who assist them with their work. The ERRC has forged good links with local and transnational NGOs, and it has become an important resource for organisations with an interest in the human rights of Roma in Europe.

The ERRC was established at a time when many Eastern and Central European countries had signed or were contemplating signing the ECHR (which is, of course, a precondition of admission to the Council of Europe and an important step towards eventual membership of the European Union); the founders recognised that this provided a potentially important opportunity to establish an international public interest law project to help improve the human rights situation of the Roma. In order to achieve its aims the ERRC has, therefore, been involved in generating a body of ECtHR 'Roma rights' jurisprudence, and this forms a considerable part of its litigation work. Prior to *Velikova*, it made a lengthy written intervention in the first Roma case heard by the Court against an Eastern and Central European country, *Assenov and Others v Bulgaria*.[16] The basis of that intervention was a belief that it was necessary to outline for the Court 'the broader context of discrimination and disadvantage which Roma face throughout Bulgaria and much of Europe'.[17] Since then the ERRC has developed a versatile multi-strategy approach to ECtHR cases: it sponsors cases through a legal funding scheme; it funds and jointly litigates cases with local lawyers (as happened in the *Velikova* case); it litigates cases itself with its in-house lawyers; and it has also continued to act as third party intervener.[18] Furthermore, it provides training, advice and information to other organisations taking Roma cases to the ECtHR. The ERRC is also involved in domestic human rights litigation and in applications before other international human rights bodies, and alongside its legal campaigns it runs educative, research and publication projects.

The *Velikova* case, therefore, formed part of the ERRC's litigation strategy to highlight, and to effect improvement of, the situation of the Roma. Although at the time that I undertook research at the offices of the ERRC there was no one working there who had been involved with the *Velikova* case from the outset, the files of the organisation show that it had contributed to that case from at least September 1997. In other words, it was involved throughout the Strasbourg proceedings, but not during the domestic proceedings. The ERRC was not the applicant's representative in this case, and therefore does not warrant a mention

---

[15] That is the number of staff listed at December 2002 in European Roma Rights Centre, *Biannual Report: 2001–2002* (Budapest, ERRC, 200?) Index I.

[16] *Assenov v Bulgaria* ECHR 1998-VIII, (1999) 28 EHRR 652.

[17] European Roma Rights Centre, *Assenov & Ors v Bulgaria: Written Comments of the European Roma Rights Center* (29 April 1998, unpublished) 1.

[18] These are not mutually exclusive roles. The ERRC have, for example, both funded and acted as third party intervener in the same case.

in the Court's judgment; however, the correspondence between Yonko Grozev (the lawyer who was authorised to take the case) and the Court's Registry mentions that the case was brought 'in co-operation' with the ERRC.[19] Although the role of the ERRC in the *Velikova* case was played out largely behind the scenes, it is clear from interviews conducted at the ERRC and from reading its case files that it was integral to the litigation of this case when it was taken to the ECtHR. First – and crucially – the ERRC funded the proceedings before the ECtHR, which means it was paying the fees of the lawyers on the case and covering all litigation costs. All correspondence between Yonko Grozev and the Court was consequently copied to the ERRC. It was also responsible, together with the named lawyer in this case, for drafting the applicant's pleadings as well as for providing much of the background material that was relied upon in them.

Because it is based in Budapest, the ERRC, in common with all transnational human rights NGOs, is inevitably at some distance from many of those people whose rights it seeks to protect.[20] In fact, although they played such a central role in the Strasbourg proceedings in the *Velikova* case, ERRC staff appear to have had no contact with the applicant herself. However, as an organisation with a public interest litigation strategy to pursue, the ERRC obviously needs to be aware of specific incidences of rights violations. In the words of its founder and then Executive Director, Dimitrina Petrova, 'a good case doesn't come through the door. You construct and build a case'.[21] The ERRC in fact has field-workers in many countries in Eastern Europe who travel around reporting on situations of human rights abuse. But equally, if not more important, are the relationships and networks that it has developed with other like-minded NGOs.

The Human Rights Project of Sofia (HRP) was the first organisation to hear about the death of Mr Tsonchev and to identify its potential as a 'public interest' case.[22] Assisted by lawyers from the Bulgarian Helsinki Committee (BHC), it unsuccessfully pursued domestic remedies before bringing the case to the attention of the ERRC in order that it could be taken to the ECtHR.[23] The HRP, which is no longer in existence, was also a public-interest law organisation that focused on the rights of Roma; it had offices throughout Bulgaria and aimed to work at a grass-roots level within Roma communities. It was therefore an important part of

---

[19] Letter from Yonko Grozev to Registry, 12 February 1998 (on file with the ERRC).

[20] At the time of my research visit the ERRC had only one Roma lawyer working in its offices. The organisation itself was not established by Roma.

[21] Interview, Dimitrina Petrova, 20 September 2002.

[22] It is noteworthy that Dimitrina Petrova also founded the HRP. For more details of that organisation's involvement in the *Velikova* case, and the difficulties it experienced trying to secure an adequate investigation in to the death of Mr Tsonchev, see (July–August 1996) 1(3) *Focus: The Newsletter of the HRP* 7–8.

[23] Under Article 188 of the Bulgarian Code of Criminal Procedure in force at the time, a request for the institution of a criminal investigation could be made by any third party. See European Roma Rights Centre, *Assenov & Others v Bulgaria* (1998) fn 8.

the chain in generating and selecting 'Roma rights' cases. Indeed, I was told in interview that all Roma cases against Bulgaria taken to the ECtHR up to that point had originated with the HRP.[24]

Although it is not clear how Anya Velikova first came to be in contact with the HRP, it is quite likely that it was as a result of the network of Roma volunteers established by the HRP to report on situations of human rights abuse, or the field workers that the HRP instituted in various parts of Bulgaria.[25] Workers from the HRP conducted the original interviews with the applicant (transcripts of these were later produced as evidence before the ECtHR) and they also found lawyers prepared to take on the case.[26] At the time of taking on the *Velikova* case the HRP had no legally qualified staff and, in fact, I was told that at that time there were no qualified Roma lawyers in Bulgaria at all.[27] Roma law students within that organisation handled all the casework as far as possible, with assistance from outside lawyers – usually from other human rights organisations – where necessary.[28] Yonko Grozev, a lawyer from the BHC, therefore acted in this case at the domestic level and continued to be the assigned lawyer before the ECtHR.[29] The BHC is a member of the International Helsinki Federation for Human Rights, which has a general interest and expertise in human rights.

Working together, these three NGOs formed a powerful and impressive trio: a large, well-resourced international organisation with expertise in the Convention; a grass-roots organisation with links to the Roma community in Bulgaria; and an organisation with experience and knowledge of the Bulgarian legal system. Together, as we have seen, they were able to bring the Bulgarian Government to account for the death of Mr Tsonchev.

III.   The Kurdish Human Rights Project: Addressing Gross Human Rights Violations Against Turkish Kurds

Within the totality of the sample cases, those suggesting a pattern of the most serious violations of the Convention were brought against the Turkish Government in respect of their treatment of persons belonging to the Kurdish minority. This group of cases involved allegations of violations of a large number of the

[24]   Interview, Ivan Ivanov, ERRC Staff Attorney, 18 September 2002, Budapest.
[25]   See Human Rights Project, *Annual Report: 1994* (Sofia, HRP, 1995) 10.
[26]   *Script of Interview with Anya Velikova: October 2 1995, Bukovlak, Pleven Region, Bulgaria* (on file with ERRC).
[27]   Interview, Ivan Ivanov, 18 September 2002. It might, perhaps, be more accurate to say that there were no lawyers in Bulgaria at this time prepared to openly acknowledge their Roma origins.
[28]   Interview, Ivan Ivanov, 18 September 2002.
[29]   Further information on the BHC can be found on its website at: www.bghelsinki.org. For a commentary on the BHC and HRP's close working relationship, see Dimitrina Petrova, *Violations of the Rights of Gypsies in Bulgaria* (Sofia, Human Rights Project, 1994) 40.

Convention's rights, but their gravity is signified by the preponderance of claims made under Articles 2 and 3. Eleven such cases were sponsored by the KHRP and formed part of its litigation strategy to highlight the extreme human rights abuses taking place in Kurdish regions of Turkey. Although it would be unwieldy to set out in detail the facts of each these 11 cases, a brief description follows to indicate their seriousness.

A. The Sample Cases Sponsored by the KHRP

Three of the KHRP-sponsored sample cases concerned the unresolved disappearance of a relative of the applicant; in each, the allegation was made that the (Kurdish) victim was last seen in the charge of Government agents.[30] A further three cases involved, respectively, the killing of a doctor, a journalist and a trade union official in which the perpetrators remained unidentified.[31] In each of these latter cases it was alleged that those killed had received threats because of their pro-Kurdish activities; it was also argued that the investigations into the deaths were inadequate and that Government agents were either directly or indirectly responsible for the killings. A further case, which echoes that of Ms Velikova, concerned a death in custody of the applicant's husband whilst he was held in detention on suspicion of involvement in pro-PKK (the Kurdistan Workers' Party) activities,[32] a death which was alleged to have resulted from deliberate police brutality.[33] Another concerned the circumstances surrounding the shooting of the applicant's son by the Gendarmerie during a raid on his flat, which was conducted to find PKK members.[34] An additional case concerned allegations of a deliberate and sustained attack on the pro-Kurdish newspaper, *Özgür Gündem*.[35] The final two cases alleged, respectively, the destruction of the applicant's home and crops,[36] and the beating of the applicant's brother with the result that he was permanently paralysed.[37] Both of these incidents were said to have been the deliberate acts of the Security Forces during raids on villages to discover PKK terrorists. Needless to say, none of these incidents were satisfactorily resolved through domestic remedies.

---

[30]   *Timurtas v Turkey* ECHR 2000-VI, (2001) 33 EHRR 6; *Taş v Turkey* (App no 24396/94) (2001) 33 EHRR 15; *Ertak v Turkey* (App no 20764/92) ECHR 2000-V.

[31]   *Mahmut Kaya v Turkey* (App no 22535/93) ECHR 2000-III; *Kiliç v Turkey* ECHR 2000-III, (2001) 33 EHRR 58; *Akkoç v Turkey* ECHR 2000-X, (2002) 34 EHRR 51.

[32]   The PKK (also sometimes known as Kongra-Gel), which was established in 1978 with the objective of achieving an independent Kurdistan, is viewed as a terrorist organisation by a number of governments, including the Turkish Government, and the EU.

[33]   *Salman v Turkey* ECHR 2000-VII, (2002) 34 EHRR 17.

[34]   *Gül v Turkey* (App no 22676/93) (2002) 34 EHRR 28.

[35]   *Özgür Gündem v Turkey* ECHR 2000-III, (2001) 31 EHRR 49. For more information on this case, see the KHRP reports, *Freedom of the Press in Turkey: The Case of Özgür Gündem* (London, KHRP and Article 19, undated) and *State Before Freedom: Media Repression in Turkey* (London, KHRP and Article 19, July 1998).

[36]   *Bilgin v Turkey* (App no 23819/94) (2003) 36 EHRR 50.

[37]   *Ilhan v Turkey* ECHR 2000-VII, (2002) 34 EHRR 36.

A reading of the Court's judgments in these cases gives us an indication of the highly contentious nature of these applications. Multiple objections were raised as to their admissibility, and in suggesting that many amounted to an abuse of process the Government went so far as to allege, inter alia, that applicants' testimony was given undue weight by the fact-finders,[38] that the applications were politically motivated and that the applicants themselves had no desire to pursue the claim.[39] The Government, at times, deliberately intimidated applicants, resulting in three findings by the Court that the Government had not complied with their obligation under former Article 25 of the Convention not to hinder the right of individual application.[40] The lack of evidence supporting the applicants' allegations was consistently relied upon by the respondent Government to show that it lacked any knowledge of, or responsibility for, the various incidents.

Despite obstructions from the Turkish Government, the 11 KHRP cases were nevertheless extremely successful: the Court found in each a violation of at least one Article of the Convention. In the eight cases that involved an allegation that the State was responsible for the death of the applicant's relative the Court found a violation of Article 2. This was either based on a finding that the State was directly responsible for the death in question, or that it had failed to protect the victim, or that it had violated the right to life through inadequate investigation of the unlawful killings. Statistically speaking, that is an extremely impressive success rate.[41] In seven cases the Court found that there had been a violation of Article 3 of the Convention. There were a further eight findings that the right to an effective remedy under Article 13 had been violated. There were also two findings of a violation of Article 5 (right to liberty and security), one of Article 8 (right to respect for private and family life), one of Article 10 (freedom of expression), and one of Article 1 of Protocol 1 (protection of property). However, allegations made in eight cases that the attacks were motivated by the victims' ethnic origin, raised under Article 14 of the Convention, were all unsuccessful.

B.   NGO Involvement in the Kurdish Cases

The KHRP, which is based in London, describes itself as 'an independent, non-political project' with a commitment to 'the protection of the human rights of all persons within the Kurdish regions'.[42] Its (Kurdish-Turkish) Executive

---

[38]   *Taş v Turkey* (App no 24396/94) (2001) 33 EHRR 15 [53].

[39]   *Bilgin v Turkey* (App no 23819/94) (2003) 36 EHRR 50 [22].

[40]   *Bilgin v Turkey* (App no 23819/94) (2003) 36 EHRR 50; *Akkoç v Turkey* ECHR 2000-X, (2002) 34 EHRR 51; *Salman v Turkey* ECHR 2000-VII, (2002) 34 EHRR 17.

[41]   Within the sample cases there were 15 admissible complaints against the Turkish Government under Art 2 of the Convention. Of these, a finding of a violation of the victims' right to life was made in nine.

[42]   Information taken from web-site at: www.khrp.org.
For a summary of the cases taken up to 2000 by the KHRP under the ECHR, see Carla Buckley, *Turkey*

Director is Kerim Yildiz who, along with a group of lawyers concerned about the situation of the Kurds, established the Project in 1992. Although Turkey ratified the ECHR in 1954, it only recognised the right of individual petition in January 1987, and the opportunity this presented to litigate strategically on behalf of the Kurdish people was very much in the mind of the KHRP's founders.[43]

At the time of my research visit from October to November 2002, the KHRP had a staff of nine, which included two lawyers (the Executive Director also has a 'legal background'), a translator and administrative staff.[44] The number of staff employed by the KHRP has remained at around 10 since then. It also (usually) has one or two legal interns at any one period. In spite of its relatively small size (the ERRC, for example, is considerably larger), the KHRP was the most prolific NGO litigating before the Court within the sample cases. During its first decade of existence, the KHRP was involved in submitting over 150 cases to Strasbourg,[45] many of which resulted in ground-breaking judgments on the prohibition of torture.[46]

Painting a precise and complete picture of the role that the KHRP played in the sample cases proved to be impossible. There were four reasons for this. First, access to the KHRP case files was not granted for the purpose of this research. Secondly, given the number of applications the KHRP has been involved in, getting comprehensive information about specific cases by means of interview was unsatisfactory. Thirdly, there was a noticeable reluctance on the part of the KHRP staff to give too much detail about their working methods and relationships with organisations in Turkey for fear of jeopardising them. Finally, as the KHRP was involved in cases on an 'informal' basis only, the Court's case files revealed almost nothing about its involvement. Nevertheless, from the information that was obtained during this research a reasonably clear description of the KHRP's involvement in the sample cases can be pieced together.

The fact that the KHRP is based in London means that in order to implement its transnational litigation project it needs information about human rights violations from a source closer to the ground. As with the ERRC, this is achieved primarily through relationships with local human rights organisations. The importance of these organisations is revealed in Kerim Yildiz's description of

and the European Convention on Human Rights: A Report on the Litigation Programme of the Kurdish Human Rights Project (London, KHRP, July 2000). Initially, the sole focus of the KHRP's litigation project was on Turkey; hence all the sample cases were taken against that country. Since the expansion of the Council of Europe, it has extended to countries such as Armenia and Azerbaijan.

[43]   Interview, Kerim Yildiz, Executive Director of KHRP, 25 November 2002, London.
On the background to the KHRP see also Buckley, *Turkey and the European Convention* (2000), para 19. On Turkey's acceptance of the individual application procedure, see Iain Cameron, 'Turkey and Article 25 of the European Convention on Human Rights' (1988) 37 *International and Comparative Law Quarterly* 887.
[44]   For a current list of staff, see: www.khrp.org/about-khrp/who-we-are/staff.html.
[45]   Interview, Kerim Yildiz, 25 November 2002.
[46]   See, for example, *Aksoy v Turkey* ECHR 1996–VI, (1997) 23 EHRR 553 and *Aydin v Turkey* ECHR 1997-VI, (1998) 25 EHRR 251.

them as 'our partners on the ground'.[47] Several interviewees from the KHRP stated that the vast majority of their cases against Turkey originated from the Human Rights Association of Turkey (HRA), and in particular from its Diyarbakir branch.[48] The HRA was established on 17 July 1986, and currently has 'over 10,000' members and 32 local branches or representative offices in Turkey.[49] It seems likely that at least nine of the 11 cases considered in this section originated from complaints made to it; in fact, in three of the cases either the applicant or the victim was a member of the HRA. However, whilst the relationship between the KHRP and HRA is no secret and is now formally acknowledged, it remained on an informal basis at the time the sample cases were taken thanks to the restrictions that operated on Turkish organisations forging formal links with international organisations.

Once a case was accepted by the KHRP, that organisation was not named as the applicant's representative in proceedings before the ECtHR.[50] Given its small number of in-house lawyers, the KHRP's role in the cases can best be described as an intermediary one: it found – and sometimes paid the fees of – lawyers, the majority of whom were from the United Kingdom, willing to represent victims of human rights violations from Kurdish regions that had come to its attention. Academic lawyers from the University of Essex with expertise in international human rights law litigated each of the KHRP cases within the sample group. In these cases all correspondence with the Court was directed to the lawyers at the University, and it was they who had rights of audience. However, neither the KHRP nor the lawyers acting on its behalf appear to have had frequent contact with applicants. The HRA (or other local contact) was usually the main point-of-contact with the applicant and it did most of the statement taking and fact-finding, with requests for further information coming from the KHRP. The KHRP had further roles in translating documents into English for the Court and researching the background material relied on in applications.

The KHRP, like the ERRC, has a supervisory role in steering the course of litigation in its sponsored cases, and in this it developed its own style, shaped both by its broad objectives in bringing cases and by the fact that direct evidence is frequently not available to prove the violations that have been alleged. The tendency in 'KHRP-cases' is to adduce evidence in the applicant's written observations of patterns of gross violations of the Convention and then to draw

---

[47] Interview, Kerim Yildiz, 3 October 2002.

[48] On the 'fruitful' and, indeed, 'crucial' KHRP-HRA relationship, see KHRP, *Ertak v Turkey, Timurtas v Turkey; State Responsibility in 'Disappearances' – A Case Report* (London, KHRP, 2001) i.

[49] Information obtained from the HRA website at: www.ihd.org.tr/english.

[50] A different practice seems to have been adopted in more recent cases, with applicants representatives named as 'lawyers of the Kurdish Human Rights Project', together with local representatives. See, for example, *Stepanyan v Armenia* (App no 45081/04), ECHR 27 October 2009, and *Amiryan v Armenia* (App no 31553/03) ECHR 13 January 2009.

inferences about the specific allegations from these more generalised observations. NGO and Inter-Governmental Organisation reports on Turkey were frequently provided to the Court and liberally referred to in support of applications. As the body of 'KHRP-cases' expands, these too have raised the Court's awareness of the situation of the Turkish-Kurds. It is interesting to recall in this respect that the KHRP, like the ERRC in *Velikova*, argued unsuccessfully in eight of the sample cases (under Article 14) that the violations in question could be attributed to the victim's ethnic origins. In nine 'KHRP-cases' the applicants also requested (again, without any success) the Court to find there was an 'administrative practice' of violating the Convention in Turkey of which the alleged violation in question formed only a part.[51]

Kerim Yildiz says of the KHRP's role in litigation: 'In a technical sense you can say we are the solicitors'.[52] However, this description does not seem entirely accurate, not least because the applicants named in their cases are not inevitably in contact with them, let alone with the lawyers who actually present their cases in Strasbourg. Indeed, this continues to be an issue for the KHRP as claims for its costs and expenses are often considerably reduced or even refused by the Court. In fact there is no word in legal terminology for the KHRP's function in these cases; as with the ERRC, its most important role is essentially an activist one, ensuring that ECtHR litigation is generated and is used to highlight violations of Kurdish human rights.

IV.   Understanding the Involvement of NGOs in the Case Studies

A.   The Wider Background of Systematic Human Rights Violations

The term Roma describes a culturally, religiously and linguistically diverse ethnic minority group that are without a State of their own, many of whom share a common experience of significant economic and social marginalisation. Bulgaria has, as a percentage figure, one of the largest Roma populations in the world,[53]

---

[51] The origin of this claim is the Court's judgment in *Ireland v United Kingdom* Series A no 25 (1979–80) 2 EHRR 25, in which the Court discussed the implications of 'administrative practices' of torture.

[52] Interview, Kerim Yildiz, 25 November 2002.

[53] European Roma Rights Centre, *Profession: Prisoner – Roma in Detention in Bulgaria* (Budapest, ERRC, December 1997) 16.

Although it is impossible to get precise statistics, Zoltan Barany estimates this figure to be about 8.5%. See Zoltan Barany, *The East European Gypsies: Regime Change, Marginality, and Ethnopolitics* (Cambridge, Cambridge University Press, 2002) 160. The European Commission estimates that there

the majority of whom lack significant formal education[54] and are illiterate.[55] In post-Communist Eastern and Central Europe, where a large proportion of Roma are to be found, a dramatic decline in respect for their rights has been well-reported by academics,[56] various NGOs[57] and Inter-Governmental Organisations (IGOs).[58] In particular, recurrent references can be found to high levels of violence against Roma during the period of transition from Communism, that frequently took place with impunity. The UN Special Rapporteur on Contemporary Forms of Racism, Racial Discrimination, Xenophobia and Related Intolerance, for example, reported in 1999 that

> [p]olice violence targeting Roma occurs in almost all countries of Central and Eastern Europe … Police abuse of Roma in custody is widespread in Bulgaria … Since 1992, at least 14 Roma men in Bulgaria have died after having last been seen alive in police custody, or as a result of the unlawful use of firearms by law enforcement officers … As a rule investigative and judicial remedies are rare.[59]

The Roma are a scape-goated and persecuted group vulnerable to racially-motivated attacks as they do not conform to popular notions of national identity.[60] Violence and discrimination against Roma flourished in the climate of

---

are between 700,000 and 800,000 Roma in Bulgaria. See European Commission, *EU Support for Roma Communities in Central and Eastern Europe* (Brussels, European Commission Enlargement Information Unit, 2003) 4.

[54] Ringold et al note that 89.6% of Bulgarian Roma have received primary school level education or less. See Dena Ringold, Mitchell Orenstein and Erika Wilkens, *Roma in an Expanding Europe: Breaking the Poverty Cycle* (Washington DC, World Bank, 2005) 42.

[55] ERRC, *Profession: Prisoner* (1997) 16.

[56] See, generally, Istvan Pogany, *The Roma Café: Human Rights and the Plight of the Romani People* (London, Pluto Press, 2004), especially ch 8, and Barany, *The East European Gypsies* (2002).

[57] See, for example, the Country Report Series of the ERRC, available at: www.errc.org.
On Bulgaria specifically see, for example, the Human Rights Watch Reports *Bulgaria: Police Violence Against Gypsies* (New York, Human Rights Watch, 1993) and *Bulgaria: Increasing Violence Against Roma in Bulgaria* (New York, Human Rights Watch, 1994).
Amnesty International has also reported extensively on the situation of the Roma. See, for example: *Bulgaria: Torture and Ill Treatment of Roma*, (London, Amnesty International, 1993); *Bulgaria: Shootings, Deaths in Custody, Torture and Ill-Treatment*, (London, Amnesty International, 1996); *Bulgaria: New Cases of Ill-Treatment of Roma* (London, Amnesty International, 1998).

[58] For a summary of various IGO reports on Roma, see Pogany, *The Roma Café* (2004) 141–6. The Court, at para 87 in the *Velikova* judgment, refers to a report of the Special Rapporteur on Torture to the United Nations Commission on Human Rights (UN Document E/CN.4/1997/7 of 10 January 1997) and the Annual Report of the United Nations Special Rapporteur on Contemporary Forms of Racism, Racial Discrimination, Xenophobia and Related Intolerance (UN Document E/CN.4/1999/15 of 15 January 1999). One might also refer, inter alia, to the UN Committee for the Elimination of Racial Discrimination's General Recommendation XXVII on the Roma (adopted at its fifty-seventh session on 16 August 2002), and the OSCE High Commissioner on National Minorities' *Report on the Situation of Roma and Sinti in the OSCE Area* (10 March 2000). See also the Parliamentary Assembly of the Council of Europe Resolution 1211 (2000).

[59] *Annual Report of the United Nations Special Rapporteur on Contemporary Forms of Racism, Racial Discrimination, Xenophobia and Related Intolerance* (UN Document E/CN.4/1999/15, 15 January 1999) para 81.

[60] Dimitrina Petrova, 'Political and Legal Limitations to the Development of Public Interest Law in Post-Communist Societies' (1996) 4–5 *Parker School. Journal of East European Law* 541, 548.

fierce nationalism that emerged during the break-up of the Soviet bloc, in which a convincing commitment to protecting the human rights of minorities was lacking.[61] Although many of these countries have impressive constitutional rights,[62] these 'float in a normative vacuum'.[63] As one journalist has noted of the Roma, '[t]heir ethnicity defines them as an underclass. It's as though Jim Crow was kicked out of America's deep south in the 60s only to land in central Europe at the start of the 21st century'.[64]

The violations in the KHRP cases outlined above occurred against a background of a bitter and bloody conflict that took place in southeast Turkey between 1984 and 1999. Although the conflict's background is complex and lengthy, at its heart is the fictitious notion of a unified and mono-ethnic Turkish State espoused by its founder, Mustafa Kemal Ataturk. The Kurdish population comprises an estimated 20 per cent of the total population of Turkey, but prior to the conflict, the policy of the Government was to deny the legitimacy of any expression of Kurdish identity.[65] Suppression inevitably bred resistance, and in 1978 the militant PKK organisation was established by Abdullah Ocalan, which explicitly sought a separate Kurdistan and by 1984 began to use violence and terror to achieve its aims. The consequence was a serious armed conflict in the predominantly Kurdish areas of Turkey between 1984 and 1999, primarily between the PKK's military wing and the Turkish Security Forces. McDowall describes the situation as follows:

> Few could dismiss the conflict in the south-east as merely a guerrilla war, as the armed forces chiefs tried to make out. On the contrary, the proliferation of the war, and the steady flow of body bags westwards was more suggestive of an incipient civil war.[66]

Of course, the degree of discrimination suffered by Roma varies from country to country. For a detailed analysis of Roma in individual European countries, see Will Guy (ed), *Between Past and Future: the Roma of Central and Eastern Europe* (Hatfield, University of Hertfordshire Press, 2001).

[61]   See Pal Dunay, 'Nationalism and Ethnic Conflicts in Eastern Europe: Imposed, Induced or (Simply) Re-emerged' in Istvan Pogany (ed), *Human Rights in Eastern Europe* (Aldershot, Edward Elgar Publishing, 1995) 21.

On 'populism' as a limitation to the pursuit of minority rights, see Petrova, 'Political and Legal Limitations' (1996). Donnelly has also noted the extremely negative impact nationalism had on human rights in post-Communist countries. See Jack Donnelly, *International Human Rights* (Boulder, Westview Press, 1998) 136–48 generally, and especially 146–8.

[62]   See Council of Europe, *The Rebirth of Democracy: Twelve Constitutions of Central and Eastern Europe* (Strasbourg, Council of Europe, 1996).

[63]   Petrova, 'Political and Legal Limitations' (1996) 558. The point should be made that the degree of discrimination suffered by Roma varies from country to country. For a more detailed analysis of Roma in individual countries, see Guy (ed), *Between Past and Future* (2001).

[64]   Gary Younge, 'Shame of a Continent', 8 January 2003 *The Guardian (G2)* 2–4, 3.

[65]   For a historical over-view of the Kurds in Turkey see: David McDowall, *The Kurds* (London, Minority Rights Group International Report 96/4, 1996); David McDowall, *A Modern History of the Kurds* (London, IB Tauris, 1997); Gerard Chaliand, *The Kurdish Tragedy*, translated by Philip Black (London, Zed Books, 1994), especially chs 1–2; Gerard Chaliand (ed), *A People Without a Country: The Kurds and Kurdistan*, translated by Michael Pallis (London, Zed Books, 1993).

[66]   McDowall, *The Kurds* (1996), 19. See also Aliza Marcus, 'Turkey's Kurds After the Gulf War: A Report from the Southeast', in Chaliand, *A People Without a Country* (1993) 238.

NGOs reported violations of humanitarian law by both sides during this large-scale and bloody conflict in which combatants were not the only victims.[67] The Turkish State tended to conflate attempts to express pro-Kurdish sentiment with separatist politics and therefore to be treated as a threat to the nation. In the 1990s (the time applicable to the KHRP cases discussed above) the Government's official response was to introduce extensive anti-terrorist laws (in particular the Law to Fight Terrorism, introduced on 12 April 1991) and to declare large areas of the south east to be under Emergency Rule.[68] Both NGOs[69] and IGOs[70] have reported widely on the unofficial State-sponsored campaign of violence, including torture, disappearances and other gross violations of the human rights of people not actively engaged in hostilities – especially, although not exclusively, Kurds – that took place with impunity and became a regular occurrence in the war against terror.

The role of the NGOs in both of the case studies discussed above can only be properly understood against a background of nationalist sentiment resulting in persistent patterns of gross human rights violations, albeit that the Roma and the Kurds experienced this at different levels of intensity. What unifies these examples is that in both situations, calls to respect the human rights of the minorities concerned struggled to gain a platform and were even seen to be contrary to national interests. Ratification by the respondent States of the ECHR, on the other hand, provided a much-needed opportunity to address deep-rooted violence and discrimination. It is noteworthy – although perhaps unsurprising, given the potentially grave diplomatic and political consequences that can follow

---

[67] See, for example, Amnesty International, *Turkey: A Policy of Denial* (London, Amnesty International, Feb 1995).

[68] There have been significant legislative improvements in the intervening years, most notably in Law No 4744 of 6 February 2002. For detailed reports of the steps taken see, for example, the annual reports of Human Rights Watch on Turkey, available at: www.hrw.org/en/europecentral-asia/turkey.

[69] See, for example, Amnesty International's reports: *Turkey: No Security Without Human Rights* (London, Amnesty International, 1996); *Turkey: Still No Proper Investigation into 'Disappearances'* (London, Amnesty International, 1998); *Turkey: Creating a Silent Society* (London, Amnesty International, 1999); *Turkey: The Duty to Supervise, Investigate and Prosecute* (London, Amnesty International, 1999); *Turkey: An End to Torture and Impunity is Overdue* (London, Amnesty International, 2001). See also Human Rights Watch, *Turkey: Violations of Free Expression in Turkey* (New York, Human Rights Watch, 1999).

[70] See, for example: Resolution No 985 (1992) of the Parliamentary Assembly of the Council of Europe on the Situation of Human Rights in Turkey, adopted on 30 June 1992; the European Committee for the Prevention of Torture and Inhuman or Degrading Treatment or Punishment's *Public Statement on Turkey* (CPT/Inf (93) 1), which refers to the 'deep-rooted problem' evident from their ad hoc visits in 1990 and 1991; the UN Committee against Torture's report on Turkey of 15 November 1993 (A/48/44/Add.1. Inquiry under Article 20), which at para 59 confirms 'the existence and systematic character of the practice of torture'; reports of UN Working Group on Enforced and Involuntary Disappearances, particularly the 1994 report (UN Doc E/CN.4/1995/36); and the report of UN Special Rapporteur on Torture of 12 January 1995 (E/CN.4/1995/34) paras 746–826.

Although the situation has now greatly improved, the legacy of unrestrained violence remains. On the on-going issues of concern, see, for example, the *Report to the Turkish Government on the visit to Turkey Carried out by the European Committee for the Prevention of Torture and Inhuman or Degrading Treatment or Punishment from 7 to 15 September 2003* (doc CPT/Inf (2004) 16).

from revealing a fellow Contracting State to be a human rights violator and exposing it to the glare of international scrutiny – that even these serious and repeated violations of the Convention were not addressed through inter-State litigation.[71] As Reidy et al note, the individual application procedure has been turned to in order to fill this void:

> The inter-State mechanism under the Convention is more readily designed to raise these larger issues. However, because the political will is absent on the part of other States to become involved in such an application against Turkey, it is in the context of the individual complaints mechanism that efforts have been made to raise complaints of such a large scale violation ... Individual applications as a means of highlighting a general situation of violation and forcing a judicial investigation of State policies in the context of an emergency may have considerable long term potential, especially if States remain reluctant to call each other to account for violations of their commitments under the Convention. But the experience of these Turkish applications to date, underline the difficulties.[72]

That ECHR litigation is used in this way is unsurprising given that legal strategies, as Eskridge notes, are most effective when the main issue for a social movement is the 'politics of protection for its members against a brutalizing state'.[73] Practical and evidential hurdles surmounted, success is obviously a foregone conclusion in cases that point to unarguable violations of basic human rights standards. Furthermore, it may be that resort to the ECtHR is the best available remedy where access to other political and legal processes is denied to certain groups.

While lodging an application with the ECtHR is not necessarily *the* most effective way of addressing serious human rights violations (for NGOs it inevitably takes place alongside advocacy, publishing and educative programmes), it is certainly recognised as *an* effective means of doing so. This perception is primarily based upon the impressive reputation of the Court. As one senior ERRC lawyer said, '[its judgments] get a lot of media attention; you can use that

---

[71]   Dunay argues in relation to the Roma – and here analogies can be drawn with the situation of the Kurds – that because they are a stateless group, they 'cannot count on the effective support of a nation represented by a state' to assist them when their rights are violated. Dunay, 'Nationalism and Ethnic Conflict (1995) 27.

[72]   Aisling Reidy, Francoise Hampson and Kevin Boyle, 'Gross Violations of Human Rights: Invoking the European Convention on Human Rights in the Case of Turkey' (1997) 15(2) *Netherlands Quarterly of Human Rights* 161, 172. These authors note, at 164, that one of the two inter-State applications that has been brought against Turkey was settled partly on the basis of Turkey agreeing to accede to the individual petition system.
See also Menno Kamminga, 'Is the European Convention on Human Rights Sufficiently equipped to Cope with Gross and Systematic Violations?' (1994) 12(2) *Netherlands Quarterly of Human Rights* 153.

[73]   William Eskridge, 'Some Effects of Identity-Based Social Movements on Constitutional Law in the Twentieth Century' (2002) 100 *Michigan Law Review* 2062. For a discussion of the use made of the Inter-American system to address gross human rights violations, see Juan E Mendez and José Miguel Vivanco, 'Disappearances and the Inter-American Court: Reflections on a Litigation Experience' (1990) 13 *Hamline Law Review* 507.

to lobby and change the law'.[74] Each favourable ECtHR judgment adds credibility to allegations that human rights violations are widespread and that systemic reform is required. The more that such knowledge exists, the harder it is for such violations to continue with impunity as domestic and international attention is drawn to the situation. In April 1995, the Parliamentary Assembly of the Council of Europe passed a resolution calling for the suspension of Turkey's right of representation unless its human rights record in relation to the Kurdish population improved,[75] and the Committee of Ministers passed an interim resolution as recently as July 2002 expressing its concern about Turkey's human rights record.[76] Membership of the European Union, to cite another example, is a carrot that has been dangled under the nose of the Turkish Government for a considerable length of time, but continues to be denied them. Violations of human rights continue to be a cause of concern in the European Commission despite the considerable improvements that have taken place in Turkey since the late 1990s.[77] In relation to Bulgaria's accession process, the European Commission each year remarked upon the continuing and little improved marginalisation of, and discrimination against, Roma.[78]

Addressing structural issues that concern discrimination against minority groups as a whole is a weighty expectation to place on individual applicants. What emerges from the case studies is the remarkable fact that the principal initiators of pressure for structural reform through individual applications are NGOs, who use the political leverage provided by ECtHR judgments as a means of publicising to a wide audience the treatment that minorities receive in these countries. While this activist function of civil society is well documented in the context of other human rights bodies, it has been less readily acknowledged that ECtHR litigation is used for aims that are, ultimately, transformative.

B. Resources

Viewed in the harsh light of economic realities, it is clear why comparatively well-resourced NGOs have a role in activating litigation that highlights systematic violations of the Convention. It was noted in the previous chapter that litigation, even before the ECtHR, can be a financially costly process. It goes without saying that the Roma and Kurds are both economically disadvantaged groups, and it would clearly be unrealistic to imagine that the individual applicants were in a position to fund the type of successful pioneering litigation

---

[74] Interview, Branimir Plese, Senior Staff Attorney at the ERRC, 20 September 2002, Budapest.

[75] Recommendation 1266 (1995).

[76] Interim Resolution ResDH (2002) 98 of 10 July 2002, which was itself a follow-up to Interim Resolution DH(99)434.

[77] The European Commission's documents on Turkey's accession process can be obtained via: ec.europa.eu/enlargement/candidate-countries/turkey/key-documents/index_en.htm.

[78] On Roma and the accession process of Eastern and Central European countries generally, see European Commission, *EU Support for Roma Communities* (2003).

exemplified in the case studies.[79] In this chapter we have gained some idea of the sheer number of people, expert in their field, that it took to ensure that the litigation in question was successful; the preparation of each relied upon a considerable network of human rights activists.[80] This preparation involved, inter alia: unearthing violations of the Convention; preparing evidence, such as medical reports; conducting interviews; translating materials; understanding domestic law provisions; ensuring that domestic remedies were exhausted; and drafting legal applications.

Considerable resources were also employed in the cases discussed above to ensure that the Court was, through various IGO and NGO reports, fully aware of the political and social background to specific human rights violations. Systematic violations were also highlighted through the introduction of numerous reiterative applications, which involved 'consistently urging that there is a practice of violation of the Convention'.[81] This sort of information served not only the broader aims of the litigation, but also as a partial remedy for the paucity of information – and the comprehensive denials – provided by respondent Governments in answer to the allegations made. Without the co-operation of the Government concerned, gathering evidence to prove the violation of fundamental rights can be almost impossible. It is therefore a sensible litigation tactic to ensure that the Court is made aware of patterns of human rights abuse and patterns of subsequent denial.[82] Particularly in circumstances of disappearances and deaths in custody, it is hard to see what alternative strategy would be successful given the total absence of any effective investigation. In these situations, an approach to litigation that focuses on an isolated violation of human rights, without placing it in its wider context, is unlikely to be successful.

With litigation strategies that involve taking multiple cases, these NGOs also gain experience and specialist knowledge which enable them to anticipate what issues are likely to be problematic before the Court and to plan their litigation accordingly. They can develop innovative arguments and litigation strategies as a result of their experience as 'repeat players'. To take one example from the sample cases, the issue of working out pecuniary damage in the *Velikova* case might have caused difficulties for a lawyer unversed in Romani culture and lifestyle, because Mr Tsonchev's employment had not been formal and documented and the applicant was therefore unable to prove his income. As the ERRC has instigated the application, however, the phenomenon of casual Roma employment conditions could be explained to the Court, and the argument made that to refuse to

---

[79]   Pogany, *The Roma Café* (2004) 2–4.

[80]   On the significance of NGO networks generally, see Margaret Keck and Katherine Sikkink, *Activists Beyond Borders: Advocacy Networks in International Politics* (Ithaca NY, Cornell University Press, 1998).

[81]   Buckley, *Turkey and the European Convention* (2000) 34.

[82]   On this point, see Reidy et al, 'Gross Violations of Human Rights' (1997) 169.

award compensation for loss of income on this basis 'would make impossible any award of pecuniary compensation to Romanies or other persons who live in a strictly cash economy'.[83]

Similarly, the KHRP has contributed to significant developments in the Court's jurisprudence, in particular in relation to its rules of evidence. The 'KHRP case' of *Timurtas v Turkey*,[84] for example, in which the Court found a violation of Article 2 as a result of a disappearance, was particularly important in challenging an earlier decision in which the Court held that the best way to consider a 'disappearance' was under Article 5 (the right to liberty and security).[85] To this end, the KHRP is also in a position to draw on the expertise of others. In *Timurtas*, the KHRP asked CEJIL (a Washington DC based NGO) to provide written comments on the Inter-American Court of Human Rights' jurisprudence on disappearances. This intervention helped persuade the Court to adapt its rules for situations of gross and systematic violations of human rights. As Buckley notes of the KHRP's litigation in general:

> While the cases have generally been valuable in developing Convention jurisprudence, they can also claim to have broken new ground and laid the foundations for future claims under the Convention involving internal armed conflict and gross violations of human rights.[86]

By developing a long-term litigation strategy, the KHRP has been successful in getting the Court to develop practices more appropriate to dealing with situations of gross and systematic rights violation. Knowledge and experience of international human rights litigation ensure that NGOs are in a better position to challenge gross violations of human rights than an individual, with or without a lawyer, would be.

C.   Access to Justice

Assuming that an applicant is in a position to use the Strasbourg system to challenge her Government, the notion of the individual rights-bearer presupposes that she will be able to find a lawyer willing to act as her representative. In most systems of justice individuals do not fully understand the language of law and do not know how to engage with the legal system; lawyers are commonly used to bridge that divide and to make systems of justice accessible. But accessing legal assistance is not always straightforward. One former employee of the HRP whom I interviewed noted that Roma who suffer a human rights violation frequently 'don't know … where to go, how to file a complaint, [or] get medical

---

[83]   *Anya Velikova v Bulgaria* (App no 41488/98) ECHR 2000-VI, [100].
[84]   *Timurtas v Turkey* ECHR 2000-VI, (2001) 33 EHRR 6.
[85]   *Kurt v Turkey* ECHR 1998-III, (1999) 27 EHRR 373.
[86]   Buckley, *Turkey and the European Convention* (2000) para 421.

certificates'.[87] The HRP writes that most Roma complaints are made 'in oral form to some local authority. These complaints are never documented and their legal value is equal to zero'.[88] A further point made to me in interview was that Roma simply 'don't have the money to travel' in order to be able to consult with lawyers.[89] Members of staff of the HRP therefore frequently travel to (potential) clients to conduct interviews and fact-finding. In relation to the first case study discussed in this chapter, the inaccessibility of lawyers to remedy violations of human rights would undoubtedly have been exacerbated by a general lack of knowledge about the Convention system amongst Bulgarian lawyers, as the Convention only entered into force for Bulgaria on 7 September 1992.[90]

Even had she known where to turn, Ms Velikova might have had trouble finding a private lawyer willing to represent her. It has already been remarked that at the time of Mr Tsonchev's death there were no qualified Roma lawyers in Bulgaria, and Istvan Pogany has written more recently that there are still 'very few Romani lawyers who can take up claims on behalf of their people'.[91] In this circumstance, it is particularly troubling to note that in post-Communist Bulgaria there are few non-Roma lawyers willing to take on Roma cases.[92] Lawyers appear to fear that Roma clients would be unable to pay fees in cases that in any event offer little prospect of adequate financial reward.

Lawyers, moreover, have reason to be reluctant to defend unpopular causes. The HRP has suggested that in the context of increased nationalist sentiment, taking a human rights case against the Government can be seen as unpatriotic and contrary to the national interest:

> It is a matter of serious concern that 'human rights' are once again becoming dirty words in the Bulgarian society, very much like they were during communist rule. Once the human rights advocates were seen as traitors of the Communist order and agents of the world imperialism, now—as traitors of the Nation and agents of 'foreign interests'.[93]

In extremis, hostility towards human rights defenders is manifested in violence. The HRP, for example, reports that it has been the subject of threats by neo-Nazis.[94] Similarly, human rights litigation on behalf of Kurds is clearly seen by the Turkish Government as part of a pro-Kurdish political campaign, inspired

---

[87]   Interview, Ivan Ivanov, 18 September 2002.
[88]   (May–June 1996) 1(2) *Focus: The Newsletter of the HRP* 11.
[89]   Interview, Ivan Ivanov, 18 September 2002.
[90]   On the lack of knowledge of Bulgarian lawyers about human rights laws at this time, see Petrova, *Violations of the Rights of Gypsies* (1994) 41.
[91]   Pogany, *The Roma Café* (2004) 46.
[92]   Interview, Ivan Ivanov, 18 September 2002. See also Petrova, *Violations of the Rights of Gypsies* (1994) 5.
[93]   Human Rights Project, *Annual Report: 1994* (Sofia, HRP, 1995) 24.
[94]   *ibid*, 22.
The European Commission notes that between October 2003 and August 2004 there were 98 court cases and investigations launched against members of the HRA in Turkey. See *2004 Regular Report on Turkey's Progress Towards Accession* 6 October 2004, Com(2004) 656 final, 42

by separatist ideals. For example, in the Government's observations in one of the KHRP cases discussed above it is claimed that the application was

> prepared with racial implications …[which] have been consistently used by the representatives of applicants in nearly all applications originating from the south eastern part of Turkey. The aim of this effort the respondent State believes is to establish a belief that the south eastern part of the Turkish State should be considered as a Kurdish territory, which was also clearly defined and accepted by the leader of the terrorist organization PKK during the trials at the Ankara State Security Court which held its sessions at Invah Island in May 1999. Thus a parallel could easily be seen with the aims of the so called Diyarbakir-London line and the theoretical claims and practices of the PKK.[95]

During the course of the conflict in Turkey, lawyers seeking to bring abuses of the human rights of Kurds to the attention of domestic and international tribunals were rewarded with criminal convictions and prison sentences under Anti-Terror Laws.[96] An indictment against 16 Diyarbakir lawyers for membership of the PKK actually included the making of applications to the ECmHR as evidence of this charge.[97] There have been regular closures of branches of the HRA,[98] harassment of its lawyers,[99] and seizure of documents relating to its cases.[100] Indeed, a number of 'KHRP cases' relate to harassment of human rights defenders.[101] Of greatest concern are reports that lawyers have been the victims of 'unknown perpetrator killings'.[102] In this climate, it is not surprising that the HRA and the KHRP operate on the simple principle of safety in numbers:

---

[95]   *Turkish Government's Observations in Timurtas v Turkey*, undated, received 1 July 1999 (on file with the Court's Registry).

[96]   See generally, Louise Christian *et al*, *The European Convention Under Attack: The Threat to Lawyers in Turkey and the Challenge to Strasbourg – A Report of Delegations to Turkey Between February and May 1995* (London, KHRP [etc], August 1995); Buckley, *Turkey and the European Convention* (2000) 154.
Amnesty International has highlighted the plight of several lawyers and human rights defenders in Turkey. See, for example: *Turkey: Creating a Silent Society: The Turkish Government Prepares to Imprison Leading Human Rights Defender* (1 February 1999, AI Eur 44/05/99); *Turkey: Fear for Safety/Fear of Arrest of Human Rights Defenders* (16 January 2001, AI Eur 44/003/2001); *Turkey: Ocalan Lawyers at Risk* (26 February 1999, AI Eur 44/20/99); *Turkey: Lawyers Severely Ill-Treated Outside Buca Prison in Izmir* (London, Amnesty International, 1996).

[97]   Indictment dated 12 January 1995, reproduced in Christian *et al*, *The European Convention Under Attack* (1995) appendix 4.

[98]   The Diyarbakir branch of the HRA, for example, was shut down in May 1997. See Amnesty International Press Release, *Turkey: Authorities Shut Down Key Human Rights Branch* (23 May 1997, AI Index: Eur 44/39/97).

[99]   Sezgin Tanrikulu of Diyarbakir has, for example, been a particular target of persecution. See Amnesty International *Harassment of Human Rights Foundation, Diyarbakir, Turkey* (18 February 2002, AI Index: EUR 44/009/2002).

[100]   Christian et al, *The European Convention Under Attack* (1995) 4.

[101]   See, for example, *Elci and Others v Turkey* (App nos 23145/93 and 25091/94) ECHR 13 November 2003.

[102]   Christian et al, *The European Convention Under Attack* (1995) 4.
The HRA's web-site names several of their members who have been assassinated at: www.ihd.org.tr/english/index.php?option=com_content&view=article&id=141&Itemid=48.

> The Human Rights Association were brave enough to insist on taking these cases. It was not individual lawyers ... It was safer for us to take cases, safer for the documents.[103]

The comparative strength of NGOs means that they are better able to withstand any backlash that occurs after calls for human rights to be respected have been made. Furthermore, being located outside of Turkey has meant that the KHRP has not suffered problems of harassment, and in this respect it has clearly been beneficial to have an organisation outside of Turkey dealing with applications and drawing attention to the Turkish Government's violations.

D.   Lack of Litigious Consciousness

The supposition that individuals will contemplate resort to legal remedies when faced with (what lawyer's would name) a human rights violation might be based more on lawyerly optimism than on sociological realism. The vision of the independent litigant fails to take into account the fact that individuals can experience systematic violations of human rights without necessarily naming them as such.[104] In fact, oppression and marginalisation – not to mention the increasingly technocratic nature of human rights – can operate to ensure that the forceful and demanding language of human rights does not come readily to minorities like the Roma and Kurds. It has been stated already that at the time of Mr Tsonchev's death violations of the rights of Roma were taking place with impunity in Bulgaria. It is not surprising, therefore, that at that time Roma tended to avoid resort to legal remedies and the assertion of their rights. In such situations, the expectation that the individual rights-bearer will be the driving force behind litigation is inadequate.

The view of those working in the field is that NGOs are needed to take an active role in such situations in order to create a culture of human rights and to generate a litigious consciousness. As an HRP report explains,

> [t]he presumption that the client is the active party in the lawyer-client relationship – which in Bulgaria has been always part of the cultural stereotypes – is counterproductive in the case of representing Roma minority clients. The legal representation of Roma victims of human rights abuse requires the defense lawyer to take up the leading role, and to be not only trusted, but followed, i.e. to urge the client to cooperate with him and not to despair. The passivity of the Roma people, which is part of their submissive role in society, makes the task of the lawyer rather different as compared to 'normal' practice. The human rights lawyer is there to motivate the victim to seek redress through the law.[105]

---

[103]   Interview, Kerim Yildiz, 25 November 2002.
[104]   Petrova, *Violations of the Rights of Gypsies* (1994) 4.
On the same point in the context of Uganda, see Susan Dicklitch and Doreen Lwanga, 'The Politics of Being Non-Political: Human Rights Organizations and the Creation of a Positive Human Rights Culture in Uganda' (2003) 25(2) *Human Rights Quarterly* 482, 492.
[105]   Human Rights Project, *Annual Report: 1994* (Sofia, HRP, 1995) 15.

Where the cost to the individual of pursuing a case is so potentially high, NGOs have found that clients need to be sought out and encouraged to litigate.[106] As Ivan Ivanov, a former member of staff at the HRP, said, '[l]awyers aren't keen to go in to the field. But victims are not coming to you. If you want them to know their rights, you have to go to them and ask them what is their problem'.[107] Whilst it would be inaccurate and too simplistic to emphasise the passivity of all Roma,[108] the HRP have noted that despite experiencing serious discrimination in the post-Communist era, for the Roma 'the law and the judiciary in particular were not foreseen as a tool for change'.[109] This can be at least partly explained by the tradition in Roma culture of scepticism and reserve towards the State and its associated bureaucracy, which are seen as alien and serving the interests of 'Gadje' (non-Roma). Pogany makes the further point that 'low levels of literacy have meant that most ordinary Roma lack the skills needed to communicate effectively with non-Roma society'.[110] NGOs like the ERRC therefore reject the traditional approach to lawyering, in favour of pro-actively developing a relationship with (potential) applicants. The language of human rights is used to legitimise this struggle for political recognition on behalf of the Roma.[111]

Although when it was first established in 1992 the KHRP had something of an awareness-raising role in relation to the Convention, the situation in which it operates is somewhat different. The Kurds of Turkey form a large group, many of whom are educated, live in cities, and are very politically aware; many of the applicants and victims involved in KHRP cases are highly educated Kurdish intellectuals, including journalists, doctors and teachers. Many are also politically active and, particularly as Turkey ratified the Convention in 1954, aware of their human rights. The human rights message of the KHRP-HRA has therefore been preached to a receptive and eager audience, and the sheer number of cases instigated against the Turkish Government stands testimony to this. However, it is clear from the case law of the ECtHR that there has been severe intimidation of applicants and lawyers who attempt to challenge the Turkish Government's human rights record,[112] and numerous successful applications concerning its

---

[106]   For an interesting account of the HRP's difficulties in getting a Roma applicant to co-operate in litigation, see N Ghughinski, 'Roma Wins a Lawsuit Against the Ministry of Internal Affairs' (January–April 1996) 1(1) *Focus: The Newsletter of the HRP* 7.

[107]   Interview, Ivan Ivanov, 18 September 2002.

[108]   For an account of the rise of pressure politics amongst the 'gypsies' of England and Wales, see Thomas Acton, *Gypsy Politics and Social Change: The Development of Ethnic Ideology and Pressure Politics Among British Gypsies from Victorian Reformists to Romany Nationalism* (London, Routledge & Kegan Paul, 1974), especially parts 3–5 & 7.

[109]   (May–June 1996) 1(2) *Focus: The Newsletter of the HRP* 10.

[110]   Pogany, *The Roma Café* (2004) 46.

[111]   See, generally, Nicolae Gheorghe and Thomas Acton, 'Citizens of the World and Nowhere' in Guy (ed), *Between Past and Future* (2001) 57.

[112]   On governmental interference with the applicant's right to petition, see, for example: *Kurt v Turkey* ECHR 1998-III, (1999) 27 EHRR 373; *Akdivar v Turkey* ECHR 1996-VI, (1997) 23 EHRR 143; *Mentes v Turkey* ECHR 1997-VII, (1998) 26 EHRR 595.

interference with the right to petition.[113] Perhaps the most striking case is that of *Aksoy v Turkey*,[114] which was the first case against Turkey concerning Article 3 of the Convention, in which the applicant was killed in suspicion circumstances before judgment was delivered. The role of the KHRP, together with the HRA, in these circumstances is to ensure that a space is provided in which the burgeoning litigious consciousness can thrive, and to provide as much encouragement and safety as possible for applicants who are potentially putting themselves at risk.

V. Recent Developments

It goes without saying, and it is something of a measure of the KHRP's success, that the human rights situation of the Kurds in Turkey has improved in the past decade.[115] Many see Europe – and especially Turkey's candidacy for accession to the EU – as a major instigator of these reforms.[116] But the reforms appear fragile and Çali is dubious, given the considerable resistance amongst the Turkish political elite to European interference, as to how much of a part the ECtHR has played in bringing them about:

> The Southeast Turkey cases were quickly reduced to a schema of 'cases lost' and compensation paid rather than taken as an opportunity to engage with the Kurdish question by coming to grips with the causes of violence and addressing state account-ability.[117]

Despite such scepticism, and despite a certain shift in focus beyond traditional civil and political rights, the KHRP continues to litigate a great number of ECHR cases that highlight gross and systemic human rights violations. In particular, expanded membership of the Council of Europe has opened up new sites for strategic litigation: in 2009 the KHRP submitted nine applications to the Court and received six favourable judgments in cases against Armenia.[118] For the KHRP, the ECHR clearly continues to be a significant tool in its struggle on behalf of the Kurds.

---

[113] See, generally, Human Rights Watch, *Violations of the Right of Petition to the European Commission of Human Rights* (New York, Human Rights Watch, April 1996).

[114] *Aksoy v Turkey* ECHR 1996-VI, (1997) 23 EHRR 553.

[115] Çali says that by 2004, 'a total of 490 laws had been adopted or amended'. See Başak Çali, 'The Logics of Supranational Human Rights Litigation, Official Acknowledgement, and Human Rights Reform: The Southeast Turkey Cases Before the European Court of Human Rights, 1996–2006' (2010) 35(2) *Law and Social Inquiry* 311.

[116] Charles G MacDonald and Carole A O'Leary, *Kurdish Identity: Human Rights and Political Status* (Gainesville FL, University Press of Florida, 2007).

[117] Çali, 'The Logics of Supranational Human Rights Litigation' (2010) 334.

[118] *Amiryan v Armenia* (App no 31553/03), ECHR 13 January 2009; *Sapeyan v Armenia* (App no 35738/03) ECHR 13 January 2009; *Gasparyan v Armenia (No 1)* (App no 35944/03) ECHR 13 January

The ERRC too continues to litigate regularly before the Court. Since *Velikova*, ERRC cases have continued to improve the protection offered by the Convention against racial violence by State actors and other forms of discrimination.[119] Perhaps most noteworthy in recent years are its cases that have successfully challenged the assignment of Romani students to schools for children with special learning needs.[120] The impact of such work is that human rights is now the dominant discourse in which injustice against Roma populations is framed. O'Nions has recently described the ERRC's work using legal strategies to 'empower the Roma at a grass-roots level' as 'particularly significant',[121] adding that the Roma voice is 'getting louder'.[122] She also remarks upon the rise of NGOs with Roma participation, arguing that this signifies 'that a public space for Roma is beginning to emerge'.[123] Reflecting on this trend and the 'success of 'the discourse of rights amongst Romani activist in particular', Vermeersch describes the ERRC as 'one of the central supportive organizations for the Romani movement'.[124] But it is noteworthy that these activist voices, whilst raised, can still appear remarkably easy to ignore. Vermeersch and Ram remarked in 2009 that the Roma movement shows 'little sign of progress'.[125] Rechel says the ECtHR rulings on the Roma 'seem to have been ignored by both the European Commission and the Bulgarian Government',[126] while Goldston and Adjani note the continued police violence against Roma in Bulgaria.[127] The ERRC itself has said that in spite of its success in challenging the education of Romani children in

---

2009; *Gasparyan v Armenia (No 2)* (App no 22571/05) ECHR 16 June 2009; *Stepanyan v Armenia* (App no 45081/04) ECHR 27 October 2009; *Karapetyan v Armenia* (App no 22387/05), ECHR 27 October 2009.

[119] See, for example, *Balogh v Hungary* (App no 47940/99) ECHR 20 July 2004, *Nachova v Bulgaria* ECHR 2005-VII, (2006) 42 EHRR 43, and *Stoica v Romania* (App no 42722/02) ECHR 4 March 2008.

[120] See, *DH v Czech Republic* (App no 57325/00) (2008) 47 EHRR 3 and *Oršuš v Romania* (App no 15766/03) ECHR [GC] 16 March 2010. The Court's enhancement of the Convention's prohibition of indirectly discriminatory measures in these cases was heavily influenced by the EU's Racial Equality Directive. See Council Directive implementing the principle of equal treatment between persons irrespective of racial or ethnic origins, Council Directive 2000/43/EC of 29 June 2000, OJ L180/22.

[121] Helen O'Nions, *Minority Rights Protection in International Law: The Roma of Europe* (Aldershot, Ashgate, 2007).

[122] *ibid*, 22.

[123] *ibid*, 273.

[124] Peter Vermeersch, *The Romani Movement: Minority Politics and Ethnic Mobilization in Contemporary Central Europe* (New York, Berghahn Books, 2006) 157–8.

[125] Peter Vermeersch and Melanie H Ram, 'The Roma' in Bernd Rechel (ed), *Minority Rights in Central and Eastern Europe* (London, Routledge, 2009) 66.

[126] Bernd Rechel, 'Bulgaria: Minority Rights Light' in Rechel (ed), *Minority Rights* (2009) 85.

[127] James A Goldston and Mirna Adjani, 'The Opportunities and Challenges of Using Public Interest Litigation to Secure Access to Justice for Roma in Central and Eastern Europe', in Yash Ghai and Jill Cottrell (eds), *Marginalized Communities and Access to Justice* (Abingdon, Routledge, 2010) 214.

Indeed, the ERRC continues to litigate cases that highlight police brutality. See, for example, *Sashov v Bulgaria* (App no 14383/01) ECHR 7 January 2010.

specialist schools, 'the practice of segregation continues unabated'.[128] There is plenty of evidence that the Roma of Europe continue to face exceptional levels of exclusion and discrimination.[129] But the ECtHR, although clearly limited in its impact, has not been abandoned by activists seeking to improve the situation of excluded minorities: quite the reverse.

The litigations strategies outlined in this chapter are perceived to have continued relevance as new struggles are brought before the Court. The vast majority of the successful applications lodged against Russia that result from the bitter conflict in Chechnya, for example, have been, and continue to be, initiated by human rights NGOs.[130] Philip Leach, who was once Legal Director of the KHRP, now heads the European Human Rights Advocacy Centre, a London-based organisation established in December 2002 that is involved in the majority of these cases.[131] Together with a number of Russian- and Georgian-based NGOs (Memorial, in particular), EHRAC is currently working on 'around 250' cases before the ECtHR.[132] It is also involved in training and awareness-raising.

The parallels with the KHRP's and the ERRC's work described in this chapter are really striking. Like those organisations, EHRAC identifies lack of knowledge and understanding of the Convention system as a reason for its establishment (Russia ratified the Convention in 1998, Georgia in 1999). EHRAC uses its legal skills and knowledge to create credible cases – cases of the most serious kind – that are designed to mobilise, shame and contribute to political reform. The Russian Government has responded to these by intimidating applicants,[133] failing to co-operate with the Court's proceedings,[134] and denying all knowledge of or involvement in the alleged wrong-doing. In many respects KHRP and ERRC cases have smoothed the way for this kind of litigation, and the success rate of EHRAC's cases is remarkable. The Court delivered its first judgments concerning the Chechen situation in February 2005, which concerned torture, indiscriminate bombings and extra-judicial killings. In each case it reached a finding of a violation of the right to life. EHRAC has since taken numerous cases concerning

---

[128]   Anon, 'ERRC Representative Opens the First Decade Meeting under the Slovak Presidency' (Nov 2009) 6 *Roma Rights News* 4.

[129]   EU-MIDIS, *European Union Minorities and Discrimination Survey: Data in Focus 1 – The Roma* (European Union Agency for Fundamental Rights, 2009); Commissioner for Human Rights, *Final Report on the Human Rights Situation of the Roma, Sinti and Travellers in Europe* (15 February 2009) CommDH(2006); UNDP, *At Risk: Roma and the Displaced in Southeast Europe* (Bratislava, UNDP, 2006); UNICEF, *Breaking the Cycle of Exclusion: Roma Children in South East Europe* (Belgrade, UNICEF Serbia, February 2007).

[130]   See Philip Leach, 'The Chechen Conflict: Analysing the Oversight of the European Court of Human Rights' (2008) 6 *European Human Rights Law Review* 732, 735.

[131]   For further information about EHRAC can be found on its website at: www.londonmet.ac.uk/ research-units/hrsj/affiliated-centres/ehrac/home.cfm.

[132]   Information from EHRAC website.

[133]   EHRAC, *Annual Report: 2006* (London, EHRAC, 2007) 16.

[134]   Leach, 'The Chechen Conflict' (2008) 738, 744 and 746.

disappearances and unacknowledged detention,[135] arbitrary executions,[136] the killing and wounding of civilians,[137] unjustified detention and inhumane conditions of detention.[138] There have also been numerous findings of a violation of the requirement on States to co-operate with proceedings in Article 38(1)(a), exposing, in Leach's words, 'a policy of legal nihilism of the domestic authorities towards Chechnya and its inhabitants'.[139] Tragically echoing the HRA's experiences, Natalia Estemirova, a Memorial board member, was abducted and murdered in July 2009.

Whilst following in the footsteps of other organisations, EHRAC's litigation strategy has managed to break new ground. Together with Planet of Hopes, EHRAC has successfully argued, at the national level, environmental cases concerning pollution from nuclear plants. EHRAC has also made innovative use of the Committee of Ministers' new Rules for the Supervision of the Execution of Judgments,[140] which allow the Committee to consider communications from NGOs.[141] EHRAC and Memorial have submitted memoranda to the Committee of Ministers concerning Russia's non-compliance with the first 'Chechen judgments'.[142] With Protocol 14 introducing new and better mechanisms for enforcing judgments, enforcement issues are likely to be of increasing interest to NGOs seeking to secure the Convention's rights for marginalised communities. In short, the limited gains on offer from an ECHR litigation strategy in terms of immediate social transformation are not off-putting to some NGOs. In fact, new ECHR litigation strategies continue to be developed. But, in light of the pioneer's experiences, NGOs are more aware now that any benefits brought to the communities concerned are, at best, future ones. Furthermore, NGOs are aware that the impact of litigation strategies will be greater if they are treated as part of a much wider effort to engender change.

---

[135] See, for example, *Magomadov and Magomadov v Russia* (App no 68004/01) ECHR 12 July 2007 and *Alikhadzhiyeva v Russia* (App no 68007/01) ECHR 5 July 2007.

[136] See, for example, *Tangiyeva v Russia* (App no 57935/00) ECHR 29 November 2007.

[137] See, for example, *Musayev & Ors v Russia* (App no 57941/00) ECHR 26 June 2007.

[138] See, for example, *Bitiyeva & X v Russia* (App no 57953/00) ECHR 21 June 2007.

[139] Leach, 'The Chechen Conflict' (2008) 760.

[140] Rule 9.2, Rules of the Committee of Minsters for the Supervision of the Execution of Judgments and of the Terms of Friendly Settlements, Adopted 10 May 2006. The ERRC has recently used this procedure too. See *Memorandum Concerning The Implementation And State Of General Measures In The Judgment Of D.H. And Others v The Czech Republic (Application No 57325/00)*, available at: www.errc.org/cms/upload/media/03/47/m00000347.pdf.

[141] Philip Leach, 'The Effectiveness of the Committee of Ministers in Supervising the Enforcement of Judgments of the European Court of Human Rights' [2006] *Public Law* 443.

[142] Anon, 'Implementation of ECtHR Judgments in Chechen Cases' (2008) 10 *EHRAC Bulletin* 6.

VI. Conclusion

Both the ERRC and the KHRP see themselves as having a role to play in addressing the patterns of discrimination that underlie the litigation in which they are involved and being a means by which concepts such as the Rule of Law and Human Rights are promoted. The cases discussed in this chapter can be described as deliberate NGO constructions that are instigated for the purpose of highlighting systematic violations of human rights on behalf of marginalised groups who are ordinarily excluded from conventional politics.[143] However, such transformative litigation programmes inevitably raise questions about who is intended to benefit from the litigation. In both case studies, the respondent Governments raised the argument that the litigation in question was not brought for the applicants' benefit, but rather to benefit the NGOs. In the *Velikova* case, for example, the Bulgarian Ministry of Justice referred to

> the disturbing tendency, which the Bulgarian government has noted before as well, that the act of having a procedure in the European Court turns itself into a profitable business, and – not for the clients, who have the right to seek their rights – but for their defenders who, after the procedure is forwarded and it became evident that the state – not the client – is going to pay, the lawyer easily get the claiming clients' signature on agreements of juridical assistance on paper, containing unpaid artificially extended sums. The approval of such pretensions by the Court acts extremely demoralizing to the Bulgarian society, throwing a shadow of doubt over the human goals sought through the [Convention].[144]

To some extent, such criticisms of NGO litigation programmes have a basis in truth. Because the NGOs discussed in this chapter have such ambitious aims for their litigation, their cases are selected not on the basis of their value to the individual litigant, but for their utility in addressing wider issues of concern. Cases of uncompromising violations of the Convention are selected not only because of their urgency, but also for their effectiveness in generating international mobility. It is therefore obvious that NGOs' aims in bringing such cases to the Court's attention might differ in certain respects from those of individual applicants. The prioritisation of the NGOs' aims in these circumstances is perhaps made more likely when the organisations funding and directing litigation strategies have little or no contact with the applicants in whose name cases are brought.

---

[143] Of course, litigation can empower the individual. One of the aims of the ERRC is to raise awareness amongst the Roma people of their rights in order that they can use them themselves. See, for example, Claude Cahn, 'Justice and Empowerment' (2001) 1 *Roma Rights* editorial, available at: www.errc.org/cikk.php?cikk=654.

[144] Undated fax to the European Court of Human Rights, received on 17 August 2000 (on file with the Court's Registry). Criticism of the role of NGOs has also been raised during domestic proceedings. See, for example, the police criticism mentioned in (May–June 1996) 1(2) *Focus: The Newsletter of the HRP* 11.

Criticisms of NGO litigation strategies are particularly serious when they highlight the tenuous links between the organisation and the communities they profess to serve, and in particular when they suggest that these organisations are driven by the imperatives of their funding bodies.[145] Indeed, the ERRC are somewhat self-critical about this point:

> It would be better if Roma lawyers were doing this. We are not a Roma dominated organisation. It makes a difference if you are from the affected community. We can't forget why we are here. Lawyers aren't interested in people. We have a bias towards law, not Roma.[146]

Vermeersch goes further and argues that Romani organisations miss out on large grants because funding bodies favour 'professionalised' organisations whose working language is English.[147] The institutionalisation of rights leaves these professionalised organisations at once with some degree of international leverage but at a distance from the communities on whose behalf that leverage is applied. Certainly, these organisations do not have empowerment of the people they profess to represent as a *direct* primary goal: rather, they hope this will follow when sufficient national and international attention is focused on their plight. The accusation that organisations like the ERRC and the KHRP seek to have a significant transnational impact on States' domestic policies is of course right. Not only is technical knowledge about the Strasbourg system introduced through their litigation programmes, but along with it the ideology of human rights and the rule of law. A consequence of this, of course, is that the real needs of the communities in question might be overlooked as the struggle for rights takes place without the close involvement of those intended to be its beneficiaries. As Pogany notes in relation to the Roma, 'observance of the basic rights of the Roma will not, of itself, resolve many of the underlying problems that the minority is currently facing'.[148]

Whilst these criticisms are undoubtedly valid, and should indeed be taken seriously by the NGOs involved in pro-active litigation strategies, the case studies discussed in this chapter strongly suggest that they should not be a cause for paralysis of these organisations' work. The Convention's mechanisms have been designed on the basis of a presumption of autonomy on the part of the individual applicant, yet years of oppression, and the comparative strength of the potential opponent in litigation, can make such freedom illusory for those most in need of the Convention's protection. It is apparent that the liberal ideal of the independent and empowered actor (applicant) who is free to take her complaint against the Government to Strasbourg – an ideal reflected in the Court's procedures – is inadequate to describe the actual practice of human rights litigation in extreme

---

[145] For a critical view of Roma NGOs see Nidhi Trehan, 'In the name of the Roma? The role of private foundations and NGOs' in Guy (ed), *Between Past and Future* (2001).

[146] Interview, Dimitrina Petrova, 20 September 2002.

[147] Vermeersch, *The Romani Movement* (2006) 143.

[148] Pogany, *The Roma Café* (2004) 150.

situations of rights abuse. Commentators have noted that the Court's individual mechanisms are not an effective means of dealing with systematic violations of the Convention.[149] The examples discussed in this chapter emphasise the failure of both domestic remedies and inter-State litigation in such situations. Indeed, the same pattern is emerging in countries that have ratified the Convention more recently.

Those clamouring for minority rights in these situations face enormous popular and official resistance, and given the extent of the violations and nature of the human rights violations outlined and the lack of political and economic clout of the minority groups concerned, it is perhaps not surprising that organisations from the outside have attempted to create a space for these communities to articulate their rights. The limitations of the individualistic model of litigation have left a clear – albeit narrow – 'gap' for NGOs to develop litigation strategies on behalf of excluded communities, a gap that they are attempting to exploit. The prevalence of NGO activity in litigating such situations suggests that it is through collective action that governments are effectively challenged and held to account. It is unarguable that these NGOs create cases that almost certainly would never exist without their activating them; it is equally unarguable that without their involvement, some of the most extreme violations of the Convention would go unanswered. However, given their distance from the ground, the utility of these NGOs is ultimately of limited value; the projects discussed in this chapter can expect to be seen as unnecessary – and perhaps irrelevant – as the communities use the space that has been created on their behalf to articulate the next stage of their struggle.

Finally, what of the question of whether by raising such broad issues NGOs unduly politicise the work of the Court? Dunay writes that complaints that address systemic problems place courts in something of a conundrum:

> If these bodies continue to focus on individual violations they may become politically irrelevant. If they react to the challenge posed by political conflicts they may well become over-politicized. The choice is not easy, particularly in light of the possible further extension of the membership of the Council of Europe to include countries facing even more severe minority conflicts.[150]

I suggest that the way forward is to recognise that the litigation of the Court in such circumstances is *inherently* political; NGOs are not *making* it political. NGOs have recognised that the Court is one instrument that has the potential to tackle systemic human rights violations, and their strategies demand that the Court be made aware of the context in which rights violations occur. As Reidy et al note,

> [t]he existence of a situation of widespread violation has significant impact on the likelihood of an individual being exposed to human rights abuses as well as on the

---

[149]　Reidy et al, 'Gross Violations of Human Rights' (1997) 162.
[150]　Dunay, 'Nationalism and Ethnic Conflict (1995) 41.

character of such abuses. To ignore the context in which an individual has suffered a violation in such circumstances is to fail to address the nature of the violation.[151]

Demonstrating respect for human rights might require a State to address deep-rooted issues of discrimination within society, and the Court should have a role in encouraging this. This, it has been seen, is something of an uphill battle, as the Court has proved itself reluctant to tackle political disputes head on.[152] Nevertheless, NGOs such as the ERRC and KHRP have, by making generalised arguments about gross and systematic human rights violations, persistently asked the Court to address these fundamental issues. It is suggested that in doing so they have made an important contribution towards the Court becoming an effective instrument.

---

[151] Reidy et al, 'Gross Violations of Human Rights' (1997) 164.
[152] *ibid*, 172.

5

'The Fight that is Never Done': the Role of 'Pure Human Rights' Organisations

'Liberty fluctuates; there is no simple progression towards greater and greater freedom'.[1]

I. Introduction

THE PREVIOUS CHAPTER highlighted the role that NGOs play in litigation that addresses serious human rights violations taking place in emerging democracies and in situations where respect for the rule of law is placed under extreme and persistent pressure. However, it is not only during times of significant political upheaval that NGOs become involved in human rights litigation. Many ECtHR cases are litigated or supported by NGOs which have a long-standing commitment to the general protection and promotion of human rights laws, regardless of the political climate in which violations occur. This chapter considers in particular the role that NGOs play in societies where human rights ideology and human rights norms are entrenched. In it, I focus on two London-based organisations that have a considerable history of involvement in ECHR litigation, namely the AIRE Centre and Liberty.

Both the AIRE Centre and Liberty perceive their role in litigation to be very different from that of the more overtly political and issue-orientated groups discussed in chapter four. These 'pure human rights' organisations – that is, organisations that work towards the general promotion and protection of human rights and do not represent a particular constituency – take particular care to present themselves as independent, apolitical and disinterested legal experts. They would argue that they act in the general interest to ensure that human rights arguments are well presented. In this chapter, however, I suggest that it is

---

[1] Barry Cox, *Civil Liberties in Britain* (Harmondsworth, Penguin, 1975) 19.

somewhat deceptive to describe the legal activities of organisations like Liberty and the AIRE Centre as politically neutral. An examination of the work of these self-appointed 'guardians of the Convention' reveals that their struggle for rights is simply one that is usually carried out in less overtly political and confrontational circumstances than that of, for example, the KHRP and the ERRC. Their success is frequently dependent upon legalistic and technocratic knowledge and skill, as opposed to more overt political campaigning. This chapter discusses the implications that this has for understanding the role that 'pure human rights' organisations play in the Court's litigation.

II. The AIRE Centre

The Advice on Individual Rights in Europe Centre (AIRE Centre) is housed in a cramped office space at the top of a ramshackle building in central London. Its two founders established the organisation in May 1993 in order to provide a free legal advice and representation service on European rights.[2] They perceived that most British lawyers were remarkably unaware of important rights available to British people under the ECHR and European Union laws, and they felt that there was a role for an NGO with specialist knowledge of international human rights law to fill this gap. The AIRE Centre continues to maintain an exclusive focus on European, rather than domestic, legal rights.

At the time of my research visit to the AIRE Centre in August 2002, there were between seven and 12 volunteers and two in-house lawyers dealing with requests for advice at the organisation. For 10 years the AIRE Centre's advisory service was available to members of the public, but by the end of 2002 this service had resulted in the opening of 5000 files and the organisation found that it was staggering under the weight of this work. It consequently decided in June 2003 to offer its direct advisory services only to legal professionals, those advising on human rights, and NGOs.[3] Because of the AIRE Centre's geographical location (it has only one office, in London) the majority of requests for advice the organisation receives come from within the United Kingdom. However, the organisation occasionally provides assistance to those in other European countries, and it has a network of European lawyers whose help it can call upon in this respect.

Given the experience and expertise that it has developed, it is perhaps unsurprising that the AIRE Centre has gone on to adopt a training role in European human rights law. When the Human Rights Act 1998 came into force, the organisation became heavily involved in training programmes on the ECHR both for private practitioners in the United Kingdom and for the Judicial Studies

---

[2] Interview, Nuala Mole, Director of AIRE Centre, 8 April 2003, London.
[3] See AIRE Centre, *The AIRE Centre: A Decade of Rights, 1993–2003* (London, AIRE Centre, 2003) 5.

Board.[4] As knowledge of the Human Rights Act spread, the AIRE Centre's training programme began to extend to other countries, most notably to the Balkans.[5] The AIRE Centre's opinion is still, however, 'regularly sought by both UK Government Departments and Parliamentary Committees on proposed changes in legislation or constitutional reforms, or by the Council of Europe or the European Commission on various comparable matters'.[6]

The AIRE Centre is a small organisation with a small budget, and consequently it is able to represent individuals directly before the ECtHR (and the European Court of Justice) in only a select number of cases. Because the organisation has maintained a focus on European Union and ECHR law, it does not become directly involved in domestic litigation. A publication documenting its first 10 years of work, *The AIRE Centre: A Decade of Rights, 1993–2003*,[7] offers the best idea of the scale of its involvement in ECHR litigation. This report reveals that by 2003 the AIRE Centre had been involved in 77 applications to the monitoring bodies of the ECHR. In 30 of these the AIRE Centre acted as primary legal representative; in 37 it acted in an advisory capacity and in seven it acted in both capacities during the course of the litigation. In the other three cases it was a third-party intervener. Although the majority of its applications are made against the United Kingdom (46), the AIRE Centre has been involved in complaints made against a remarkable range of other State parties, most recently focusing on litigation against Armenia, Georgia and Russia.[8] Within the research sample, the AIRE Centre was the primary representative in one case in which Austria was the respondent and it also intervened as a third party in a further case. Those two cases are both examined below.

A.   Legal Advice and Representation in *Cooke v Austria*[9]

Mr Cooke, a British national, was found guilty of murdering his companion during a holiday in Austria. The applicant lodged a plea of nullity with the Austrian Supreme Court, and both he and the Public Prosecutor's Office appealed against sentence. The applicant was not permitted to attend the hearing of the nullity plea, as section 286(2) of the Austrian Code of Criminal Procedure permitted appearance through counsel only for appellants held under arrest. He also did not appear in person for the appeals against sentence, as section 296(3) of the Code of Criminal Procedure provided that a detainee may only attend these hearings on request, which he failed to do, or 'if his personal appearance appears necessary in the interests of justice', which it apparently did not. After the

[4]   *ibid*, 4.
[5]   *ibid*, 12–15.
[6]   *ibid*, 4.
[7]   *ibid*.
[8]   Information taken from the Table of Cases in AIRE Centre, *A Decade of Rights. ibid*, 10–11.
[9]   *Cooke v Austria* (App no 25878/94) (2001) 31 EHRR 11.

domestic proceedings in his case were concluded, Mr Cooke contacted the AIRE Centre personally (on the recommendation of Prisoners Abroad, an NGO whose aim is to assist Britons held in detention overseas[10]), seeking help with various complaints he wished to make to the ECmHR.[11] Although Mr Cooke had had an Austrian lawyer appointed to him, he was dissatisfied with his work; consequently, the AIRE Centre agreed to represent him. It did so assisted by a German-speaking lawyer based in the United Kingdom[12] and Mr Cooke's Austrian lawyer.

The initial application to the Commission in Mr Cooke's case raised multiple issues under Article 6 of the Convention (the right to a fair trial) concerning procedures adopted at his trial and at the subsequent appeal hearings. The Commission declared the complaints relating to the trial proceedings inadmissible, but found the complaints concerning the applicant's non-attendance at his appeal hearings to be admissible.[13] On this point, the Austrian Government maintained that Mr Cooke had been adequately represented before the Supreme Court and that, as the issues to be decided on appeal were legal in nature, there was nothing to be gained from him attending the hearings in person. In its Report, the Commission accepted the Government's argument in part and held that the applicant's absence from the hearing of the plea of nullity did not violate the Convention.[14] However, the Commission found that the hearing of the appeals against sentence did involve an evaluation of the applicant's character and personality and therefore the Supreme Court should have taken positive measures to ensure his presence. The Commission therefore found (by 15 votes to one) that there was a violation of Article 6(1) and (3)(c) of the Convention,[15] and in its judgment of 8 February 2000 the Court unanimously agreed with this finding.

In contrast to the litigation strategies adopted by the NGOs discussed in chapter five, the AIRE Centre did not actively seek out Mr Cooke's case: the applicant himself instigated the complaint to the ECmHR and it was he who approached the AIRE Centre for assistance. Once the AIRE Centre agreed to represent him, Mr Cooke was regularly contacted over his application's progress and he was actively involved in drafting the memorial on the issues in the case that was submitted to the Court on his behalf. The issues raised by his case before

---

[10] Further information about Prisoners Abroad can be found on its web-site at www. prisonersabroad.org.uk.

[11] Letter from M Cooke to AIRE Centre, 29 March 1994 (on file with the AIRE Centre).

[12] See AIRE Centre, *A Decade of Rights* (2003) 21–2.

[13] *Cooke v Austria* (Cm dec) (App no 25878/94) ECHR 10 April 1997, (1997) 23 EHRR CD70.

[14] *Cooke v Austria* (Cm rep) (App no 25878/94) ECHR 20 May 1998.

[15] The relevant provisions of Art 6 read: '(1) In the determination of his civil rights and obligations or of any criminal charge against him, everyone is entitled to a fair and public hearing within a reasonable time by an independent and impartial tribunal established by law … (3) Everyone charged with a criminal offence has the following minimum rights … (c) to defend himself in person or through legal assistance of his own choosing or, if he has not sufficient means to pay for legal assistance, to be given it free when the interests of justice so require …'.

the Court were rather narrow, and it was certainly not a 'test case' brought by the AIRE Centre specifically in order to challenge the relevant provisions of the Austrian Code of Criminal Procedure (the issue of non-attendance of appellants at appeal hearings in Austria had already been successfully argued before the Court in an earlier case[16]).

It is tempting to conclude, therefore, that the AIRE Centre's involvement in Mr Cooke's case did not form part of a strategic and overtly political litigation campaign. Certainly, AIRE Centre staff themselves do not emphasise the potential social, political or legal impact that their cases might have. Rather, they prefer to present the AIRE Centre, in contrast to other NGOs involved in ECtHR litigation, as a 'pure human rights' organisation that is not 'issue driven' or partisan. Nicola Rogers, then Assistant Director of the AIRE Centre, referred disparagingly to the practice of 'ambulance chasing' for potential cases, and was at pains to distance her organisation from such activities:

> When we get involved in cases we get involved as direct representatives, and there I see our role as no different from a lawyer. We're not campaigning. We don't do test cases. We are not looking for a particular type of case. We're not looking for a particular issue to be resolved at an international level. We are simply offering representation in a case that we believe has a good prospect of success, and that is our only criteria. So it could be on an issue that has already been resolved by the European Court, it could be on an issue that has never been resolved. It can be an issue that we've thought about fifteen million times, or an issue that we've never thought about before. That's not the defining criteria. That is how we are different from other organisations, I think. We don't search out test cases at all.[17]

The professed lack of political purpose behind the AIRE Centre's litigation leads one to question what motivates its involvement in ECtHR cases. Certainly, in seeking to have his complaints heard by the Court, Mr Cooke did not have before him the considerable social, economic and political hurdles that were faced by the Roma and Kurdish applicants discussed in the previous chapter. Although Mr Cooke undoubtedly experienced some difficulty as a prisoner in a foreign country who felt unable to communicate adequately with his Austrian lawyer,[18] he nevertheless had legal representation and was aware of his rights prior to being assisted by the AIRE Centre.

The AIRE Centre's rationale for acting as representatives in cases like Mr Cooke's seems to be the positive qualities, or the 'added value', that it brings to litigation. At the same time as arguing that her organisation simply acts like a law

---

[16] *Kremzow v Austria* Series A no 268-B (1994) 17 EHRR 322 [57]–[69].

[17] Interview, Nicola Rogers, Assistant Director of the AIRE Centre, 15 August 2002, London.

Catharina Harby, a consultant who has worked closely with the AIRE Centre for a number of years, makes a remarkably similar point in her review of the AIRE Centre's experience before the Court. See Catharina Harby, 'The Experience of the AIRE Centre in Litigation Before the European Court of Human Rights' in Tullio Treves et al (eds), *Civil Society, International Courts and Compliance Bodies* (The Hague, TMC Asser Press, 2005) 43.

[18] Letter from Mr Cooke to AIRE Centre, 28 July 1994 (on file with the AIRE Centre).

firm when representing a client, Nicola Rogers acknowledged that the two are not motivated by the same aims and priorities:

> If we can recover our costs, all well and good, but you'll be aware that legal aid in Strasbourg is absolutely appalling. I mean it doesn't even cover the photocopying, let alone any other aspect of the litigation … And therefore we are not tainted by what a commercial law firm would be tainted by, which is the commercial prospects of the case. We are only interested in taking cases that have a good prospect of success because we do not want put our very small amount of resources into cases that are going nowhere.[19]

Its handling of Mr Cooke's case clearly demonstrates that the AIRE Centre puts a great deal of effort and resources into cases in which it acts as representative. The memorial submitted to the Commission on the applicant's behalf in that case was an impressive piece of legal research and, at 23 pages in length, the product of considerable effort.[20] A lawyer from the AIRE Centre and counsel visited Mr Cooke in person even though legal aid had not been granted for this purpose, and after the Strasbourg proceedings were exhausted they found him an Austrian lawyer to pursue residual issues.

In effect, the AIRE Centre staff would say their representation of applicants in litigation is merited because, as apolitical, disinterested and independent human rights law experts, they are in a strong position to meet the general interest in having human rights issues capably and professionally argued. Consequently, the language adopted by the AIRE Centre to describe its role in litigation is reassuringly apolitical and balanced. The organisation takes a cautious approach to litigation because:

> We also have a reputation to preserve in the Strasbourg court and against the responding governments that we bring cases against, and I think if you spoke to the Government they would acknowledge that our applications always raise a sensible point. If we ultimately fail, it's not because it wasn't a sensible litigation. And public officials, civil servants, have told me this. They know that we bring sensible cases. And we have that reputation to bring because your credibility in this kind of world is quite important.[21]

The AIRE Centre recognises that it would be 'naïve' not to acknowledge that as a human rights organisation it attracts people with non-legal problems; it argues that by litigating only in 'sensible' cases (and putting off 'hopeless' cases) it actually assists the Court by acting as a filter for inadmissible applications.[22] The AIRE Centre also believes that it has a responsibility to litigate in a manner that is not 'damaging' to others. Nuala Mole, Director of the AIRE Centre, notes that a

---

[19]   Interview, Nicola Rogers, 15 August 2002.
[20]   Memorial submitted 12 August 1994 (on file with the AIRE Centre).
[21]   Interview, Nicola Rogers, 15 August 2002.
[22]   *ibid.*

lost case has implications for people other than the individual client and that, as a result, human rights NGOs 'have to litigate responsibly so you don't knock the jurisprudence back'.[23]

While the organisation is somewhat opaque about how it chooses the cases upon which to confer its expertise, Nuala Mole did note of *Cooke v UK* that she would 'not have chosen that as being representative of AIRE Centre cases'.[24] I understood her to mean that it is not one of the more important cases in which the organisation has been involved. Part of the AIRE Centre's reputation as experts in human rights law is secured by litigating in high-profile cases, so staff there are particularly proud of their involvement in landmark cases such as *Osman v UK*[25] (in which positive obligations under Article 2 of the Convention were elaborated upon and expanded) and *D v UK*[26] (in which the deportation of a person terminally-ill with AIDS to a situation where he was unlikely to receive adequate care was held to be a violation of Article 3). Whilst professing to have few selection criteria beyond a case's prospects of success,[27] it appears that the AIRE Centre's understandable preference is for jurisprudentially significant cases which merit, and indeed bear testimony to, its legal expertise. Consequently, there are certain areas of human rights law for which the AIRE Centre has developed specialist knowledge and upon which its litigation has concentrated.

B.   Third-Party Interventions: *Ignaccolo Zenide v Romania*

One of the AIRE Centre's areas of expertise is the intersection between family law and human rights law. As well as litigating in a steady stream of cases that have concerned this area,[28] the AIRE Centre also intervened as a third party in a 'family rights' case before the ECtHR that fell within the sample group, *Ignaccolo Zenide v Romania*.[29] That case concerned a French mother and a Romanian father who were involved in a protracted dispute over custody of their two children. Despite a ruling by the French courts giving the mother custody, the father had not returned the children to their mother and had kept the children in Romania. In its intervention (which was made jointly with Reunite, a child

---

[23]   Interview, Nuala Mole, 8 April 2003.
[24]   *ibid.*
[25]   *Osman v United Kingdom* ECHR 1998-VIII, (2000) 29 EHRR 245.
[26]   *D v United Kingdom* ECHR 1997-III, (1997) 24 EHRR 423.
[27]   Interview, Nuala Mole, 8 April 2003. See also AIRE Centre, *A Decade of Rights* (2003) 9.
[28]   For details, see AIRE Centre, *A Decade of Rights* (2003) 17–18. More recent cases include *MAK & RK v United Kingdom* (App nos 45901/05 and 40146/06) ECHR 23 March 2010, *AD & OD v United Kingdom* (App no 28680/06) ECHR 16 March 2010 and *RK and AK v United Kingdom* (App no 38000/05) (2009) 48 EHRR 29.
[29]   *Ignaccolo Zenide v Romania* ECHR 2000-I, (2001) 31 EHRR 7.
The AIRE Centre has also intervened in a case that related to asylum, see *Chahal v United Kingdom* ECHR 1996-V, (1997) 23 EHRR 413, and another on the right to fair trial in proceedings under canon law, see *Pellegrini v Italy* ECHR 2001-VIII, (2002) 35 EHRR 2.

abduction organisation also based in the United Kingdom[30]) the AIRE Centre provided the Court with information concerning the Hague Convention on the Civil Aspects of International Child Abduction. The AIRE Centre believed that providing this information was necessary and important because this was the first case to be decided on its merits before the Court which raised issues under that treaty. Remarking on this intervention, Nuala Mole said:

> We wrote twenty-two pages, but got it to ten by using font size eight! It was jolly lucky as the applicant's lawyers only put in eight pages, and that was double-spaced. We were very frightened that they wouldn't understand about the Hague Convention, a lot of people think that a Hague Convention return [to the country from which a child has been abducted] is a permanent return.[31]

The intervention related purely to legal issues, and was motivated by a desire to equip the Court with adequate information on the relevant aspects of the Hague Convention. In that respect it was a success. The court addressed the Hague Convention issues raised by the case in detail, and reached a finding that the applicant's right to family life had been violated.[32]

Nicola Rogers's views on the AIRE Centre's role when intervening are revealing: 'I see us like an impartial observer, and not really to comment on the facts of any particular case, but to deal with the principles'.[33] Echoing its careful approach to selecting cases, Nicola Rogers explained that the AIRE Centre tries to ensure that its interventions are likely to be of benefit to the 'human rights movement':

> We do work on the principle that we would never interfere in a case unless it would be helpful for us to do so. We're not interfering busybodies who go around looking for third party interventions.[34]

Nuala Mole also referred in interview to the 'responsibility' human rights organisations have to the parties in litigation when intervening and her belief that 'it can be dangerous for people to jump into litigation'.[35] Consequently, the AIRE Centre will usually contact the parties to the litigation to consult them before intervening in a case. As with cases in which it acts as representative, the best rationale that one can offer for the AIRE Centre's interventions is that the wealth of specialist legal knowledge and experience that it is able to draw upon makes it particularly well placed to present human rights arguments before the Court. Indeed, this was implicit in Nuala Mole's letter to the Court's registry seeking permission to intervene in *Ignaccolo Zenide*, in which she was at pains to outline her organisation's considerable experience of ECHR litigation.[36]

---

[30] Further information about Reunite can be found on its website at www.reunite.org.

[31] Interview, Nuala Mole, 8 April 2003. More recently, the AIRE Centre represented the applicant in a Hague Convention case. See *Carlson v Switzerland* (App no 49492/06) ECHR 6 December 2008.

[32] *Ignaccolo Zenide v Romania* ECHR 2000-I, (2001) 31 EHRR 7, especially [95] and [113].

[33] Interview, Nicola Rogers, 15 August 2002.

[34] *ibid.*

[35] Interview, Nuala Mole, 8 April 2003.

[36] Letter from Nuala Mole to ECtHR Registry, 13 May 1999 (on file with the Court's Registry).

C.   The AIRE Centre as Expert Litigants

The AIRE Centre's primary role in litigation is to ensure that human rights arguments – which in the sample cases discussed above took the form of rather narrow points of legal interpretation – are presented (at least from a lawyer's point of view) in a coherent, reasoned and sophisticated manner. As a human rights organisation whose very *raíson d'être* is the legal expertise it offers, it is unsurprising that the AIRE Centre's approach to litigation is professional and co-operative rather than politically partial and conflict-driven. If at first this seems to place it at some distance from the NGOs discussed in the previous chapter, this distance – which undoubtedly exists – should not be exaggerated. While the AIRE Centre strives to be a 'helpful' litigator, there have been occasions when its involvement in ECtHR cases has nevertheless been unwelcome. For example, at the time when she was interviewed Nicola Rogers was particularly concerned about the procedure that the Court had developed in *Akman v Turkey* for striking out cases in which applicants had not wished to accept a friendly settlement.[37] The AIRE Centre sought to intervene in that case because,

> for us it's a point of principal that the Court does not act in that way; and we bring our expertise in so far as we are expert litigants before the European Court and we try to bring that to our third party intervention.[38]

When asked why its request to intervene in the *Akman* case had been denied, Nicola Rogers replied without hesitation: 'Political. I've no doubt about it'.[39] The AIRE Centre was subsequent denied permission to intervene in two other 'striking off' cases against Turkey, and it is the only 'RP' I am aware of that has met such refusal.[40] That the AIRE Centre has more recently turned its attention towards entrenching human rights ideology in newer Member States of the Council of Europe through training programmes also suggests common ground between the AIRE Centre and the NGOs discussed in the previous chapter.

Nevertheless, it can be deduced from their comments in interview that AIRE Centre staff believe themselves to be an integral part of the human rights legal system, rather than agitators working from outside it. The AIRE Centre does not usually find itself singing from an entirely different hymn sheet from governments that have professed a serious commitment to the ECHR. Indeed, Nicola Rogers referred to the 'working relationship' and 'mutual respect' that the AIRE Centre has with the UK Government and its 'very good relationship' with British lawyers at the Court's Registry.[41] Two members of the Court's Registry that the author spoke with acknowledged the latter point, and both referred to the AIRE

---

[37] *Akman v Turkey* (striking out) (App no 37453/97) ECHR 2001-VI.
[38] Interview, Nicola Rogers, 15 August 2002.
[39] *ibid.*
[40] See *TA v Turkey* (striking out) (App no 26307/95) ECHR 9 April 2002 and *Toǧcu v Turkey* (striking out) (App no 27601/95) ECHR 9 April 2002.
[41] *ibid.*

Centre's involvement in litigation extremely positively. That, when I visited, AIRE Centre staff sat at desks discarded from, and donated by, the Treasury Solicitor's Office is suggestive of the close nature of their relationship with the UK Government.[42] It is also revealing that before establishing the organisation the founders of the AIRE Centre – one of whom had previously worked at the ECmHR – thought to turn first to Nicolas Bratza, then the UK member of the European Commission on Human Rights, for his opinion on the need for the service they proposed to offer.[43] The consequences of human rights NGOs being so closely associated with government bodies and the formal organs of international human rights law, and the impact that this has on their approach to litigation, are returned to for further consideration below.

III.   Liberty: Challenging Criminal Justice Reforms

The National Council for Civil Liberties (NCCL), which was renamed 'Liberty' in January 1989, has a venerable tradition of protecting human rights within the United Kingdom. It was established in 1934 by a journalist called Ronald Kidd who resolved to create an organisation that would defend 'traditional freedoms against the encroachments of a repressive government'[44] after he witnessed police *agents provocateurs* inciting violence during the Hunger Marches of November 1932.[45] Despite having a certain reputation for political radicalism, Liberty has expertise in human rights law and, in fact, performs similar work to the AIRE Centre, albeit on a considerably larger scale and occasionally involving more deliberate activism.[46] In contrast to the AIRE Centre, however, Liberty is a national organisation that is concerned with human rights within the UK. In its early years, therefore, Liberty's focus was exclusively on domestic law. However, the emergence of the ECHR as a mechanism through which the rights of Britons could be upheld, and through which national laws could be influenced, brought a new international dimension to Liberty's work.

In furtherance of its aim to promote human rights, Liberty has human rights telephone advice lines both for individual members of the public in England and Wales and for lawyers and rights advisers. The organisation conducts research

---

[42]   AIRE Centre, *A Decade of Rights* (2003) 2.

[43]   *ibid.*

[44]   Cox, *Civil Liberties* (1975) 12.

[45]   For a history of Liberty see: Brian Dyson, *Liberty in Britain 1934–1994: A Diamond Jubilee History of the National Council for Civil Liberties* (London, Civil Liberties Trust, 1994); Cox, *Civil Liberties* (1975); Mark Lilly, *The National Council for Civil Liberties: the First Fifty Years* (London, The Macmillan Press, 1984); Sylvia Scaffardi, *Fire Under the Carpet: Working for Civil Liberties in the Thirties* (London, Lawrence and Wishart, 1986); Peter Wallington (ed), *Civil Liberties: 1984* (Oxford, Martin Robertson & Co, 1984).

[46]   Further information about Liberty's work is available from its web-site at: www.liberty-human-rights.org.uk/about/index.shtml.

projects and produces publications on various aspects of human rights law, and it is also involved in human rights training. Liberty is, in addition, a campaigning organisation that lobbies Parliamentary, Governmental and Inter-Governmental bodies, and its staff are careful to maintain a high profile in the media. Most significantly for the purposes of this research, Liberty is also directly involved in both domestic and ECHR litigation.

Almost immediately after the NCCL was established, and no doubt as a consequence of the significant number of lawyers involved in the operation of the organisation from its early days, it began to offer representation in cases that challenged violations of human rights (or 'civil liberties', to adopt the termin-ology of the day).[47] Of course its early litigation campaigns took place before domestic tribunals, but as the ECmHR and ECtHR gained competence to receive complaints from individuals against the United Kingdom the NCCL lost little time in using this means to further its aims.[48] Liberty's test case strategy before the ECtHR has 'proved most effective and newsworthy',[49] and it now has a lengthy history of involvement in cases taken under the Convention. Because the ECtHR is 'more liberal than the domestic courts' and because 'governments can't appeal to Strasbourg', John Wadham, Director of Liberty from 1995 to 2003, described it as the 'the perfect system from our point of view'.[50]

Although initially the scale of Liberty's litigation campaigns was very small and relied solely on legal volunteers, human rights casework is now a central part of the organisation's work. In October 2001, Liberty launched 'a remodelled legal unit targeted specifically at leading the way in European test case litigation, taking cases both domestically and to the European Court of Human Rights'.[51] As well as employing 'about seven full-time lawyers' at the time of my research visit in January 2003, Liberty also had a network of over 150 lawyers prepared to act on its behalf.[52] Typically, Liberty's involvement in a case means that its own lawyers act (pro bono) as representatives themselves, although it does occasionally jointly litigate cases with other legal representatives.

---

[47]   For a discussion of Liberty's test cases, see Barbara Cohen and Marie Staunton, 'In Pursuit of a Legal Strategy: The National Council for Civil Liberties' in Jeremy Cooper and Rajeev Dhavan (eds), *Public Interest Law* (Oxford, Basil Blackwell, 1986) and Richard J Maiman, '"We've had to Raise our Game": Liberty's Litigation Strategy under the Human Rights Act 1998' in Simon Halliday and Patrick Schmidt (eds), *Human Rights Brought Home: Socio-Legal Perspectives on Human Rights in the National Context* (Oxford, Hart Publishing, 2004).

[48]   See, for example, the table in Carol Harlow and Richard Rawlings, *Pressure Through Law* (London, Routledge, 1992) 257. This identifies that the NCCL sponsored several of the early cases heard by the ECtHR, including *Golder v United Kingdom* Series A no 18 (1979–80) 1 EHRR 524, and *Tyrer v United Kingdom* Series A no 26 (1979–80) 2 EHRR 1. Lilly's study contains several references to early NCCL cases taken to the ECmHR and ECtHR. See Lilly, *The National Council for Civil Liberties* (1984).

[49]   Dyson, *Liberty in Britain* (1994) 52.

[50]   Maiman, '"We've had to Raise our Game"' (2004) 104.

[51]   Liberty, *Liberty/The Civil Liberties Trust: Annual Review 2001* (London, Liberty/The Civil Liberties Trust, 2001) 3.

[52]   Interview, John Wadham, Director of Liberty, 20 January 2003, London.

Liberty's cases emerge either directly through its advisory service or, if there is a case in which it has a particular interest (it monitors all cases that reach the appeal courts), Liberty will contact a solicitor directly and offer to assist. Although Liberty does not keep accurate records of the number of cases in which it is involved, in 2003 John Wadham estimated that it was handling about 20 applications to the ECtHR at any one time.[53] Given the length of time which its involvement in ECHR cases has spanned, that would make them one of the most, if not *the* most, prolific 'repeat players' in litigation before the Court (not including, of course, respondent States). As well as representing applicants directly, Liberty has also intervened in several ECtHR cases.[54]

Liberty was involved in the second largest number of cases within the research sample, with only the KHRP involved in more. Liberty directly represented applicants in six of the sample cases, and it also intervened in a further two sample cases. Liberty's test cases that fell within the sample, all of which related to criminal justice issues within the United Kingdom, are the focus of this case study.

A.   Liberty's Test Cases

Three of the sample cases in which Liberty acted as representative, *Rowe and Davis v UK*,[55] *Fitt v UK*[56] and *Jasper v UK*,[57] addressed the non-disclosure of prosecution material during criminal proceedings. Each of the applicants in those cases had been convicted of serious criminal offences, and before the Court they all complained about 'sensitive' prosecution material being withheld from them on 'public interest' grounds during their trials and subsequent appeals. The Court, sitting as a Grand Chamber, heard all of these cases together and considered all of the applicants' complaints under the general 'right to a fair hearing' provision of Article 6(1). In *Rowe and Davis* it found a violation of that provision because the decision to withhold prosecution material was, at the time of the applicants' original trial, a matter for the prosecution itself, and the trial judge did not have the opportunity to see the material in question.[58] Crucially,

---

[53]   Interview, John Wadham, 20 January 2003.
[54]   Examples of ECtHR cases in which Liberty has intervened are: *Karner v Austria* (App no 40016/98) ECHR 24 July 2003, (2004) 38 EHRR 24; *Goodwin v United Kingdom* ECHR 1996-II, (1996) 22 EHRR 123; *Sheffield and Horsham v United Kingdom* ECHR 1998-V, (1999) 27 EHRR 163; *McGinley & Egan v United Kingdom* ECHR 1998-III, (1999) 27 EHRR 1; *Halford v United Kingdom* ECHR 1997-III, (1997) 24 EHRR 523; *Chahal v United Kingdom* ECHR 1996-V, (1997) 23 EHRR 413; *Saunders v United Kingdom* ECHR 1996-VI, (1997) 23 EHRR 313; *Brannigan and McBride v United Kingdom* Series A no 258-B (1994) 17 EHRR 539.
[55]   *Rowe and Davis v United Kingdom* ECHR 2000-II, (2000) 30 EHRR 1.
[56]   *Fitt v United Kingdom* ECHR 2000-II, (2000) 30 EHRR 480.
[57]   *Jasper v United Kingdom* (App No 27052/95) (2000) 30 EHRR 441.
[58]   *Rowe and Davis v United Kingdom* ECHR 2000-II, (2000) 30 EHRR 1 [65]–[66]. Following this judgment, the Court of Appeal found the applicants' conviction (together with that of their original co-defendant) to be unsafe. See *R v Johnson, Rowe and Davis (No 3)* [2001] 1 Cr App R 8.

however, the Grand Chamber went on to find in the same case that an ex parte hearing before the Court of Appeal, at which the matter of non-disclosure of prosecution material was put before a judge, did not violate the Convention.[59] That finding was confirmed in both *Jasper* and *Fitt*, in which the Grand Chamber held – by a knife-edge vote of nine to eight – that ex parte hearings in which the non-disclose of prosecution material to the defence was judicially supervised did not violate the Convention.

The danger of not disclosing to a defendant any prosecution material that is relevant to an issue in a criminal trial, or that might assist the defence, is obvious.[60] Rowe and Davis's high-profile case was one of many miscarriages of justice in Britain that came to be synonymous with the dangers of non-disclosure.[61] However, when public interest immunity is claimed as a reason for non-disclosure, the conflict between individual rights and the wider public interest is clear.[62] Liberty's test cases, outlined above, were a means for it to address some of those difficulties and to propose reforms of the law governing disclosure.[63] In particular, Liberty argued in them that a 'special counsel' should be appointed in ex parte disclosure hearings to represent the interests of the defendant.[64] This echoed arguments that it had raised as a third-party intervener in an earlier ECtHR case, which concerned the inability of the applicant to effectively challenge a deportation order that had been made on national security grounds.[65] In its disclosure cases Liberty argued that special counsel should be appointed in order to satisfy the requirements of Article 6, and its submissions were primarily directed towards achieving a judgment which required such measures to be introduced in ex parte disclosure hearings.[66] In support of this

[59]   At the time of Rowe and Davis' original trial prosecuting authorities had responsibility for applying the Attorney General's Guidelines (1981), which determined what material should be disclosed to the defence. Consequently, there was prosecution material that was withheld both from the defence and from the trial judge. These guidelines were superseded by the Court of Appeal's decision in *R v Ward* [1993] 1 WLR 619, a judgment in force by the time of the appeal hearings in this case, in which it was held that court and not the prosecutor should decide where the balance lay in relation to public interest immunity is claimed in relation to the non-disclosure of material.

[60]   The importance of prosecution disclosure is implicit, of course, in the right to adequately prepare a defence (Art 6(3)(b)) and the principle of equality of arms (Article 6(3)(d)) that are enshrined in the Convention. See *Edwards v United Kingdom* Series A no.247-B (1993) 15 EHRR 417.

[61]   Among the well known miscarriages of justice arising from the non-disclosure of prosecution material are: *R v Ward* [1993] 1 WLR 619; *R v Stefan Kiszko*, *The Times*, 19 February 1992; *R v Taylor and Taylor* (1994) 98 Cr App R 361. McConville et al found evidence of habitual suppression of evidence that weakens the prosecution's case. See Mike McConville, Andrew Sanders and Roger Leng, *The Case for the Prosecution* (London, Routledge, 1991), especially 65–75.

[62]   See *Goodwin v United Kingdom* ECHR 1996-II, (1996) 22 EHRR 123.

[63]   See Anon, *Liberty Newsletter* (London, Liberty, Autumn 2000) 8.

[64]   Following the Court's judgments in *Chahal v United Kingdom* ECHR 1996-V, (1997) 23 EHRR 413 and *Tinnelly & Sons Ltd v United Kingdom* ECHR 1998-IV, (1999) 27 EHRR 249, the UK had introduced legislation making provision for special counsel in certain situations involving national security under the Special Immigration Appeals Commission Act 1997 and Northern Ireland Act 1998.

[65]   *Chahal v United Kingdom* ECHR 1996-V, (1997) 23 EHRR 413, especially [144].

[66]   See *Rowe and Davis v United Kingdom* ECHR 2000-II, (2000) 30 EHRR 1 [55].

argument Liberty attached an affidavit to the applicants' memorial from Anne Owers, who was at that time the director of JUSTICE – another 'legally-orientated' British human rights NGO that had an interest in the rules governing disclosure – which also called for the appointment of special counsel in ex parte disclosure hearings.[67] The British Government was clearly unhappy with Liberty submitting this unusual form of written submission, which it argued was 'simply a vehicle for making, in a slightly different form, the same argument already advanced by the applicants'.[68] In any event, Liberty's arguments about the appointment of special counsel were ultimately unsuccessful, although, given the division of the Court, they had clearly been persuasive.[69]

The fourth sample case that was litigated by Liberty, *Condron and Condron v UK*,[70] related to the provisions governing the right to silence in criminal proceedings in the United Kingdom. The applicants in that case had both been arrested and charged with offences relating to the supply and possession of heroin. At their trial both gave evidence in their defence that they had not revealed when questioned by the police, and both said they had not answered police questions on their solicitor's advice. Pursuant to section 34 of the Criminal Justice and Public Order Act 1994 the previous common law rules on the right to silence were significantly amended to allow for the drawing of inferences from an accused's silence during police questioning. The applicants' silence was consequently used in evidence against them and they were found guilty of the charges. Their subsequent appeals against conviction were unsuccessful. In its judgment of 2 May 2000 the Court held in this case that there was a violation of Article 6(1) on the basis that the trial judge had not directed the jury to give sufficient weight to the applicants' explanation for maintaining their silence during police questioning, particularly as this had followed legal advice to decline to answer questions. The Court held that the jury should have been invited to draw an inference from the applicants' silence if it 'could only sensibly be attributed to their having no answer or none that would stand up to cross-examination'.[71]

It goes without saying that in taking the *Condron and Condron* case Liberty sought to redress, or at least to mitigate, the highly contentious reforms of the law governing the accused's right to silence that had resulted in one of Liberty's biggest campaigns of 1994.[72] Although the right to silence had not been abolished by the Criminal Justice and Public Order Act 1994, the fact that inferences

[67] Affidavit of Anne Owers, 6 October 1999, para 4 (on file with the Court's Registry).

[68] Government's Memorial, 15 December 1999, para 4 (on file with the Court's Registry).

[69] The dissenting judgments were explicit that the 'special counsel' measure was necessary and took the view that 'because there is a less restrictive measure which is available and adaptable the Government is in violation of the applicant's right to a fair trial'.

[70] *Condron and Condron v United Kingdom* ECHR 2000-V, (2001) 31 EHRR 1.

[71] *ibid*, [61].

[72] See Liberty, *The Right to Silence: Liberty Parliamentary Briefing December 1993* (London, Liberty, 1993). For academic commentary on the reforms see, for example, Di Birch, 'Suffering in

might be drawn from an accused's refusal to answer questions obviously had severe implications for the exercise of this right in practice. While the right to silence and the associated privilege against incrimination are not explicitly recognised in the Convention, the Court has described these as 'generally recognised international standards lying at the heart of the notion of a fair procedure under Article 6'.[73] The Court's jurisprudence in this area has, however, been somewhat contradictory.[74] Consequently, Liberty has made repeated efforts to ensure that the right to silence is interpreted as broadly as possible.[75] In *Murray v UK*, an earlier case in which Liberty intervened, the Court made clear that the right to silence is not absolute and found that the drawing of an inference from an accused's silence did not violate the Convention in the context of a trial conducted by a judge, sitting without a jury, who delivered a reasoned judgment. Liberty's conclusion, and its motive for taking *Condron and Condron* as a test case, was that an inference drawn by a jury that did not give reasons for its decision might be found to violate Article 6. As we saw, the Court was not inclined to agree with this argument. It was implicit in the Court's judgment that, had the trial judge given adequate direction to the jury, a satisfactory balance between the defendant's rights and the public interest could have been achieved under section 34, and Article 6 would not have been violated.[76]

The applicant in *Caballero v UK*,[77] Liberty's fifth test case within the sample, had been charged with attempted rape in January 1996. Under the terms of section 25 of the Criminal Justice and Public Order Act 1994 there was no discretion for him to be granted bail as he had a previous conviction for a serious offence.[78] To the Commission, Mr Caballero alleged, inter alia, that the automatic denial of bail was a violation of Article 5(3) and (5) of the Convention.[79] The majority of the Commission – in a decision consistent with its 'long and

---

Silence: A Cost-Benefit Analysis of Section 34 of the Criminal Justice and Public Order Act 1994' [1999] *Criminal Law Review* 769, and Anthony Jennings, 'Silence and Safety: The Impact of Human Rights Law' [2000] *Criminal Law Review* 879.

[73]   *John Murray v United Kingdom* ECHR 1996-I, (1996) 22 EHRR 29 [45].

[74]   See, for example, *Funke v France* Series A no 256-A (1993) 16 EHRR 297, *John Murray v United Kingdom* ECHR 1996-I, (1996) 22 EHRR 29, and *Saunders v United Kingdom* ECHR 1996-VI, (1997) 23 EHRR 313.

[75]   Liberty intervened in *John Murray v United Kingdom* ECHR 1996-I, (1996) 22 EHRR 29 and *Saunders v United Kingdom* ECHR 1996-VI, (1997) 23 EHRR 313 on this issue. More recently, it represented the applicants in *O'Halloran and Francis v United Kingdom* (App nos 15809/02 and 25624/02) ECHR 29 June 2007, (2008) 46 EHRR 21.

[76]   For a case commentary, see Andrew Ashworth, 'Human Rights: Adverse Inferences from Failure to Answer Police Questions' [2000] *Criminal Law Review* 679.

[77]   *Caballero v United Kingdom* ECHR 2000-II, (2000) 30 EHRR 643.

[78]   For a discussion of this provision, see Philip Leach, 'Automatic Denial of Bail and the European Convention' [1999] *Criminal Law Review* 300.

[79]   Article 5 provides for the right to liberty and security. The relevant provisions read as follows: (3) Everyone arrested or detained in accordance with the provisions of paragraph 1.c of this article shall be brought promptly before a judge or other officer authorised by law to exercise judicial power and shall be entitled to trial within a reasonable time or to release pending trial. Release may be conditioned by guarantees to appear for trial.

reasonably robust line of … decisions upholding suspects' rights during pre-trial detention'[80] – agreed with the applicant's arguments. By the time his case reached the Court, and as a direct result of the Commission's decision, section 25 had been amended to allow for bail to be granted in 'exceptional circumstances' where it would have been automatically refused under the original formulation of that section. Although the parties did not reach a friendly settlement, the Court accepted the Government's concession that there had been a violation of Article 5 and the applicant was awarded £1000 damages.

At the heart of this case was a highly contentious issue. The Law Commission note that section 25 of the Criminal Justice and Public Order Act 1994 'was introduced as part of a "package of measures" intended to reduce the incidence of offending by people on bail, then estimated by the Government at 50,000 offences a year'.[81] Liberty, on the other hand, was keen to ensure that an accused's rights under Article 5 were forcefully asserted; in particular it argued that judges should always have discretion to grant bail. While the majority of the Commission agreed with Liberty's arguments, it was nevertheless a controversial issue that divided the Commission by 19 votes to 12. Although section 25 of the 1994 Act had already been amended after the Commission's decision in the *Caballero* case, this case left some issues unresolved. First, the Law Commission suggested that the reformulation of section 25 might still conflict with the rights of the defendant as it created a presumption that bail will not be granted, and it worried that there seemed 'to have been no discussion of a possible conflict with the Convention'.[82] Furthermore, six judges expressed concern about the Court's acceptance of the Government's concession without itself considering the merits of the applicant's arguments, because 'it makes the judgment unclear as to the Court's position'.[83] Subsequently in *SBC v UK*[84] – which was not a 'Liberty case' – the Court held that section 25 (in its original form) violated Article 5 of the Convention, thereby resolving an issue left undecided by *Caballero*.

The applicant in *Foxley v UK*,[85] Liberty's sixth and final test case that fell within the sample, had been found guilty of 12 counts of corruption and, pursuant to Part VI of the Criminal Justice Act 1988, a confiscation order in the amount of £1.5 million was made against him. As a result of bankruptcy proceedings a Redirection Order was made for all postal packets addressed to the

---

(5) Everyone who has been the victim of arrest or detention in contravention of the provisions of this article shall have an enforceable right to compensation.

[80] Leach, 'Automatic Denial of Bail' (1999) 300. For a summary of these decisions, see Karen Reid, *A Practitioner's Guide to the European Convention on Human Rights* (London, Sweet & Maxwell, 1998) 304–10.
[81] The Law Commission, *Criminal Law: Bail and the Human Rights Act 1998*, Law Commission Consultation Paper No 157, para 9.3.
[82] *ibid*, para 9.30.
[83] *Caballero v United Kingdom* ECHR 2000-II, (2000) 30 EHRR 643, 663.
[84] *SBC v United Kingdom* (App no 39360/98) (2002) 34 EHRR 21.
[85] *Foxley v United Kingdom* (App no 33274/96) (2001) 31 EHRR 25.

applicant to be forwarded to the trustee-in-bankruptcy, including letters from his legal advisers. All of this correspondence was copied to file by the trustee-in-bankruptcy before being forwarded to the applicant. The applicant complained that the confiscation order against him constituted a violation of Article 7(1) of the Convention (which prohibits punishment without law). He further complained that the interception of his mail was a violation of Articles 6, 8 (the right to respect for private life), and 34 (the right to individual application) of the Convention. The Court concluded that the application under Article 7(1) was made out of time (he was not, when this application was submitted, represented by Liberty) and held, moreover, that documents produced by the applicant to prove otherwise were not genuine. Indeed, the Court held that this application 'could equally be rejected as an abuse of the right of application'.[86] In its judgment of 20 June 2000, however, the Court held that there had been a violation of Article 8 in relation to the opening of the applicant's privileged mail and also to the opening of mail after the Redirection Order had expired. The applicant was not awarded damages.

Although the *Foxley* case had some significance as the 'first case to come before the court in which the Court has addressed the powers of the trustee-in-bankruptcy under English law',[87] by the time it reached the Court it was, in all likelihood, no longer the case that Liberty had intended to take. Given the pattern that emerges from this sample of Liberty's test cases, which clearly points to the fact that Liberty uses targeted litigation strategies to challenge specific legislative provisions, it appears likely that the primary purpose of *Foxley* had been to test Part VI of the Criminal Justice Act 1988 concerning confiscation orders.[88] Needless to say, Liberty would also undoubtedly have been embarrassed to find itself – through no fault of its own – representing an applicant whose claims the Court exposed as fraudulent. Consequently, this case at least highlights the point that deliberately targeted test cases are vulnerable to forces that are outside of the control of the NGOs that initiate them.

B.   Liberty's Watchdog Role

Liberty's purpose in litigating cases before the ECtHR is best understood by re-visiting the intentions of its founders. Kidd was keen that the NCCL should be an independent, non-partisan organisation that could take positive action where human rights were threatened:

> This determination to preserve our democratic rights must be translated into concrete action. We must challenge any encroachment, however small, by legal action in the

---

[86]   *Foxley v United Kingdom* (dec) (App no 33274/96) ECHR 12 October 1999.

[87]   Letter from Adrian Marshall Williams, Legal Officer at Liberty, to the ECtHR Registry, 16 November 1999 (on file with the Court's Registry).

[88]   This was repealed by the Proceeds of Crime Act 2002 in March 2003.

courts, by the mobilisation of public opinion through all democratic organisations, or by whatever means lies ready to hand at the moment. The individual acting alone can do only a little, but great things can be accomplished through united action through trade unions, peace societies, political parties, cultural and religious societies – and, above all, through the National Council for Civil Liberties, which stands on a solid, non-party basis and devotes all its energies to these specialised problems.[89]

Indeed, the written histories of Liberty's campaigns provide an interesting picture of key political issues in the United Kingdom of the past 70 years.[90] From its early opposition to the Sedition (Incitement to Disaffection) Bill of 1934, to its concern with the rights of servicemen and women during the Second World War, to its treatment of race and immigration issues in the 1960s and anti-discrimination issues in the 1970s, up to its most recent concern with repressive legislation designed to tackle the threat from terrorists, Liberty has responded to many of the important political and legal issues of the day. Liberty is therefore essentially a 'reactive' organisation that acts as a watchdog to guard against the encroachment of liberties and the erosion of human rights. The organisation perceives this to be a permanent function. On reaching its 60th anniversary, Liberty made clear that it was 'not contemplating retirement. There will always be a need for organisations like Liberty which act as independent watchdogs in defence of our freedoms'.[91]

Liberty's cases that fell within the sample were targeted to address concerns about some of the major criminal justice reforms of the 1990s. In particular, they were a response to regressive policies of a government that was keen to be 'tough on crime' and efficient in the administration of justice. Roger Leng remarked at the time of the direction that these reforms were taking:

> Efficiency now rules, and in criminal justice terms efficiency requires unquestioning confidence in the law enforcers whatever their previous form. To those familiar with the traditional model of adversarial criminal justice in which prosecution is something which happens to a non-volunteer, who is fully entitled to devote his energies to defending himself, the theme of the defendant as a participant with responsibilities in connection with the efficient running of the system is disturbing.[92]

It is clear that the six cases outlined above were deliberately chosen by Liberty for their potential to respond to those repressive measures. When questioned in interview, John Wadham was explicit about the rationale that Liberty uses when selecting cases:

---

[89]   Ronald Kidd, *British Liberty in Danger: An Introduction to the Study of Civil Rights* (London, Lawrence & Wishart, 1940) 255.

[90]   See, for example, Dyson, *Liberty in Britain* (1994); Cox, *Civil Liberties* (1975); Lilly, *The National Council for Civil Liberties* (1984).

[91]   Liberty, *Annual Report 1993* (London, Liberty/Civil Liberties Trust, 1993) 1.

[92]   Roger Leng, 'Losing Sight of the Defendant: The Government's Proposals in Pre-Trial Disclosure' [1995] *Crim LR* 704, 711.

We are obviously trying to change the law. We are obviously looking to expand the law to protect human rights. The more important the issue, the more likely we are to take the case.[93]

If John Wadham is making a rather trite point, re-iterating it nevertheless serves as a useful reminder that Liberty's aims are not in any way 'neutral' or 'impartial'. Rather, in its litigation Liberty engages with legal issues that it perceives to have considerable political significance. As Liberty's current Director, Shami Chakrabarti, has said, '[t]hough I am a lawyer working at Liberty ... I want the litigation to serve the campaign ... I want everything we do to serve the human rights campaign'.[94]

While the work of Liberty's is inherently politically engaged, it is interesting to note that there has been a remarkable change in how Liberty has been perceived by the British authorities. Despite Kidd's claims for his organisation, he was clearly a politically conscious person who was, in particular, concerned about the threat to liberty posed by the growing popularity of far-right political ideology.[95] Consequently, at certain times during Liberty's history, its agenda has been seen as left-wing, anti-establishment and radical.[96] Patricia Hewitt has noted: 'By the Cold War years, NCCL was widely regarded as a communist "front", and a number of Communist Party members were indeed prominent on the Executive Committee'.[97] Accusations of Communist allegiance were made 'fairly regularly' from the NCCL's early years ('although much less so after the 1970s'[98]), which led to resignations from high-profile members. Members of Liberty were also routinely kept under surveillance by the security services,[99] and it continues to battle fiercely to protect privacy rights.[100] This early experience of Liberty

---

[93]   Interview, John Wadham, 20 January 2003.

[94]   Quoted in Maiman, '"*We've had to Raise our Game*"' (2004) 99.

[95]   Kidd, *British Liberty in Danger* (1940) 168.

[96]   Patricia Hewitt, 'The NCCL Fifty Years on' in Wallington (ed), *Civil Liberties* (1984) 32.

[97]   *ibid*, 32.

[98]   Dyson, *Liberty in Britain* (1994) 33.

[99]   *ibid*, 23–4.

[100]   On the subject of the UK Government's excessively wide powers under the (repealed) Interception of Communications Act 1985, see also *Liberty & Ors v United Kingdom* (App no 58243/00) ECHR 1 July 2008, (2009) 48 EHRR 1.

On the lack of regulation protecting privacy rights in the UK, see *Copland v United Kindgom* (App no 62617/00) ECHR 3 April 2007, (2007) 45 EHRR 37 and *Peck v United Kingdom* ECHR 2003-I (2003) 36 EHRR 41, in which Liberty represented the Applicants.

For Liberty's successful challenge to the retention of DNA and fingerprints in the absence of a criminal conviction, see *S and Marper v United Kingdom* (App nos 30562/04 and 30566/04) ECHR 4 December 2008, (2009) 48 EHRR 50.

For an example of Liberty's on-going engagement with the issues raised by the Regulation of Investigatory Powers Act 2000, see Anon, 'Council spied on family over school catchment area, hearing told' (5 November 2009) *The Guardian (online edition)*, available at www.guardian.co.uk/society/2009/nov/05/council-spying-school-catchment-area.

For a proposed legal challenge from Liberty to plans to retain information gathered from automatic number plate recognition cameras, see Paul Lewis, 'Legal Fight Over Muslim Suburbs Spy Cameras' (12 June 2010) *The Guardian* 7.

suggests that merely using the term 'human rights' to describe its aims does not provide an organisation with some kind of divine neutrality and immunity from political engagement: human rights discourse can be deeply political and fractured.

However, while some parallels can be drawn between the suspicion and mistrust that marked the first decades of Liberty's existence and the recent experiences of the organisations working for the rights of minorities that were discussed in chapter four, those parallels are not readily apparent at the present time. Liberty's work has been progressively better thought-of as human rights discourse has become an increasingly common feature of British politics. In effect, working in a political climate in which the validity of human rights is at least tacitly accepted has given legitimacy to Liberty's 'pure human rights' agenda. Liberty appears to have recognised the advantages that 'respectability' brings, and it has come to share many of the AIRE Centre's characteristics as it too emphasises the expertise and experience that it brings to human rights litigation. John Wadham declared himself 'appalled at the level of [representatives'] incompetence in ECHR cases, cases involving important issues'.[101] He also argued that applicants are 'better off with a repeat player' because of the experience they bring to litigation.[102]

Liberty has developed a number of constructive relationships that befit a 'respectable' human rights organisation. One place in which these relationships are particularly evident is in Liberty's third-party interventions, many of which are made jointly with other organisations. For example, Liberty and JUSTICE submitted a joint intervention in one of the sample cases concerning the use in criminal trials of evidence obtained as a result of a violation of the right to privacy.[103] Both organisations found in that case, as they have done several times before and since,[104] that – despite the existence of an 'interesting tension between co-operation and competition' among NGOs[105] – working together enabled them to better serve their aims.[106] Nevertheless, by co-operating closely with JUSTICE, an organisation that counts several judges and senior lawyers amongst its members, Liberty puts very little distance between itself and 'the establishment'.

---

[101]   Interview, John Wadham, 20 January 2003.

[102]   *ibid.*

[103]   *Sultan Khan v United Kingdom* ECHR 2000-V, (2001) 31 EHRR 45.
Within the sample, Liberty also intervened alone in the case of *Kingsley v United Kingdom* [GC] ECHR 2002-IV, (2002) 35 EHRR 10, in which it argued that where the Court has found a violation of Article 6, and where it was impossible to speculate what the outcome of a trial would have been had Article 6 not been violated, an applicant should be given the benefit of the doubt when costs are awarded.

[104]   For example, a number of recent reports and submissions co-authored by JUSTICE and Liberty are mentioned on JUSTICE's website. See: www.justice.org.uk/ourwork/humanrights/index.html.

[105]   Interview, Eric Metcalfe, JUSTICE's Director of Human Rights Policy, 10 April 2003, London.

[106]   It is worth noting, however, that the ECtHR has occasionally compelled Liberty to conduct joint-interventions with JUSTICE to avoid a deluge of interventions. Interview, John Wadham, 20 January 2003.

As with the AIRE Centre, Liberty has also developed positive relationships with both the British government and Strasbourg institutions. John Wadham referred to 'the very good relationship' that Liberty has with the UK lawyers at the Registry, and he noted that its 'relationship with the Foreign Office lawyers is good'.[107] Moreover, staff move fluidly between Liberty and posts within the administration: for example, the current Director of Liberty, Shami Chakrabarti, worked as a lawyer for the Home Office before joining Liberty, and John Wadham is currently Legal Director of the Equality and Human Rights Commission.

The reason for the emphasis on 'professionalism' and 'expertise' by organisations like Liberty can best be understood by considering the context in which they operate. In effect, these organisations are riding on the crest of the human rights wave. They work in environments in which their aims have such a broad support-base that they can describe themselves as apolitical without much fear of contradiction. Nevertheless, while Liberty's test cases might raise violations that are less immediately shocking that those of the KHRP and ERRC, they do serve as a reminder that in countries such as the United Kingdom human rights can be gradually eroded beneath a veneer of legal sophistry.[108] As Liberty's challenge to the UK's criminal justice reforms of the 1990s show, it can be alarmingly easy in countries that have a long-standing commitment to the ECHR for vulnerable groups to be the victims of repressive, populist measures. Liberty's human rights work has attempted to promote the human rights of a number of such vulnerable groups, including those with mental health problems, sexual minorities, immigrants, and defendants in the criminal justice system. Recent legislation that has arisen in response to 'the war against terror' serves only to highlight the continued importance of Liberty's work.

In the context of countries like the United Kingdom, in which the Government professes a commitment to upholding human rights laws and where law is still a primary arena for the development of human rights discourse, there are enormous benefits to be had in having NGOs, sophisticated in their use of legal arguments, who are able to manipulate this tool for positive change. Although the work of 'pure human rights organisations', like Liberty, in litigating before the ECtHR is inherently political, its success is largely dependent upon those organisations having the ability to respond to repressive measures with legal skill and technical ability. Liberty's test cases discussed above appear to have met with only moderate success: they are, therefore, far from being a panacea. However,

---

[107]   Interview, John Wadham, 20 January 2003.

[108]   Of course that is not to say that gross violations of human rights do no happen in countries that have a long-standing commitment to the ECHR; cases such as *McCann and Others v United Kingdom* Series A no 324 (1996) 21 EHRR 97 and *Selmouni v France* ECHR 1999-V, (2000) 29 EHRR 403 stand testimony to this. However, the work of the NGOs discussed in this chapter is not typically directed at finding evidence of patterns of systematic and gross violations of the Convention that take place with impunity.

Liberty's ability to mount a coherent and sustained challenge to repressive laws in a way that combines legal professionalism with political idealism should not be under-valued.

IV. Recent Developments

Liberty, it goes almost without saying, continues its struggle for human rights and maintains a significant presence before the ECtHR. In recent litigation it has addressed a range of human rights issues, but its key focus is responding to legislative measures introduced in 'the fight against terrorism'. This has raised the stakes in litigation considerably. In the United Kingdom, the executive's response to the perceived threat from terrorists continues to challenge the boundaries of human rights laws, and the Human Rights Act 1998 and ECHR have been at the centre of a flurry of on-going legal challenges by NGOs. The impact of these campaigns has been such that the abolition of the Human Rights Act is now a matter of serious debate.

In *A & Others v Secretary of State for the Home Department*, Liberty successfully intervened in a case before the House of Lords to challenge the indefinite detention without charge of non-nationals under the Anti-Terrorism, Crime and Security Act 2001.[109] It also intervened (jointly with 13 other organisations, including the AIRE Centre) in a second House of Lords case concerning the same 'Belmarsh detainees' that established that evidence obtained by torture is inadmissible, regardless of where or under whose authority the torture is committed.[110] In *Al-Skeini*,[111] Liberty intervened (again, successfully) in a case which established that the Human Rights Act extends to the activities of public authorities (British troops) within the jurisdiction, but outside the territory, of the United Kingdom. In *Al Jedda*, which concerned a detainee held by British forces in Iraq, Liberty and JUSTICE were unsuccessful in their argument that the ECHR's protections were not qualified by UN Security Council Resolution 1546.[112] In *E v Secretary of State for the Home Department*, Liberty intervened (again, unsuccessfully) to argue that the making of non-derogating control orders issued under the Prevention of Terrorism Act 2005 involves the determination of a criminal charge under Article 6 of the Convention.[113] In *Al Rawi*, in which the claimants sought to sue the Security Services and others for damages relating to their detention and mistreatment in Guantánamo Bay and elsewhere, Liberty and JUSTICE argued jointly and successfully before the High Court that

---

[109]   *A and Others v Secretary of State for the Home Department* [2004] UKHL 56.
[110]   *A and Others v Secretary of State for the Home Department* [2005] UKHL 71.
[111]   *R (on the application of Al-Skeini) v Secretary of State for Defence* [2007] UKHL 26.
[112]   *R (on the application of Al-Jedda) v Secretary of State for Defence* [2007] UKHL 58. See n 117 below.
[113]   *E and S v Secretary of State for the Home Department* [2007] UKHL 47.

it was not within the court's jurisdiction to order a closed material procedure in relation to the trial of an ordinary civil claim.[114]

The time-scale of litigation is such that cases challenging the UK's 'post-9/11' legislative responses to terrorism are starting now to be heard by the ECtHR. Unsurprisingly, Liberty is to be found at the centre of these cases too. In *A & Ors v United Kingdom,* Liberty continued their fight against detention without charge and argued (unsuccessfully) in an intervention that the Government was precluded from raising an argument that had not been raised before the House of Lords, namely that the indefinite detention of terrorist suspects was lawful and permissible under Article 5(1)(f) of the Convention.[115] In *Gillan and Quinton v UK,* Liberty, as the applicants' representatives, successfully challenged the broad 'stop and search' (without suspicion) powers introduced under section 44 of the Terrorism Act 2000.[116] Finally, in *Al Jedda v UK,* which is currently before the Grand Chamber, Liberty has intervened jointly with JUSTICE to argue once again that international law obligations cannot displace substantive ECHR obligations.[117]

The AIRE Centre litigation in recent years has been, as one would expect, somewhat less focused than Liberty's, but the impact of repressive terrorism laws has been a shared point of concern.[118] The AIRE Centre has made a particular niche for itself defending the principle of non-refoulement. In *Ramzy v Netherlands* the AIRE Centre, together with eight other organisations, intervened to argue (successfully) that where a person is at risk of torture of ill-treatment if returned to their country of origin, the principle of non-refoulement is absolute.[119] Those interventions were submitted in response to a joint intervention from four governments, steered by the United Kingdom, which argued that the prohibition on return should be modified where the person concerned is considered to present a risk to national security. In *Mamatkulov and Askarov v Turkey*[120] and *Ismoilov and Others v Russia,*[121] the AIRE Centre and Human

---

[114]   *Al Rawi & Others v The Security Service & Others* [2010] EWCA Civ 482.

[115]   *A & Others v United Kingdom* (App no 3455/05) ECHR 19 February 2009, (2009) 49 EHRR 29.

[116]   *Gillan and Quinton v United Kingdom* (App no 4158/05) ECHR 12 January 2010, (2010) 50 EHRR 45.

[117]   *Al Jedda v United Kingdom* (App no 27021/08). A copy of Liberty's intervention can be found at www.liberty-human-rights.org.uk/publications/pdfs/al-jedda-strasbourg-submissions-final.pdf.

[118]   Notable cases not related to terrorism in which the AIRE Centre has intervened in recent years are: *Rantsev v Cyprus & Russia* (App no 25965/04) ECHR 7 January 2010, (2010) 51 EHRR 1 (human trafficking); *Sejdić and Finci v Bosnia and Hertzegovina* (App nos 27996/06 and 34836/06) ECHR 22 December 2009 (religious and ethnic discrimination); *Hirst v United Kingdom (No 2)* [GC] ECHR 2005-IX, (2006) 42 EHRR 41 (right to vote).

[119]   *Ramzy v Netherlands* (App no 25424/05) ECHR 27 May 2008 (admiss dec).

This case was overtaken by the Court's judgment in *Saadi v Italy* (App no 37201/06) ECHR 28 February 2008, (2009) 49 EHRR 30 (the UK government once again intervening), in which the absolute nature of the principle of non-refoulement was affirmed.

[120]   *Mamatkulov & Askarov v Turkey* [GC] ECHR 2005-I, (2005) 41 EHRR 25.

[121]   *Ismoilov & Ors v Russia* (App no 2947/06) ECHR 24 April 2008, (2009) 49 EHRR 42.

Rights Watch jointly intervened to argue (successfully) that diplomatic assurances do not provide sufficient protection where reliable evidence suggests a person is at real risk of torture if extradited to her country of origin. Finally, in *Saadi v UK*, the AIRE Centre and Liberty were among four organisations that intervened (unsuccessfully) to argue that the detention of an Iraqi man for the duration of expedited asylum proceedings was a violation of the Convention and, specifically, that detention under Article 5(1)(f) should be viewed as exceptional.[122]

This remarkable series of recent cases shows that NGOs are currently at the forefront in the legal battle against excessive legislative and executive zeal. In the present climate, the need for such organisations is felt all the more acutely. However, given the seriousness of the issues at stake, it has to be noted that their misses in court have been at least as remarkable as their hits. This uneven record suggests that NGOs' capacity to restrain executive excess using polite and incremental legislative strategies is limited: when the stakes are highest, the best efforts of these 'defenders of the Convention' resemble the roars of toothless tigers. Furthermore, in these cases, repressive and violent acts carried out in the name of the 'war on terror' tend to be reduced to surprisingly anodyne and technocratic legal points of law, thereby stripping them of their capacity to shock.

V. Conclusion

While there would probably be some consternation on the part of Liberty and the AIRE Centre if they were likened to one another too closely, the differences between them should not be exaggerated. The main differences are that Liberty's primary concern is with domestic law whereas the AIRE Centre is focused exclusively on European rights, Liberty litigates a much greater number of cases than the AIRE Centre, and Liberty has a more clearly targeted litigation strategy. However, both Liberty and the AIRE Centre see themselves as human rights law experts, working to ensure that rights are effectively realised. Both organisations tend to emphasise their 'neutrality' and 'disinterestedness', in particular by focusing upon their legal 'expertise' and 'professionalism', and their work derives almost exclusively from a western, liberal attachment to, and understanding of, civil and political rights.

The liberal idea of human rights developed as a phenomenally important strain of European political discourse in the second half of the twentieth century. However, Liberty's test cases demonstrate that even in democracies with a long-standing commitment to the ECHR, respect for individual freedoms competes constantly with other political imperatives. Mature democracies such as the

---

[122]   *Saadi v United Kingdom* (App no 13229/03) [GC] ECHR 29 January 2008, (2008) 47 EHRR 17.

United Kingdom cannot afford to be complacent; the enjoyment of rights depends upon a thriving civil society. Writing in 1984, John Griffith emphasised the importance of having an active civil movement to protect human rights:

> It cannot be said that civil liberties are a general concern in this country. Positive promotion of the cause is limited to a small number of people. Nor is it easy to arouse support for any but the most flagrant examples of infringements of civil liberties. There is not, and never has been, a civil liberties movement.[123]

NGOs like Liberty and the AIRE Centre fight a continuous battle to secure hard-won freedoms, but it is a battle that is usually fought in courts of law over the legal minutiae of Convention interpretation. Through their systematic challenges to repressive legislation, through raising awareness amongst lawyers and the public about human rights issues, and through engaging governments in debate that focuses attention on human rights concerns, the organisations discussed in this chapter perform a function that is important to a supposedly thriving democracy that respects the rule of law. Their tenacity in presenting sober, constructive and thoughtful legal analyses of human rights issues, particularly on behalf of those at the margins of society, provides NGOs like the AIRE Centre and Liberty with a clear answer to anyone who would question their importance.

However, if human rights work cannot be devoid of political purpose, what each of the case studies discussed in this chapter demonstrates is that it *can* be devoid of confrontationalism. The NGOs discussed in this chapter work within political and legal environments that are comparatively open to human rights discourse and in which they usually face little serious opposition to their work. They have adapted to their reasonably hospitable environment, tailoring themselves as politically-neutral legal experts. Given the ease with which they can be brushed aside when perceived to be seriously disruptive or too radical, this is perhaps understandable. However, the legitimacy that has been conferred on them as a result of this does not come without cost. In order to be a watchdog one's actions are generally responsive to the actions of those being watched, and there is an inevitable symbiosis in the relationship that develops. On occasion, the impression one gathers is not just of a close relationship between these organisations and the legal and administrative system of the States they are concerned with, but of a relationship that borders on the claustrophobic. It is almost inevitable that organisations engaging in human rights debate with governments through the medium of legal systems will become a part of that system to a certain extent. This is not without practical implications: it is inevitable that these organisations tend to think and work reactively. It has been noted that Liberty's history 'is written around the campaigns against legislative proposals put forward by Governments and Private Members',[124] and that their

---

[123]   John Griffith, 'The Democratic Process' in Wallington (ed), *Civil Liberties* (1984) 86.
[124]   *ibid*, 101.

work, and that of other organisations like them, 'has been essentially conserva-tive'.[125] Organisations like those discussed in this chapter are locked into close relationships with administrative bodies, relationships that leave little space to consider new meanings that might be given to human rights.

Organisations dominated by lawyers, such as Liberty and the AIRE Centre, are particularly prone to conservatism. I would echo Eskridge's view that lawyers tend towards integrationism by nature, and 'the more their social movement becomes committed to constitutional litigation the more integrationalist it will be'.[126] These strategies, often successful enough in legal terms, lead to enormous amounts of energy being devoted to what arguably can only ever amount to incremental changes. Such strategies assume and affirm the legitimacy of the institutions in play, and at worse, critical voices maintain, may absorb radical energy from social movements, taming them with the 'illusion of change'.[127]

It has been seen throughout this chapter that these organisations capitalise on the legal expertise that they bring to human rights litigation. However, while legal expertise enables organisations like Liberty and the AIRE Centre to engage in human rights dialogue with administrative bodies, the case studies discussed in this chapter demonstrate that this expertise also implicates them in the increas-ingly technocratic and elitist nature of human rights discourse. Issues such as the right to silence, to take just one example, are placed for resolution before the ECtHR as a matter of technical interpretation of Article 6 rights. As a result, important political debates are conducted within specialist legal systems and in specialist legal language; it goes without saying that this can have an alienating effect on those not versed in the language of law. Key political debates become rather narrowly defined as they are squeezed in to the corset of the Convention's rights, with the associated danger that they become of little interest to anyone outside the legal profession. Ultimately, both Liberty and the AIRE Centre espouse a human rights ideology that has come of age; but this has the potential to undermine the future relevance of their work, and might lead to something of a 'crisis of utility'. As activists without a specific political agenda and without a significant constituency, they are particularly vulnerable to this. Mary Cunneen, formerly of Liberty, observed: 'In the outside world there's a debate on whether western organisations are too focused on rights as opposed to other mechan-isms'.[128] Her comment seems to have particular relevance for the organisations discussed in this chapter, for whom human rights are an end in themselves. Of course the limits of ECtHR litigation as a tool for effecting change is partly to be found in the nature of the Convention itself – which, when compared with other

---

[125] Cox, *Civil Liberties* (1975) 23.

[126] Willian Eskridge, 'Some Effects of Identity-Based Social Movements on Constitutional Law in the Twentieth Century' (2002) 100 *Michigan Law Review* 2062, 2395.

[127] Gerald N Rosenberg, *The Hollow Hope: Can Courts Bring About Social Change?* (Chicago, University of Chicago, 1991) 341.

[128] Interview, Mary Cunneen, former legal officer with Liberty, 8 April 2003, London.

regional human rights treaties, contains a very restrictive range of rights – and in the cautious judgments that the Court often delivers. A significant number of important ECHR cases are filtered through a close-knit community of 'pure' human rights NGOs whose influence is considerable. The case studies discussed in this chapter suggest, however, that these NGOs are prone to a natural conservatism and have so far spent little effort imagining and realising the radically transformative potential of human rights.

6

'A Desire that Never Ends':[1] Pressure Groups and the European Convention on Human Rights

'For the extraordinary flowering of human spirit always allows new questions to be raised and to see new or different aspect of truth'.[2]

I. Introduction

HUMAN RIGHTS ARE a constantly developing set of norms that, to some degree, reflect evolving cultural values. As Donnelly notes:

> There are few political issues more important than establishing the exact extent of the political space allowed to autonomous individuals in the exercise of their rights. Dominant understandings have changed over time and will continue to change.[3]

Our understanding of the rights protected under the ECHR is therefore subject to continual change. The ECtHR's adopted process of teleological interpretation requires it to pronounce upon legal, social, political and cultural developments as it establishes the scope of the Convention's rights, regardless of whether or not it is adequately equipped to do so. In 2002, for example, the Court was asked to decide whether the right to life, protected under Article 2 of the Convention,

---

[1] Costas Douzinas, *The End of Human Rights: Critical Legal Thought at the Turn of the Century* (Oxford, Hart Publishing, 2000) 261.

[2] *Collected Edition of the "Travaux Préparatoires" of the European Convention on Human Rights* (Dordrecht, Martinus Nijhoff, 1985) vol II, 62 (M De la Vallee-Poussin).

[3] Jack Donnelly, 'The Social Construction of International Human Rights' in Tim Dunne and Nicholas J Wheeler (eds), *Human Rights in Global Politics* (Cambridge, Cambridge University Press, 1999) 99.

encompasses the right of a terminally ill person to die as they choose.[4] In the same year the Court was asked whether the right to respect for family life (Article 8) and the right to marry and to found a family (Article 12) extend to transsexual people in their new gender.[5] The questions raised by cases such as these – which serve only as examples of the myriad important and complex issues that have been placed before the Court for resolution – have no immediately obvious answer that can be derived from universally accepted human rights standards. In delivering judgment upon such issues, therefore, the Court has the potential to play a dynamic role in sculpting the social landscape of Europe.

NGOs in particular recognise that the ECtHR's judgments have the potential to foster social transformation – albeit on a modest and incremental scale – and several organisations have become involved in applications to the Court with this aim in mind. It is particularly noteworthy that groups that have a narrow political focus and a clear agenda to promote social change ('pressure groups' or 'single-issue groups') have a tendency to instigate litigation that demands a (re)interpretation of the Convention's rights. This chapter focuses on three pressure groups that were involved in one or more of the sample cases. Through these examples further consideration is given to the role that such groups play in the Court's litigation.

II.   'PESUE' and The Right to Family Life

PESUE (The Association for Family Rights in Finland) is the name of a tiny Finnish organisation concerned with certain aspects of the right to family life.[6] At the time of writing, it is inactive. It was established in August 1994 by Anu Suomela – its (unpaid) Executive Manager – and her husband, together with an anthropologist friend of theirs and the parents of a child who had been taken in to care as a result of accusations of sexual abuse. Anu Suomela appears to have been the driving force behind the organisation's operations; so much so that it is difficult, and somewhat artificial, to distinguish her own aims from those of PESUE.[7] In interview, Anu Suomela described PESUE's principal aim as being to help 'families against authorities, as experts in their own life'.[8] In practice, its

---

[4]   *Pretty v United Kingdom* ECHR 2002-III, (2002) 35 EHRR 1.

[5]   *Christine Goodwin v United Kingdom* ECHR 2002-VI, (2002) 35 EHRR 18.

[6]   As a small, national, organisation, the limited information available about PESUE is almost entirely in Finnish. Much of the following is therefore based upon information obtained from its Executive Manager, Anu Suomela, who was happy to answer questions about the background to PESUE's involvement in ECtHR cases. A questionnaire, based on the (primarily open-ended) questions used in interviews, was sent to Anu Suomela by e-mail. Her answers were also sent by e-mail.

[7]   PESUE receives no government funding and is funded principally by Anu Suomela herself.

[8]   Anu Suomela, response to questionnaire, 14 September 2002.

activities have been primarily directed towards supporting the relatives of children taken from their families and placed in public care, often as a result of sexual abuse allegations.

Although PESUE was not established by lawyers (Anu Suomela herself is a qualified social worker), litigation has been an important means for it to challenge care orders. Consequently, PESUE members acted as unqualified representatives in several family law cases before domestic tribunals[9] and they also acted on behalf of applicants in both a representative and advisory capacity in a number of ECtHR cases.[10] Despite its very small size, Anu Suomela described PESUE as a relatively high-profile organisation in Finland that had generally been contacted directly by the families seeking its assistance. PESUE's legal advice and assistance service was supported by a network of sympathetic lawyers, of which Anu Suomela described herself as 'the spider in the middle'.[11] Two of the ECtHR cases that PESUE was involved in fell within the sample group of cases and are discussed below.

A.   PESUE's Involvement in the Sample Cases

(i)   K and T v Finland[12]

K's second child (M) was voluntarily placed in public care in May 1993, primarily due to K's repeated hospitalisation for mental illness. K's third child (J), the father of whom was the second applicant, was born in June 1993 and was immediately taken in to care by emergency order. The reasons given for taking J into care focused on K's poor mental health and the lack of guarantees for J's development and safety. Days after J's birth and removal from her family, M was also placed in compulsory care pursuant to an emergency order. After the emergency care orders were executed the Social Welfare Board prohibited all unsupervised visits between K and her children, and when M and J were placed in a permanent foster home by normal care orders access continued to be restricted to monthly supervised visits.[13] A fourth child was born to the two applicants in 1995 without being taken into care. Continuous reviews and appeals of the situation did not lead to any fundamental changes in the children's care plan and the Social

---

[9]   It was possible under Finnish law for unqualified persons to act as representatives in such situations until 2002. Under the Code of Judicial Procedure (Oikeudenkäymiskaari), Chap 15, s 2 (amendment 259/2002), the general rule was adopted that a layperson cannot represent another in court.

[10]   PESUE has been significantly involved in seven applications lodged with either the ECmHR or ECtHR. Anu Suomela states that she has also given 'behind the scenes' assistance in a further four applications.

[11]   Anu Suomela, response to questionnaire, 14 September 2002.

[12]   K and T v Finland [GC] ECHR 2001-VII, (2003) 36 EHRR 18.

[13]   The children's care plan was subsequently altered in November 2000 to allow for unsupervised monthly visits and some over-night stays during the holidays.

Director had concluded by December 1998 that 'the reunification of the family was not in sight as the substitute family was now the children's factual home'.[14]

Before the Court the applicants raised complaints under Articles 8 (the right to respect for family life) and 13 (the right to an effective remedy).[15] In its initial judgment the Court held that there was a violation of Article 8 in relation to the placing of the children in care[16] and also in relation to the refusal to terminate their care arrangements.[17] On the other hand, the Court found that the continuing access restrictions did not exceed the national authorities' margin of appreciation, as the children had been in care for seven years by the time judgment was delivered;[18] nor did the Court find Article 13 had been violated.[19]

The Finnish Government, in what was the first successful referral of a case to the Grand Chamber under Article 43, requested the re-examination of the Court's judgment in relation to Article 8 only. The Grand Chamber considered that such a partial re-hearing would not be compatible with the language of the Convention[20] and that the correct interpretation of Article 43 required that on referral to the Grand Chamber the entire case should be re-heard, a new judgment delivered and the original judgment set-aside.[21] The Grand Chamber went on, therefore, to deliver a new judgment in *K and T*. In this second judgment the Court found that while there had been a violation of Article 8 in respect of the emergency care order relating to J (by 14–3 votes), there was no violation in respect of M who was already at the time physically separated from the family (by 11–6 votes).[22] In relation to J, the Court said that

> the taking of a new-born baby into public care at the moment of its birth is an extremely harsh measure. There must be extraordinarily compelling reasons before a baby can be physically removed from the care of its mother, against her will, immediately after birth as a consequence of a procedure in which neither she nor her partner has been involved.[23]

The Grand Chamber also held (unanimously) that there was a violation of Article 8 arising from the authorities' failure to try and reunite the family, reiterating that care orders should normally be regarded as temporary measures.[24] On the other hand, the Court (again, unanimously) found that the

---

[14]   *K and T v Finland* (dec) (App no 25702/94) ECHR 8 June 1999, 12.

[15]   Various other complaints were declared inadmissible on the basis that they were manifestly ill-founded or because they were incompatible *ratione materiae* with the Convention as the Finnish Government had entered a relevant and valid reservation.

[16]   *K and T v Finland* (App no 25702/94) ECHR 27 April 2000, (2001) 31 EHRR 18.

[17]   *ibid*, [164].

[18]   *ibid*, [176].

[19]   *ibid*, [179].

[20]   Article 43(3) reads as follows: 'If the panel accepts the request [for referral of a case to the Grand Chamber], the Grand Chamber shall decide the case by means of a judgment.'

[21]   *K and T v Finland* [GC] ECHR 2001-VII, (2003) 36 EHRR 18 [140].

[22]   *ibid*, [168]–[170].

[23]   *ibid*, [168].

[24]   *ibid*, [179].

authorities had acted within their margin of appreciation when adopting the normal care orders[25] and access restrictions,[26] and they concurred with the original judgment that Article 13 had not been violated.[27]

(ii)   L v Finland[28]

The applicants in the second sample case in which PESUE was involved were the father and grandfather of two girls (P and S) who had been taken into provisional care in January 1992 on the grounds that there was suspicion that they had been sexually abused or were at risk from sexual abuse. During their time in provisional care S's whereabouts were disclosed to neither of her parents and parental visits to P were permitted only twice a week. Although the suspicions of sexual abuse could not be proven, the children were formally placed in public care in March 1992 on the basis that their parents could not look after them adequately. Once both the children were placed in a new foster home access between them and their parents was restricted to infrequent supervised meetings, despite numerous appeals by the parents. Access between the children and their grandfather was prohibited, as it was found to be disruptive.

The applicants complained under Article 8 in conjunction with Article 13 about the interference with their family life.[29] Specifically, the applicants argued that under the factual circumstances of the case, taking P and S into care was a disproportionate measure. They complained that no attempts had been made to reunite the family; rather, access had been prohibited in the case of the grandfather and severely restricted in the case of the father.[30] The Court was reluctant to interfere with the authorities' decisions concerning P and S, and noted that in these circumstances the Finnish authorities were best placed to make an assessment of the children's best interests.[31] It consequently found that the Government had acted within its margin of appreciation under Article 8 in placing the children in care,[32] refusing to terminate the care order[33] and in restricting parental access.[34] The applicants also complained that they had not been granted

---

[25]   *ibid*, [173]–[174].

[26]   *ibid*, [194].

[27]   *ibid*, [199].

[28]   *L v Finland* (App no 25651/94) ECHR 27 April 2000, (2001) 31 EHRR 30.

[29]   Subsequent to the children being taken into care, the children's parents divorced. Before the Court the Government alleged that the children's mother was happy with their care arrangements.

[30]   Other complaints concerning the care proceedings were held to be manifestly ill-founded. See *L v Finland* (dec) (App no 25651/94) ECHR 8 June 1999.

[31]   *L v Finland* (App no 25651/94) ECHR 27 April 2000, (2001) 31 EHRR 30 [118].

[32]   *ibid*, [121].

[33]   *ibid*, [123].

[34]   *ibid*, [128].

an oral hearing before the County Administrative Court when it reviewed the care orders in March 1997,[35] in relation to which the Court reached a unanimous finding of a violation of Article 6.[36]

B.   Understanding PESUE's Role

Anu Suomela is described in the Court's judgments in both *K and T* and *L* as an 'adviser' to the applicants and their representatives, which does not adequately reflect the level of her involvement in the litigation.[37] In both cases the applicants had contacted PESUE in 1994 seeking help, and Anu Suomela had represented them in domestic legal proceedings to challenge the care orders. When Anu Suomela realised that the circumstances of *K and T* potentially raised issues under the Convention she instigated the application to the Commission by herself – with minimal advice on relevant case-law from a friendly lawyer – despite the fact that she had no prior experience of the Convention's mechanisms. Anu Suomela estimates that she personally wrote 90 per cent of the correspondence to the Court in both *K and T* and *L*, with some assistance from the applicants' formal representatives (who were lawyers from PESUE's legal network). Despite their significant involvement in the Strasbourg litigation, PESUE's costs in *K and T* were not granted, as they were 'not a party to the present proceedings' and their costs were 'not actually incurred by the applicants themselves'.[38] The same decision was reached in *L*.[39]

The involuntary placement of children into public care is intervention into family life of a most serious nature, which can require Solomon-like wisdom in balancing the rights of the family (traditionally understood to mean the rights of the parents) and the best interests of the children concerned. It is a divisive and complex issue that has troubled many States and, when placed before the Court, has resulted in split judgments.[40] The partly dissenting opinion of Judge Bonello

---

[35] The same complaint concerning earlier hearings had been declared incompatible *ratione materiae* with the Convention as the Finnish Government had adopted a valid reservation. See *L v Finland* (dec), (App no 25651/94) ECHR 8 June 1999, 28–29.

[36]   *L v Finland* (App no 25651/94) ECHR 27 April 2000, (2001) 31 EHRR 30 [133].

[37]   As the Court's files in both cases were confidential, much of the following information is based on information obtained directly from PESUE.

[38]   *K and T v Finland* (App no 25702/94) ECHR 27 April 2000, (2001) 31 EHRR 18 [186]. See also *K and T v Finland* [GC] ECHR 2001-VII, (2003) 36 EHRR 18 [207].

[39]   *L v Finland* (App no 25651/94) ECHR 27 April 2000, (2001) 31 EHRR 30 [140].

[40]   The inherent difficulties when such issues are dealt with by a human rights tribunal are highlighted if one contrasts the *K and T* decision with that of the Court in *Z and Others v United Kingdom* ECHR 2001-V, (2002) 34 EHRR 3. The latter case was brought by four siblings, with assistance from the AIRE Centre, who had been brought up by their mother in circumstances of considerable abuse and neglect. The conditions of the siblings had been brought to the attention of Social Services on numerous occasions and they were being monitored regularly, but remained with their mother. They were eventually placed in care only at the insistence of the mother, who said that she was likely to do them serious harm if they were not taken away from her. The facts were the subject of some legal notoriety in the UK when the siblings were denied permission to sue the local

in *K and T* highlights how emotive this issue can be, particularly when it involves the involuntary removal of a new-born baby from its mother:

> In my view, the Finnish care services, faced with harrowing alternatives, acted soundly, in the only rational and accountable manner open to them, achieving a fair balance between wrong inflicted and wrong prevented. They who preferred to place a child beyond the reach of harm have now been branded violators of human rights. I inquire what the majority would have styled them had the infant, left with the applicant mother, suffered mischief. Had I, like the Finnish authorities, been faced with choosing whether to be cruel to the mother or to the child, I know which way I would have looked.[41]

Prior to its judgment in *K and T* the Court had been unwilling to intervene in such complex and sensitive issues and had persistently refused to find that the placement of children in public care violated the Convention.[42] Consequently, Anu Suomela is right when she describes the case of *K and T* as a 'historical success in many ways'.[43] Certainly, it was an important development in the Court's jurisprudence because it had taken 'the unprecedented step of finding that the national authorities had acted outside of their wide margin of appreciation' when taking children into care.[44]

---

authority for the psychological damage that had befallen upon them by the failure of Social Services to act sooner in placing them in local authority care. See *X and Others v Bedfordshire County Council* [1995] 3 All ER 353. The Court found that these facts disclosed a violation of Article 3.

Judge Pettiti has argued that in some situations it would be desirable for a separate lawyer to be appointed to represent the interests of the children concerned. See separate concurring opinion in *X Y & Z v United Kingdom* ECHR 1997-II, (1997) 24 EHRR 143.

[41]   *K and T v Finland* [GC] ECHR 2001-VII, (2003) 36 EHRR 18. On the issue of emergency removal of children from their parents, see Judith Masson, 'Human Rights in Child Protection: Emergency Action and its Impact' in Peter Lødrup and Eva Modvar (eds), *Family Life and Human Rights: Papers Presented at the 11th World Conference of the International Society of Family Law* (Oslo, Gyldendal, 2004).

[42]   See, generally, Adriana Opromolla, 'Children's Rights Under Article 3 and 8 of the European Convention: Recent Case Law' (2001) 26 *European Law Review Supp (Human Rights Survey)* 50.

[43]   Anu Suomela, response to questionnaire, 14 September 2002.

[44]   Mitchell Woolf, 'Coming of Age? The Principle of the "Best Interests of the Child"' (2003) 2 *European Human Rights Law Review* 205, 211.

For the Court's earlier jurisprudence see, for example, *Olsson v Sweden (No 1)* Series A no 130 (1989) 11 EHRR 259 and *Johansen v Norway* ECHR 1996-III, (1997) 23 EHRR 33. In both of those cases the Court held that the taking of children into care did not violate the Convention, but the implementing of the care orders in each case did violate Article 8 as they were not aimed at reuniting the families in question.

It is apparent that the judgment in *K and T* has led to a change of direction in the Court's jurisprudence. In the more recent case of *P, C & S v United Kingdom* ECHR 2002-VI, (2002) 35 EHRR 31 [133] (in which the applicants were assisted by the AIRE Centre) the Court described the immediate placement of a newborn child whose mother had previous convictions relating to Munchausen Syndrome By Proxy into care as 'draconian'. Nevertheless, it is clear that the Court will not declare all emergency care orders to be in violation of the Convention, provided that the action is sufficiently considered, based on relevant and sufficient reasons, and opportunity has been given for the parents to respond. See *KA v Finland* (App no 27751/95) ECHR 14 January 2003.

It is PESUE's belief that the Finnish State has persistently exercised its power to place children in care in an excessive and draconian fashion, without taking into account the rights of parents. When asked her reasons for supporting cases such as those discussed above, Anu Suomela replied in broad terms that she would 'love to live in a constitutional State and to leave for my grandchildren a better place to live in this regard'.[45] Interestingly, PESUE's perception is that its cases reveal a deep-rooted lack of respect for human rights in Finland. Its view is that Finnish democracy is quite young (the country achieved independence from Russia in 1917) and 'the traditions of the Tsarist administration live on strongly'.[46] Moreover, Finland only ratified the ECHR in 1990. This lack of mature commitment to human rights is reflected, PESUE suggests, in the way that its clients, who are frequently poor and unaware of their rights, have been treated as 'objects of pressure and aggression by the local authorities'.[47] PESUE's support for parents whose children have been removed extends to a rejection of primacy being given to the rights of the child, which it describes as an 'undemocratic act' because it subjugates parental rights.[48] This argument, of course, does not accord with contemporary international human rights standards.[49]

Some support for PESUE's criticisms of the Finnish authorities can be found in the UN Committee on the Rights of the Child's Concluding Observations on Finland's second periodic report in 2000, in which the Committee notes with concern the 'increasing number of children placed outside their families in recent years'.[50] It appears, moreover, that this number continues to rise.[51] In the late 1980s and throughout the 1990s there had been several ECHR applications against Scandinavian countries concerning the involuntary placement of children into care,[52] which indicates that these countries have had, from a Western European view-point, particularly interventionist child welfare laws and policies. There is, nevertheless, an element of hyperbole in many of PESUE's claims. Julie Selwyn and Wendy Sturgess's statistical overview of the number of children in

---

[45]   Anu Suomela, response to questionnaire, 14 September 2002.

[46]   PESUE, *Collection of Articles Concerning the Human Rights Situation in Finnish Child Welfare* (unpublished, on file with the author) 2.

[47]   *ibid*, 3. It is somewhat ironic that in both *K and T* and *L* the applicants' complaints under Art 6(3)(c) and (d), that they had not being granted cost-free proceedings for their challenge to access restrictions, were rejected in part because they had been represented by Anu Suomela.

[48]   PESUE, *Collection of Articles* 40.

[49]   See Article 3(1) of the UN Convention on the Rights of the Child (1989).

[50]   Committee on the Rights of the Child, *Report on the Twenty-Fifth Session*, CRC/C/100 (2000) para 59.

[51]   See *Finland's Third Periodic Report to the Children's Rights Committee* (CRC/C/129/Add.5 (2003) 46. More recent data on numbers of children in alternative care in Finland can be found on the website of the Finnish National Institute for Health and Welfare at: www.stakes.fi/EN/tilastot/ statisticsbytopic/childhoodandfamily/childwelfare.htm. Comparative data can be found in Eurochild, *Children in Alternative Care*, 2nd edn (January 2010), available from www.eurochild.org.

[52]   See, for example: *Olsson v Sweden (No 1)* Series A no 130 (1989) 11 EHRR 259 and *Johansen v Norway* ECHR 1996-III, (1997) 23 EHRR 33, *KA v Finland* (App no 27751/95) ECHR 14 January 2003; *Eriksson v Sweden* Series A no 156 (1990) 12 EHRR 183.

care in 2000 shows Finland's percentage to be well within European norms, and the authors remark that both 'Norway and Finland have very high thresholds at which children are taken into care'.[53] It is also clear that the question of when the State should intervene to remove children from their families has been deeply problematic and troubling for the authorities in many European countries.

It appears that PESUE's litigation, rather than addressing gross neglect of human rights norms, represents a conscious and weighted attempt to place the Court at the centre of a difficult social debate. As Dingwall, Eekelaar and Murray note, '[d]ebates about the proper response to child abuse and neglect are, in substance, debates about the nature of the good society. They are possible only because of the clash of utopias between humanitarian and organizational moralists'.[54] PESUE's position appears to be consistent with a minimalist libertarian viewpoint. This viewpoint sees the family as an important restraint on excessive State power, and consequently tends to emphasise the value of family privacy and 'parental rights'. Goldstein, Freud and Solnit were influential in espousing such ideas in the UK in the early 1980s, and they employed psychological concepts to argue for minimalist State intervention in the relationship between parents and children:

> Though obvious once said, when left unsaid, the limitations of law often go unacknowledged in discussions about child placement. Too frequently there is attributed to law and its agents a magical power – a power to do what is far beyond its means. While the law may claim to establish relationships, it can in fact do little more than give them recognition and provide an opportunity for them to develop. The law, so far as specific individual relationships are concerned, is a relatively crude instrument. It may be able to destroy human relationships, but it does not have the power to compel them to develop. It neither has the sensitivity nor the resources to maintain or supervise the ongoing day-to-day happenings between parent and child – and these are essential to meeting ever-changing demands and needs. Nor does it have the capacity to predict future events and needs, which would justify or make workable over the long run any specific conditions it might impose concerning, for example, education, visitation, health care, or religious upbringing … The law, then, ought to and generally does prefer the private ordering of interpersonal relationships over state intrusions on them.[55]

Indeed, Goldstein et al have gone so far as to argue that parental devotion is based upon 'being the undisputed sole possessor of the child and the supreme arbiter of his fate'.[56] Thus, they draw a distinction between the private and public spheres,

[53] Julie Selwyn and Wendy Sturgess, *International Overview of Adoption: Policy and Practice* (Bristol, University of Bristol, 2000) 42.

[54] Robert Dingwall, John Eekelaar and Topsy Murray, *The Protection of Children: State Intervention and Family Life* (Oxford, Basil Blackwell Publisher Ltd, 1983) 3.

[55] Joseph Goldstein, Anna Freud and Albert J Solnit, *Beyond the Best Interests of the Child* (London, Burnett Books, 1980) 49–50.

[56] *ibid*, 25. For a further defence of minimal State intervention in family life, see Michael Wald, 'State Intervention on Behalf of "Neglected Children": A Search for Realistic Standards' (1974–75) 27 *Stanford Law Review* 985.

with responsibility for children falling into the former unless exceptionally compelling reasons for State intervention arise.[57] It is clear that these ideas have held a certain appeal for the Court, whose jurisprudence has at times appeared to give considerable weight to 'parental rights'.[58] This approach is perhaps unsurprising given that the Convention itself makes no express reference to children's rights and the language of Article 8 clearly reflects a preference for the concept of family privacy over State intervention.[59]

Nevertheless, a simple libertarian view of family life fails to adequately address the inevitable social aspect of raising children. Dingwall et al have argued:

> The peculiarly intractable difficulty presented by children, though, is their social potential, the way in which their moral and physical welfare represent matters of concern to the future survival and character of the nation but whose maintenance depends upon the invisible actions of a myriad caretakers.[60]

The concept of the privacy of family life raises particular problems when it conflicts with child welfare concerns. It is acknowledged, even by liberally minded authors, that the privacy of the home can conceal gross abuses of children and that biological parents will not always be the best guarantors of their children's basic rights. Those voicing child welfare concerns gathered momentum in the 1960s and 1970s as medical and social science literature brought to light the issue of child abuse.[61] The law's response to these developments was slow, but both international and domestic laws have now been influenced by the concept of children's rights, and have in particular emphasised that decision-making affecting children should be undertaken on the basis of the best interests of the child.[62]

The developments that led to legal status being granted to the rights of children have naturally had implications for family privacy. In the words of Dingwall et al,

---

[57]   See, for example, the well-known US Supreme Court decision in *Wisconsin v Yoder* 406 US 205 (1972), in which the removal of children from compulsory education at the age of 14 for religious reasons by Amish parents was analysed by the Court as a question of resolving parental rights against the interests of the State.

[58]   See in particular its judgment in *Nielsen v Denmark* Series A no 144 (1989) 11 EHRR 175. Fortin has been particularly critical of the Court's 'very conservative approach to family life and to the parental role'. See Jane Fortin, 'Rights Brought Home for Children' (1999) 62 *Modern Law Review* 350, 357.

[59]   *ibid*, 354.

[60]   Dingwall, Eekelaar and Murray, *The Protection of Children* (1983) 215. See also Martha Minow, 'Rights for the Next Generation: A Feminist Approach to Children's Rights' (1986) 9 *Harvard Women's Law Journal* 1.

[61]   Dingwall, Eekelaar and Murray, *The Protection of Children* (1983), vii. See also Nigel Parton, *The Politics of Child Abuse* (Basingstoke, Macmillan, 1985), especially ch 3.

[62]   See, for example, s.3(1) of the UN Convention on the Rights of the Child. In the UK a landmark House of Lords judgment, which forcefully asserted the rights of the child, was delivered in *Gillick v West Norfolk and Wisbech AHA* [1985] 3 WLR 830.

The ECtHR has made frequent reference to the concept of 'the best interests of the child' in its judgments. See, for example, *Johansen v Norway* ECHR 1996-III, (1997) 23 EHRR 33 [64] and *Hokkanen v Finland* Series A no 299-A (1995) 19 EHRR 139 [58].

[i]f we recognise such rights for children, we must accept corresponding restrictions on parents' rights and on family autonomy. We must also acknowledge, however, that if children's rights are to be taken seriously, their interpretation and enforcement must find some institutional expression.[63]

In consequence, one can see something of a compromise emerging in liberal States: family privacy is generally treated with considerable respect, but the State provides a crude – but nonetheless vital – safety net when parents appear to be unable to meet the minimal requirements for their children's welfare. As with any compromise, however, the results are somewhat uneven: liberal States will differ to a certain degree about what constitutes parental inadequacy; human frailty will operate to prejudice certain groups (such as poor families);[64] and mistakes with catastrophic consequences for the families concerned will undoubtedly be made as the authorities negotiate the difficult demands placed upon them.[65] Dingwall et al are undoubtedly right that '[w]hatever machinery is devised, however, it will always remain vulnerable to criticism from Utopian libertarians [such as PESUE] whose ideals break on the brute physical reality of children's dependence on adults'.[66]

Interestingly, the language chosen by Anu Suomela in responding to questions about her motivation in bringing these cases is the language of the battlefield. She said that she has 'fought the Finnish child welfare authorities' power and illegal practices' and that for most social workers she 'is the worst enemy'.[67] This intense rivalry has led to verbal attacks of a personal nature being directed against her by the administration:

This lady from The Ministry of Social and Health Affairs did the best she could to debase me personally. She even made to the Court two groundless allegations about my actions and my intentions to win the case … I've known her personally for years and she really is passionately against me and for the social workers. I guess I'm exceptionally tough too, but have very limited resources compared to the State. She made my life hell, but could not beat me.[68]

It is clear that antagonism may arise when the pressure applied by groups such as PESUE is met by counter-pressure from those who resist their calls for reform;

---

[63]   Dingwall, Eekelaar and Murray, *The Protection of Children* (1983) 224.

[64]   See Parton, *The Politics* (1985) 172 and Dingwall, Eekelaar and Murray, *The Protection of Children* (1983) 98.

[65]   For a vivid portrayal of the difficulties that can arise where the State intervenes in cases of child abuse, one need only refer to the 'Cleveland child abuse scandal' that took place in the UK in 1987. See: Elizabeth Butler-Sloss, *Report of the Inquiry into child abuse in Cleveland 1987* (1988 Cm 412), (London, HMSO, 1988); Stuart Bell, *When Salem Came to the Boro* (London, Pan Books, 1988); Beatrix Campbell, *Unofficial Secrets: Cleveland Sexual Abuse – The Cleveland Case* (London, Virago Press, 1988).

[66]   Dingwall, Eekelaar and Murray, *The Protection of Children* (1983) 220.

[67]   Ana Suomales, response to questionnaire, 14 September 2002.

[68]   *ibid.*

and PESUE's cases demonstrate that the dressing up of contested and multi-dimensional social issues in the language of human rights does not provide them with an immediate solution. In litigating before the Court on behalf of a specific socio-political cause, PESUE has used human rights discourse – and consequently the ECtHR – as a battlefield upon which difficult social questions are struggled over.

III. Stonewall: Lobbying for Gay Rights

Stonewall was formed in 1989 as a professional lobby organisation that would strive to achieve legal equality and social justice for lesbians, gay men, bisexual and transgender (LGBT) people in the United Kingdom.[69] The experience of those who had campaigned against the introduction of the notorious 'Section 28', which prohibited local authorities from intentionally 'promoting homosexuality', highlighted the need for such an organisation.[70] Stephen Jeffery-Poulter, in his study of the UK movement for gay law-reform, writes:

> The establishment of Stonewall as a modern, streamlined, professional non-partisan lobbying outfit designed to react quickly and effectively without being hamstrung by reference to a mass membership and yet aiming to work within the broad consensus of its constituency, suggests that the campaigning movement has finally come of age.[71]

Jeffery-Poulter suggests that the Section 28 debate was something of a water-shed as it was the 'first time, every politician opposed to Clause 28 had framed their arguments in the context of gay rights being a matter of basic civil liberties'.[72]

Stonewall certainly used rights-based arguments as a lobbying tactic from very early on, and one of its first actions was to draft an Equality Bill.[73] The adoption of a rights-based approach has led Stonewall to challenge discriminatory legislative provisions through a limited programme of human rights litigation, alongside more traditional lobbing methods. Although Stonewall is not a public interest litigation organisation, I was told that it does fund 'one or two cases a year, if that', each of which is chosen for its 'strategic importance'.[74] Stonewall does not have in-house lawyers working on its cases; it relies instead upon a network of lawyers who are prepared to do pro bono work on its behalf. Neither does Stonewall have a dedicated legal advice help-line, which might be used to

---

[69] For more information, see Stonewall's web-site at: www.stonewall.org.uk.

[70] The Local Government Act 1986 s 2A(1) (as amended by Local Government Act 1988 s 28). It was repealed in September 2003.

[71] Stephen Jeffery-Poulter, *Peers, Queers and Commons: The Struggle for Gay Law Reform, from 1950 to the Present* (London, Routledge, 1991) 260.

[72] *ibid,* 240.

[73] *ibid,* 246.

[74] Interview, Helen Marsh, Communications Officer at Stonewall, 12 August 2003, London.

identify potentially important cases. Nevertheless, it is a relatively large and high-profile organisation with a wide membership body and it is regularly contacted for help and advice by people who have faced discrimination, which appears to be the primary means by which potential test cases are identified.

In particular, Stonewall has a short but impressive history of challenging legislative provisions that criminalise homosexual activity, some of which has been done through litigation before the ECtHR. It was, for example, involved in *Wilde, Greenhalgh and Parry v UK*[75] and *Sutherland v UK*,[76] both of which challenged the higher age of consent for sexual activity between men.[77] *ADT v UK*, a Stonewall case which fell within the sample group of cases and is discussed in detail immediately below, followed this pattern of challenging specific pieces of discriminatory legislation through human rights litigation.[78]

A.   Sponsoring Cases: *ADT v United Kingdom*[79]

The ADT case arose following the applicant's conviction for gross indecency between men contrary to Section 13 of the Sexual Offences Act 1956. Although sexual acts between men in England and Wales were partially decriminalised under the Sexual Offences Act 1967, this did not extend to acts committed when more than two persons take part or are present. The applicant's conviction was primarily based on videotapes that showed him and up to four other men engaging in sexual acts, which were found during a police search of his home. Although the acts in question were consensual and had taken place in a private residence, because they involved more than two men they fell foul of the Sexual Offences Act. Following his conviction the applicant was sentenced and conditionally discharged for two years and he was advised that there were no prospects for a successful appeal. He immediately turned to Stonewall for help. The application to the ECmHR and the resulting proceedings before the ECtHR were financed by Stonewall, which was assisted by lawyers acting pro bono. By this

---

[75]   *Wilde, Greenhalgh and Parry v United Kingdom* (Cm dec) (App no 22382/93) ECHR 19 January 1995, (1995) 19 EHRR CD86.

[76]   *Sutherland v United Kingdom* (Cm dec) (App no 25188/94) ECHR 27 March 2001, (1997) 24 EHRR CD22.

[77]   Stonewall also took the case of *Lustig-Prean and Beckett v United Kingdom* (App nos 31417/96 and 32377/96) ECHR 27 September 1999, (2000) 29 EHRR 548) to the Court concerning the dismissal of gay personnel from the military on the grounds of their sexual orientation. *Karner v Austria* ECHR 2003-IX, (2004) 38 EHRR 24, which concerned property rights for people in same-sex relationships, was taken by the 'Austrian version' of Stonewall, and Stonewall notes that it 'fed into' this case 'through the Lesbian, Gay and Bisexual network' (Interview, Helen Marsh, 12 August 2003). Stonewall was also involved in *Grant v South West Trains* [1998] ECR I-621 before the European Court of Justice.

[78]   As with PESUE's cases, the Court's file on the *ADT* case was confidential at the applicant's request. However, Stonewall gave the author permission to see many of its documents on the case and interviews were conducted with the then Executive Director, Angela Mason, and Communications Officer, Helen Marsh.

[79]   *ADT v United Kingdom* ECHR 2000-IX, (2001) 31 EHRR 33.

stage of the proceedings the domestic lawyer, although named as the applicant's representative, was 'not really involved'.[80] Angela Mason, then Executive Director of Stonewall, is referred to in the judgment as 'adviser' to the applicant.

Before the Court the applicant complained that his conviction amounted to a violation of his right to privacy under Article 8 of the Convention. He also complained of discriminatory treatment under Article 14 of the Convention, as there were no equivalent laws pertaining to sexual acts between adult women or between heterosexuals. The UK Government argued that the matter did not relate to the applicant's private life because the offence involved a number of people and the sexual acts had been recorded.[81] This argument was dismissed by the Court on the grounds that there was no evidence that the video tapes in question were intended for distribution and, on the contrary, the applicant had sought to maintain his anonymity at all stages of the proceedings. As the Court found that there had been an interference with the applicant's private life, it turned next to consider the Government's contention that this interference was lawful. In particular the Government argued that they were entitled to control 'group, potentially public and therefore unacceptable homosexual activity (between more than two men)'.[82] It claimed a considerable margin of appreciation in regulating sexual acts of a group nature, particularly where the activities had been videotaped.[83] The Court rejected that argument and referred to the 'narrow margin of appreciation afforded to national authorities in the case, the absence of any public health considerations and the purely private nature of the behaviour in the present case'.[84] It found unanimously that the existence of the legislation and the applicant's conviction under the relevant provision amounted to a violation of Article 8 (finding it unnecessary to consider the matter under Article 14).

B.   Understanding Stonewall's Role

Repeal of section 13 of the Sexual Offences Act 1956 was a central part of Stonewall's 'Equality 2000' campaign that was launched in June 1997 to eradicate specific areas of legislative discrimination against gay people. Gross indecency laws, Stonewall argued, 'led to the use of "pretty policemen" acting as agents provocateurs and often poisoned relationships between the police and the gay community'.[85] Angela Mason said that the purpose of the *ADT* case was 'to show that the gross indecency laws were in breach of the Convention, therefore having

---

[80]   Interview, Angela Mason, Executive Director of Stonewall, 7 October 2002, London.
[81]   *ADT v United Kingdom* ECHR 2000-IX, (2001) 31 EHRR 33 [21].
[82]   *ibid,* [27].
[83]   *ibid,* [35].
[84]   *ibid,* [38].
[85]   Stonewall Press Release, '*Anti-Gay Law Now a Dead Letter*', 31 July 2000 (on file with author).

a much stronger argument for their repeal'.[86] Indeed, the *ADT* litigation undoubtedly made a considerable contribution to the British Government's decision in January 1999 to conduct a major review of sexual offences, which was undertaken by a diverse team that included representatives from Stonewall. The review team, noting the discriminatory nature of the gross indecency laws, recommended their repeal. Behind this recommendation was a belief that 'the criminal law should not treat people differently on the basis of their sexual orientation'.[87] The review team's conclusion was based – at least in part – on the 'indications of greater openness towards and acceptance of differing sexual orientation'.[88] The Sexual Offences Act 2003, which was implemented on May 2004, repealed the gross indecency provisions of the earlier Sexual Offences Act and brought this particular campaign to its conclusion.

Although on a restrictive reading the *ADT* case addressed a rather narrow legal provision prohibiting certain sexual acts between men, it goes without saying that its significance lies in the fact that it was a small but important step in Stonewall's (on-going) journey towards eradicating all forms of discrimination against LGBT people and achieving social inclusion for this group. Whilst LGBT people in Europe are not subjected to the same levels of discrimination and marginalisation as the Roma, for example, it is clear that they have been frequently constructed as 'undesirable' and 'the other',[89] and that neither the British State nor British society have been immune to this.[90] The important contribution that law makes to the normalisation of heterosexuality is well documented.[91] Stonewall has consequently used human rights claims to challenge discriminatory laws, such as the Sexual Offences Act 1956 that was in issue in *ADT*, because such laws contribute directly towards the social exclusion of, and resultant violence against, sexual minorities.

Stonewall's use of litigation to bring about legislative reform has occasionally put them in a confrontational relationship with the Government, and it is fascinating to note that they, like PESUE, have used the metaphor of war to describe their campaigning:

---

[86]   Angela Mason, interview, 7 October 2002.

[87]   Home Office, *Setting the Boundaries: Reforming the Law on Sex Offences* vol 1 (London, Home Office Communication Directorate, July 2000) Recommendation 44.

[88]   *ibid*, 98.

[89]   Carl Stychin, *A Nation by Rights: National Cultures, Sexual Identity Politics, and the Discourse of Rights* (Philadelphia, Temple University Press, 1998) 13. Herman makes the similar point that 'the demand for "lesbian and gay rights" is a struggle for membership in the "human community"'. See Didi Herman, 'The Politics of Law Reform: Lesbian and Gay Rights Struggles into the 1990s' in Joseph Bristow and Angelina R Wilson (eds), *Activating Theory: Lesbian, Gay, Bisexual Politics* (London, Lawrence & Wishart, 1993) 250.

[90]   For a study of homophobia in British society, see Jeffery-Poulter, *Peers, Queers and Commons* (1991), and Conor Foley, Outrage and Stonewall, *Sexuality and the State: Human Rights Violations Against Lesbians, Gays Bisexuals and Transgendered People* (London, Liberty, 1994).

[91]   See, for example, Derek McGhee, *Homosexuality, Law and Resistance* (London, Routledge, 2001).

> In many ways we have been living in a war zone … As the prospect of winning the war comes closer we also have to think long and hard about winning the peace. Winning the peace will mean coming out of the ghetto.[92]

Stonewall's description of the struggle for inclusion is appropriate because, as Carl Stychin perceptively comments, the demands of LGBT people to have their human rights respected and their humanity acknowledged can have a destabilising effect on societies:

> While normalization is one side of the rights equation, the norm itself may become 'troubled' and possibly destabilized through the articulation of rights. Thus, as the dominant background norms of national identity must continually be reconstituted, rights claims are one means by which groups and individuals can play an active role in altering how the nation is imagined. In fact, given the centrality of rights discourse in the Western national imaginary, it seems an obvious arena in which to engage in that struggle.[93]

As McGhee notes, international laws and human rights standards are potentially important in this respect because they 'provide opportunities for the unsettling of law's "truths" and for the disruption, or the questioning, of the interdependency of law's discourses with intolerable power effects perpetuated within nation-states'.[94] Through targeted litigation campaigns, Stonewall can radically challenge deep-rooted social and legal norms. Consequently, it will not necessarily perceive a lost case as a failure if, for example, it contributes to social change through public debate or if it highlights 'how ridiculous the law is'.[95]

It is noteworthy that 'pure human rights' organisations – which are not immune themselves from being influenced by hetero-normative understandings of human rights – were initially hesitant to take the initiative in pursuing litigation on behalf of LGBT rights, and that much of the early pressure for recognition of sexual-orientation and gender-identity rights applied through domestic[96] and international law mechanisms emanated from 'LGBT rights' organisations.[97] This provides us with a key to understanding the significance of

---

[92]   Statement formerly on Stonewall's website, October 2002.

[93]   Stychin, *A Nation by Rights* (1998) 17.

[94]   McGhee, *Homosexuality* (2001) 176. On the Court's jurisprudence in this area see, as well as the Stonewall cases already mentioned: *Laskey, Jaggard and Brown v United Kingdom* ECHR 1997-I, (1997) 24 EHRR 39, in relation to sado-masochistic relationships; *Dudgeon v United Kingdom* Series A no 45 (1982) 4 EHRR 149, *Norris v Ireland* Series A no 142 (1991) 13 EHRR 186 and *Modinos v Cyprus* Series A no 259 (1993) 16 EHRR 485 concerning the age of consent for homosexual activity.

[95]   Interview, Helen Marsh, 12 August 2003.

[96]   The Homosexual Law Reform Society, formed on 12 May 1958, was instrumental in pushing through the reforms that decriminalised private homosexual behaviour. The National Council for Civil Liberties was sympathetic towards the HLRS's calls for reform of the criminal law in the late 1950s and 1960s and they later had a Gay Rights Officer. However, Antony Grey, who was actively involved in both, states that their support for reform was by no means automatic'. See Antony Grey, *Quest for Justice: Towards Homosexual Emancipation* (London, Sinclair-Stevenson, 1992) 165.

[97]   Jeff Dudgeon, the applicant in the first successful Strasbourg case dealing with discrimination against homosexual men in the criminal law, was the secretary of the Northern Ireland Gay Rights Association and one of the founders of the International Lesbian and Gay Association.

single-issue group litigation. By demanding that the Court re-imagines social and legal norms, organisations like Stonewall play a role in providing the Convention with vitality and dynamism, and a relevance for a greater range of actors. Although it goes without saying that Stonewall is not alone in its fight for equality for LGBT people in Europe,[98] and although many areas of discrimination remain to be addressed that will doubtless be the subject of future litigation before the ECtHR, it has made a notable contribution to the Court's jurisprudence in this area.

IV. Greenpeace and Environmental Rights

Greenpeace was established in 1971, emerging out of Canadian ecological and peace movements' concerns about the proposed US underground nuclear tests on the Aleutian Island of Amchitka.[99] It has since become an extremely high-profile global NGO, which in 2008 had 2.9 million supporters, branches in 41 countries, and an annual income of €202.6 million.[100] Its aim is to draw attention to the most serious environmental abuses, which it usually achieves through research, lobbying and 'quiet diplomacy', as well as through high-profile and media-friendly peaceful confrontations. In contrast to the other groups considered in this research, Greenpeace does not have a particular human constituency to whom it offers advice and/or legal representation: the entire earth is (potentially) its constituency. Nonetheless, Greenpeace has found that courts of law are occasionally useful arenas in which to voice specific environmental concerns. A number of Greenpeace cases have been heard before domestic courts[101] and the European Court of Justice.[102] Furthermore, both Swiss Greenpeace and Luxembourg Greenpeace have taken cases to the ECtHR,[103] one of which fell within the sample group.

---

[98]   For a discussion of the legislative steps that have been taken towards homosexual equality in Europe see, for example, the collection of essays in Part II Section E of Robert Wintemute and Mads Andenæs, *Legal Recognition of Same-Sex Partnerships: A Study of National, European and International Law* (Oxford, Hart Publishing, 2001).

[99]   On the history of Greenpeace see Michael Brown and John May, *The Greenpeace Story* (London, Dorling Kindersley, Revised Edition 1991) and Rex Weyler, *Greenpeace: An Insider's Account* (London, Rodale, 2004).

[100]   *Greenpeace: Annual Report 2004*, available at: www.greenpeace.org/international/en/about/reports.

[101]   See, for example, *R v Secretary of State for the Environment Ex parte Greenpeace Ltd* [1994] 4 All ER 352; *R v Inspectorate of Pollution Ex parte Greenpeace Ltd (No 2)* [1994] 4 All ER 329, and *Japan Whaling Association v American Cetacean Society et al*, 478 US 1986.

[102]   See, for example, *Association Greenpeace France v Ministère de l'Agriculture et de la Pêche* [2000] ECR I-1651, and *Stichting Greenpeace Council (Greenpeace International) v Commission of the European Communities* [1998] ECR I-1651.

[103]   As well as the cases discussed in detail below, see *Asselbourg and 78 Others and Greenpeace-Luxembourg v Luxembourg* (App no 29121/95) ECHR 1999 VI. See also *Geert Drieman and Others v Norway* (App no 33678/96) ECHR 4 May 2000.

A.   Litigating on Behalf of the Environment: *Greenpeace Schweiz and Others v Switzerland*[104]

As its title reveals, the case of *Greenpeace Schweiz and Others v Switzerland* was originally brought by the Swiss branch of Greenpeace in its own name, together with several other environmental groups and individuals. *Greenpeace Schweiz* concerned a Swiss nuclear power plant, Beznau II, which had been run by a private company since it was first put into operation in 1971. Although the plant is in Switzerland, it is situated only five miles from the German border. On 18 December 1991 the company running Beznau II filed a request with the Swiss Federal Council (Bundesrat) for the renewal of their operation permit for an unlimited period of time. Under Section 48 of the Federal Administrative Procedure Act, standing to object to administrative decisions is given as follows:

> whoever is affected by the contested decision and has an interest worthy of protection in the annulment or amendment thereof is entitled to file an objection.[105]

In the event, there were over 18,400 objections to the renewal of the Beznau II licence, including those lodged by the applicants requesting that the plant be closed down on safety grounds. Notwithstanding these objections, the Federal Council, against whose decisions there was no right of appeal, concluded that there were no relevant deficiencies in the safety standards of Beznau II and renewed the operating licence for a limited time period.[106] The applicants complained to the ECmHR under Article 6(1) (the right to a fair hearing) about their lack of access to a court to challenge the decision to renew the licence in this case and to have examined any violation of their rights that followed from this decision; they also complained about the unfairness of the proceedings before the Federal Council and the partiality of various witnesses.[107] The applicants further claimed under Article 13 (the right to an effective remedy) that there was no adequate means by which they could complain about the violation of their right to life and the breach of respect for their bodily integrity caused by the existence of Beznau II.

Aside from Swiss Greenpeace, the applicants in this case were: six other Swiss environmental groups; two German environmental groups; 12 individuals living

---

[104]   *Athanassoglou and Others v Switzerland* ECHR 2000-IV, (2001) 31 EHRR 13.
[105]   Reproduced in *Greenpeace Schweiz v Switzerland* (Cm dec) (App no 27644/95) ECHR 7 April 1997, (1997) 23 EHRR CD116.
[106]   The Federal Council relied upon expert opinions prepared by the Swiss Federal Nuclear Safety Inspectorate and the Section for Nuclear Technology and Safety of the Federal Office for Energy to reach its decision. Statements of the Federal Commission for the Safety of Nuclear Power Plants and of the Canton of Aargau were also taken into account.
[107]   Section 97 of the Federal Judicature Act of 16 December 1943 provides that the Federal Court hears, as a final court of appeal, administrative law appeals against decisions of the federal authorities. However, by virtue of section 100 (u) no appeal lies in matters of nuclear energy against decisions concerning licences for nuclear installations and preparatory acts (summarised in the Court's judgment at para 27)

in 'Emergency Zone I'[108] (Switzerland); five individuals living in 'Emergency Zone II'[109] (Switzerland and Germany); and five individuals living elsewhere in Switzerland. Somewhat inevitably, the question of the standing of the applicants to bring these complaints was the first obstacle to the progression of this case. Before the Commission the Swiss Government argued that the applicants' complaints were inadmissible because they had no rights to protect and their complaints merely raised hypothetical questions and not matters of a genuine and serious nature. In a decision that was obviously disappointing for those hoping that an expansive approach would be taken to the rules of standing in cases of general public importance, the Commission concluded that only the 12 applicants resident in the Zone I Emergency Area could properly be said to have rights that were affected by the licence decision. The remainder of the application was held to be incompatible *ratione materiae* with the Convention. The Commission said of the environmental organisations that they had 'failed to indicate whether they own, or lease, property within the vicinity of the nuclear power';[110] this effectively made the standing of these organisations to bring their complaint conditional upon them having a proprietary interest that was under threat.

Pursuant to the Commission's decision, the case was re-named *Athanassoglou & Others v Switzerland* and the role of Greenpeace ostensibly ended. Nonetheless, it seems clear that the applicants' lawyer in this case, Rainer Weibel, worked closely with Greenpeace Schweiz throughout the Court proceedings and continued to act, to all intents and purposes, on their behalf. The Court's case file, for example, reveals that Mr Weibel still forwarded Greenpeace press releases to the Court,[111] and continued to make general arguments in his letters to the Registry about the dangers posed by nuclear technology power, rather than focusing on the particular situation of the individual applicants.[112] A nuclear campaigner for Greenpeace Schweiz who was involved in this case confidently stated that 'without the support of Greenpeace the involved natural persons would not have taken the actions against the Swiss Federal State'.[113] It appears that while Greenpeace actually remained the driving-force behind the litigation, the Commission's restrictive decision on the issue of standing meant their role was effectively 'hidden'.

Before the Court the applicants in *Athanassoglou* continued to stress the very real risk posed by the sub-standard and aged Beznau II, and they submitted to the

---

[108] The area immediately surrounding a nuclear power plant.

[109] An area outside of Zone I, but within a radius of 20 km from the nuclear power plant.

[110] *Greenpeace Schweiz v Switzerland* (Cm dec) (App no 27644/95) ECHR 7 April 1997, (1997) 23 EHRR CD116.

[111] Letter from R Weibel to the President of the Grand Chamber, 28 February 2000 (on file with the Court's Registry).

[112] See letter from R Weibel to the President of the Grand Chamber, 8 October 1999 (on file with the Court's Registry).

[113] Leo Scherer, Nuclear Campaigner for Greenpeace Switzerland, written reply to questionnaire, 8 August 2002.

Court a report by the Institute for Applied Ecology in Darmstadt to this effect. The Government in turn referred to the reports of the Swiss Nuclear Safety Inspectorate as evidence that the plant was operating to the required safety standards. The Court, undoubtedly troubled by the nature of these arguments, held that there was a genuine dispute concerning the lawfulness of the Federal Council's decision whether or not to grant a licence. However, it went on to find that this decision was not directly decisive of the applicants' rights and that the connection between the Federal Council's decision and the domestic law rights that the applicants invoked was too remote and tenuous:

> Contrary to the view of the applicants and the fifteen dissenters in the Commission, it cannot be said that the new report of the Institute for Applied Ecology in the present case … showed that at the relevant time the operation of the Beznau II power plant exposed the applicants personally to a danger that was not only serious but also specific and, above all, imminent.[114]

The Court therefore found by 12 votes to five that Articles 6(1) and 13 were not applicable. Although the margin in favour of the Government was greater in the Court than it had been in the Commission (where 15 dissenting Commissioners were satisfied that Beznau II posed a specific and immediate danger to the applicants), the five dissenting judges were nonetheless vociferous in their opposition to the judgment. Aside from questioning the practicalities of proving to the requisite degree the existence of an imminent threat in the case of 'inherently dangerous installations', the dissenting judges argued forcefully that such issues should be capable of being the subject of domestic judicial review.[115]

B.   Understanding Greenpeace's Role

It was clearly the inherent danger associated with nuclear energy that Greenpeace was seeking to address in *Greenpeace Schweiz/Athanassoglou*. The following section of the Court's judgment in that case provides one example of the broad-ranging arguments that were raised by the applicants:

> To summarise, it needs to be said that, from the medical point of view, the operation of an atomic power plant involves a specific and direct risk to health both when the plant is working normally and when minor malfunctions occur … [I]t is necessary to take a decision of principle in respect of nuclear energy. The operation of atomic power plants involves high risks and it may – and with a considerable degree of probability will – damage the property and physical integrity of those living in the vicinity.[116]

In fact, Swiss Greenpeace had already aired these issues before the Court in *Balmer-Schafroth and others v Switzerland*, which also concerned the operation of

---

[114] *Athanassoglou and Others v Switzerland*, ECHR 2000-IV, (2001) 31 EHRR 13 [51].
[115] Joint dissenting opinion of Judges Costa, Tulkens, Fischbach, Casadevall and Maruste.
[116] *Athanassoglou and Others v Switzerland* ECHR 2000-IV, (2001) 31 EHRR 13 [52].

a nuclear power station.[117] In that case the Court, paving the way for its *Athanassoglou* judgment, held that the applicants had 'failed to show that the operation of Mühleberg power station exposed them personally to a danger that was not only serious but also specific and, above all, imminent'.[118] A case commentary in the *European Human Rights Law Review* found this to be a 'worrying development in the Court's jurisprudence in this area'.[119] Certainly, as I have already discussed, the Court's requirement that applicants show themselves to be facing a 'specific' and 'imminent' danger has significantly limited the prospect of litigating on behalf of the environment in Strasbourg.

Underlying the judgments in these Greenpeace cases is a clear reluctance on the part of the Court to be drawn into a debate on the safety of nuclear energy. In its judgment in *Athanassoglou*, the Court held that 'how best to regulate the use of nuclear power is a policy decision for each Contracting State to take according to its democratic processes'.[120] The majority of the judges undoubtedly felt that the applicants' arguments placed them in an uncomfortable position:

> To this extent, the applicants are seeking to derive from Article 6 § 1 of the Convention a remedy to contest the very principle of the use of nuclear energy, or at the least a means for transferring from the government to the courts the responsibility for taking, on the basis of the technical evidence, the ultimate decision on the operation of individual nuclear power stations.[121]

This implicitly raises the question of whether single-issue groups such as Greenpeace, when they attempt to present contentious political issues in the guise of human rights problems, seek to stretch the competence of the Court too far. It is suggested here that Greenpeace's litigation in fact raised important human rights concerns, which could legitimately have been addressed by the Court.

The adoption of nuclear energy has been recognised by several authors as having significant implications for civil liberties, which arise directly from its potential to cause catastrophic environmental damage. David Schiff, for example, argues that the move to nuclear power engenders radical socio-political changes, 'whose potential involves the deconstruction of existing conceptions of liberty and their reconstruction'.[122] He notes that the creation of the nuclear State, with its concomitant tight regulatory controls, can be linked to increased State secrecy

---

[117]   *Balmer-Schafroth and others v. Switzerland* ECHR 1997-IV, (1998) 25 EHRR 598.
[118]   *ibid*, [40].
[119]   Anon, 'Nuclear Power Plant Licence – Neighbours' Right to Fair Trial Following Challenge to Grant of Licence' (1998) 1 *European Human Rights Law Review* 94, 96.
[120]   *Athanassoglou and Others v Switzerland* ECHR 2000-IV, (2001) 31 EHRR 13 [54].
[121]   *ibid*, para 53.
[122]   David Schiff, 'Reconstructing Liberty in the Nuclear Age' in Carol Harlow (ed), *Public Law and Politics* (London, Sweet & Maxwell, 1986) 245.
As early as 1982 the Scottish Council for Civil Liberties were highlighting the link between nuclear power and the violation of liberties. See Gari Donn (ed), *Missiles, Reactors and Civil Liberties* (Glasgow, Scottish Council for Civil Liberties, 1982). See also JC Woodliffe, 'Nuclear Power: Does it Threaten Civil Liberties?' [1983] *Public Law* 440.

and a lack of participation in public life.[123] Nuclear power operates in a climate in which workers are expected to be compliant, experts are vetted and work is clouded in secrecy. Given the potential dangers posed by nuclear power, and bearing in mind the connection between nuclear power and national prestige, Schiff's argument that the use of nuclear power poses a challenge to individual liberties is extremely compelling. It also indicates the potential that (human rights) law has to address these concerns. Although Greenpeace's primary concern, for example, was with the safety of nuclear power plants, and in particular the safety of old models like Beznau II, the levels of secrecy and control that surround nuclear energy meant that Greenpeace believed that they did not have an adequate means of ensuring that their concerns were addressed. The questions raised in the *Athanassoglou* case about the safety of nuclear energy were therefore inextricably linked to issues of fundamental human rights. Judge Pettiti's view, expressed in a dissenting opinion in *Balmer Schaforth*, that in the field of nuclear power meticulous supervision of governments is required and that the Court is well positioned to undertake this role is, in my view, highly persuasive:

> If there is a field in which blind trust cannot be placed in the executive, it is nuclear power, because reasons of State, the demands of government, the interests concerned and pressure from lobbyists are more pressing than in other spheres. George Washington said that governments, like fire, are dangerous servants and fearsome masters. In the past (1939–45), as in the present, we have been only too aware of the shortcomings of which authorities and operators have been capable, regardless of people's rights. That is why, in order to protect democracy, it was sought through the European Convention to establish machinery to review any administrative acts capable of causing injustice to the individual.[124]

Numerous anti-nuclear protest movements have emerged throughout Western Europe, particularly during the cold war years;[125] several of these organisations have shown that courts of law can be used as fora in which to voice environmental and humanitarian concerns. Nelkin and Pollak note that 'ecologists in both France and Germany regard the courts as one of the more important means to influence nuclear policy, and since 1973 have brought nearly every sitting decision to court'.[126] Furthermore, numerous applications that have been lodged in Strasbourg demonstrate the impact that the adoption of nuclear power can have on human rights: these have concerned, inter alia,

---

[123]   *ibid*, 237.
[124]   Dissenting opinion of Judge Pettiti, joined by Judges Gölcüklü, Walsh, Russo, Valticos, Lopes Rocha and Jambrek, *Balmer-Schafroth and others v Switzerland* ECHR 1997-IV, (1998) 25 EHRR 598.
[125]   Dorothy Nelkin and Michael Pollak, *The Atom Besieged: Extraparliamentary Dissent in France and Germany* (Cambridge, Massachusetts, The MIT Press, 1981) 6.
[126]   *ibid*, 155.

the transport of nuclear waste;[127] the surveillance of anti-nuclear protesters;[128] and the treatment of those exposed to harmful radiation.[129]

Nevertheless, Greenpeace's litigation shows that an individualistic model of litigation is a considerable obstacle to those seeking to address broad environmental concerns through legal mechanisms. In Stuart Scheingold's words, 'Legally speaking ... air and water quality are everyone's problem, and, therefore, nobody's'.[130] As the Court's refusal to recognise Greenpeace's standing made clear,[131] organisations with eco-centric priorities like Greenpeace, which act in litigation as advocates for the environment, do not comfortably fit in with the Court's anthropo-centric focus on the individual rights-bearer.[132] In one of the earliest cases before it that raised significant environmental issues, the Court recognised that a balance needed to be struck between the individual and the community,[133] and as long ago as 1991 it held 'that in today's society the protection of the environment is an increasingly important consideration'.[134] In light of these decisions, the Court's response to the potentially catastrophic dangers posed by nuclear power has been disappointing. The upshot of the Court's approach in the *Athanassoglou* case was that the litigation was reduced to a 'battle of the experts', as each side tried to show whether or not the risk posed by Beznau II could be viewed as imminent, with the Government's experts almost inevitably poised to win in such a contest.[135] Upendra Baxi notes in relation to nuclear technology:

> The might of the state-industry combine has proved ... overwhelming for human rights theory and action ... The industry marshals language of risk-analysis and risk management to which human rights languages have yet to provide an effective response.[136]

---

[127]   *L, M and R v Switzerland* (Cm dec) (App no 30003/96) ECHR 1 July 1996, (1996) 22 EHRR CD130.

[128]   *Campaign for Nuclear Disarmament & Ors v United Kingdom* (Cm dec) (App nos 11745/85 and 13595/88) ECHR 10 March 1989 and *MPH v United Kingdom* (Cm dec) (App no 10888/84) ECHR 3 December 1986.

[129]   *McGinley and Egan v United Kingdom* ECHR 1998-III, (1999) 27 EHRR 1 and *LCB v United Kingdom* ECHR 1998-III, (1999) 27 EHRR 212 and *Burkov v Russia* (dec) (App no 46671/99) ECHR 30 January 2001.

[130]   Stuart Scheingold, *The Politics of Rights: Lawyers, Public Policy and Political Change* (New Haven, Yale University Press, 1974) 113.

[131]   For a contrasting approach, see *R v Inspectorate of Pollution and Ministry of Agriculture, Fisheries and Food, ex parte Greenpeace* [1994] 4 All ER 329, in which Otton J allowed Greenpeace standing to challenge a decision that British Nuclear Fuels could vary its activities at the Sellafield nuclear plant.

[132]   For an explanation of these terms, see Philippe Sands, 'Human Rights, Environment and the López Ostra Case: Context and Consequences' (1996) 6 *European Human Rights Law Review* 597.

[133]   *López Ostra v Spain* Series A no 303-C (1995) 20 EHRR 277 [51].

[134]   *Fredin v Sweden* Series A no 192 (1991) 13 EHRR 784 [48].

[135]   Nelkin and Pollak have noted that 'scientists in the nuclear debate have been a decisive political resource'. See Nelkin and Pollak, *The Atom Besieged* (1981) 89.

[136]   Upendra Baxi, *The Future of Human Rights* (New Delhi, Oxford University Press, 2002) 158.

In order to address adequately the intersection of human rights and environmental issues the Court must be willing to make difficult and politically sensitive decisions about where the balance between individual and community should lie, which in turn necessitates making an assessment of the environmental risk posed by government policies.[137] Furthermore, if it wants to address important environmentally-associated human rights violations, the Court must recognise the standing of a broader range of applicants. Cases such as *Greenpeace Schweiz/ Athanassoglou* suggest that in the absence of a readily identifiable 'victim' to voice concerns about (potential) environmental destruction, environmental organisations are particularly well placed to raise such issues before legal tribunals. Indeed, they may be the only entities that are disposed to do so.

V. Recent Developments

PESUE has not been involved in ECHR litigation for some time. The last of its cases was *HK v Finland*, which concerned the separation of a child from her father for a period of time with restrictions on his visits after suspicions of abuse arose. The Finnish Government appears to have learnt a lesson from the earlier cases: it admitted two violations of Article 8 in connection with the care proceedings, and the Court rejected each of the applicants' other complaints. In its Resolution concerning the enforcement measure that followed from the *K and T* judgment,[138] the Committee of Ministers notes that the Finnish government has instigated various judicial training activities as well as a review of all ECHR child custody cases.

Although PESUE's cases have been significant in shaping the Court's jurisprudence on the scope of the right to family life, they have not eradicated the difficulty facing authorities where suspicions of abuse are raised. In recent years, for example, the AIRE Centre has taken on a number of cases on behalf of parents who have been wrongly accused of child abuse and separated from their children in the United Kingdom.[139] The most significant achievement of PESUE's cases is not that they clarified the Convention's case-law on placing children in

---

[137] *Powell and Rayner v United Kingdom* Series A no 172 (1990) 12 EHRR 355. See generally, Sands, 'Human Rights' (1996), and Francoise Jarvis and Ann Sherlock, 'The European Convention on Human Rights and the Environment' (1999) 24 *European Law Review* Supp (Human Rights Survey) 15. See also Stefan Weber, 'Environmental Information and the European Convention on Human Rights' (1991) 12 *Human Rights Law Journal* 177.
[138] Resolution ResDH (2006) 50 concerning the judgment of the European Court of Human Rights of 12 July 2001 (Grand Chamber) in the case of *K and T against Finland*, 2 November 2006.
[139] *TP and KM v United Kingdom* ECHR 2001-V, (2002) 34 EHRR 2; *P, C and S v United Kingdom* ECHR 2002-VI, (2002) 35 EHRR 31, *RK and AK v United Kingdom* (App no 38000/05) (2009) 48 EHRR 29, *AD and OD v United Kingdom* (App no 28680/06) ECHR 16 March 2010, *MAK and RK v United Kingdom* (App nos 45901/05 & 40146/06) ECHR 23 March 2010.

alternative care, but rather that they placed 'parents' rights' higher up on the political and social agenda in Finland and beyond. It is, I note, apparent and somewhat surprising that NGOs have not been as active before the Court in using their resources and knowledge to protect the interests of children who have experienced abuse within their families and been inadequately protected by the State.[140]

It could be argued that Stonewall has won the legal battle for LGBT rights in the United Kingdom. Over the past 10 years in the UK there have been significant legislative developments that have opened up the way for civil partnerships (placing same-sex partnerships on a near-equal footing with opposite-sex marriage), same-sex adoption, and the prohibition of sexual-orientation discrimination in the provision of goods and services. Yet Stonewall's current work shows that even such striking and rapid legal developments can, if they take place without associated changes in social attitudes, be less than effective. Consequently, Stonewall is now targeting areas where social attitudes are lagging behind: for example, its current priorities include tackling school bullying and homophobia in sports, and promoting 'fair treatment' in the work-place.

For some, the human rights model, while having considerable strategic importance, lacks radical edge and the focus on sexual orientation discrimination simply serves to shore-up discredited binary divisions.[141] Certainly, the question of LGBT *rights* (narrowly understood) in the United Kingdom seems less urgent now than it has in previous decades. But Stonewall nonetheless sometimes still finds that a human rights framework has utility, and it occasionally finds it helpful to take its fight into the legal arena. In *Karner v Austria*,[142] it intervened jointly with Liberty and ILGA-Europe to argue that unmarried same-sex couples must at least enjoy the same rights as unmarried opposite-sex couples. This concern with anti-discrimination and partnership rights was something of a development in Stonewall's litigation, which had previously focused on privacy issues. While human rights discourse continues to play a part in opening up narrow constructs of gender and sexuality and while Stonewall continues to play in part in shaping our understanding of rights, it may well be that in coming years it will find itself less inclined to tread on the ECtHR's diminutive stage.

Various members of Greenpeace continue to use the ECHR reactively pursuant to legal proceedings brought against them in relation to campaigning activities. But none of them has met with particular success in Strasbourg. In *Greenpeace and Others v Germany*[143] the national chapter complained about the German

---

[140] The AIRE Centre represented the applicant in *Z and Ors v United Kingdom* ECHR 2001-V, (2002) 34 EHRR 3, which concerned the failure of authorities to protect children. But see *E v United Kingdom* (App no 33218/96) ECHR 26 November 2002, (2003) 36 EHRR 31 and *DP and JC v United Kingdom* (App no 38719/97) ECHR 10 October 2002 (2003) 36 EHRR 14.

[141] Julie Mertus, 'The Rejection of Human Rights Framings: The Case of LGBT Advocacy in the US' (2007) 29(4) *Human Rights Quarterly* 1036.

[142] *Karner v Austria* ECHR 2033-IX, (2004) 38 EHRR 24.

[143] *Greenpeace and Others v Germany* (admiss dec) (App no 18215/06) ECHR 12 May 2009.

authorities' refusal to take specific measures to curb emissions from diesel vehicles and Greenpeace's lack of standing to bring a legal action. Once again, the Court's response to an environmental issue was extremely deferential: in light of the Court's 'fundamentally subsidiary role with respect to issues of environmental policies', the applicants were unable to show that the State had exceeded its discretionary powers in refusing to take the enforcement action they sought.[144] The application was consequently declared inadmissible. It is perhaps unsurprising that Greenpeace – and, indeed, other environmental organisations – still do not add greatly to the Court's burden. Yet from time-to-time, it provides a platform upon which they can raise awareness of particular environmental justice campaigns.

VI. Conclusion

The single-issue groups discussed in this chapter are typically formed from grass-roots movements, and are made up of – and at least partly funded by – an active membership body. None are human rights law specialists, and none have litigation strategies at the heart of their activities. These groups are more politically oriented than legally minded and less incorporationist than NGOs discussed in previous chapters. This, as we have seen, can make courts of law an unnatural environment for them. As law is not central to their thinking, these groups in particular cannot be judged against a 'legal success' criterion: their litigation strategy is often just as concerned with raising awareness of the particular issues that are of interest to them than with winning a narrow legal point. Because they are not legally-oriented organisations that establish their expertise by taking a repeated and high-profile part in litigation, their involvement in ECtHR cases is inevitably sporadic. Furthermore, identifying and describing the role played by a particular pressure group in litigation can be hard because their activities frequently form part of a wider movement of loosely associated activists. Consequently, groups like PESUE, Stonewall and Greenpeace have been particularly overlooked by academics considering NGO involvement in ECtHR litigation because they are not perceived to be as significant, in legal terms, as the 'repeat-players' considered here in earlier chapters. Nonetheless, it can be concluded from this research that single-issue groups play an important role in the Court's litigation.

It is precisely the non-legal character of the organisations discussed in this chapter that gives their involvement in ECtHR litigation its significance: in effect, it enables them to create a momentum towards uncovering new sites of oppression and generating new understandings of human rights. Whilst it may be

---

[144]   *ibid*, 5.

discomforting to acknowledge this in a body of law that consistently asserts its universality, it is clear that human rights laws are adaptable (and fallible) creations. Each of the cases discussed in this chapter raised complex and socially-divisive issues, and each was driven by a pressure group with a particular vision of how the issue in question should be progressed. The situations involved in these cases frequently concerned competing interests and conflicting rights claims, and it is therefore not surprising that the 'grey area' of the margin of appreciation was so often prayed in aid by the respondent States in an attempt to circumscribe the Court's influence. Although we have seen that the Court has frequently deferred to the authority of States in matters of such nature, it is likely that if the ECtHR's confidence in its ability to address such issues increases more pressure groups will involve themselves in targeted litigation before it.

Because the role that pressure groups play in ECtHR litigation has received little academic attention, it has not been the subject of serious criticism. The obvious concern such cases raise is that politically and socially important decisions are being influenced by the litigation strategies of unaccountable and partisan groups (some of which have a very small membership body), thereby circumventing the democratic process. Kenneth Minogue suggests that 'the more rights we discover, each having more and greater resource implications, the more tensions will result from the strain upon the resources of a liberal-capitalist society'.[145] The claims of pressure groups can consequently be viewed as self-serving and unattractive: the ideological positioning of certain groups involved in the Court's litigation makes it clear that NGOs do not always represent a progressive liberal agenda.[146] Furthermore, the radical potential offered by 'pressure-group cases' which call for social reform through human rights mechanisms, also means that that they raise particularly strong concerns about judicial activism. This is a particularly serious issue for the ECtHR because Europe does not consist of a homogenous and static society; this stands as at least a partial explanation for the Court's exercise of extreme caution before delivering judgments that take the Convention forward into new territory.[147]

Despite these concerns, it is inevitable that rights-based claims will arise that have the capacity to change our understanding of human rights themselves. That human rights change shape is inevitable because they arise out of a process of

---

[145]   Kenneth Minogue, 'What is Wrong With Rights' in Carol Harlow (ed), *Public Law and Politics* (London, Sweet & Maxwell, 1986) 216.

[146]   One might also mention, for example, the pressure group 'UK Men's Movement', which claims to have been involved in several ECtHR cases in order to challenge what it views as the feminist agenda of the human rights movement. For information on that organisation's campaigning (which currently seems to be in something of hiatus) see: www.ukmm.org.uk.

[147]   In order to assist it with its interpretative task, the Court has developed various restrictive principles, such as the principle of proportionality and the doctrine of the margin of appreciation. See, generally, Paul Mahoney, 'Judicial Activism and Judicial Self-Restraint in the European Court of Human Rights: Two Sides of the Same Coin' (1990) 11 *Human Rights Law Journal* 57.

continuous social struggle. As Donnelly notes, the list of groups specifically protected under the United Nations' Bill of Rights

> provides a record of the successful struggles by excluded and despised groups to force full (or at least formally equal) inclusion in political society [which] implicitly raises the question of other groups currently subject to discrimination, of victims of invidious public discrimination whose suffering remains legally and politically acceptable.[148]

The groups discussed in this chapter are part of social movements, some of which have a great deal of popular support. Greenpeace, for example, is part of an environmental movement that has become truly global. These organisations also frequently forge links with similarly minded groups in order to further particular campaigns. This means that their litigation provides the Court with opportunities to reflect upon, and perhaps to reflect, developing social norms. We saw in several of the sample cases that the Court has been reluctant to engage in 'social engineering through law' (as evidenced by its approach to Greenpeace's anti-nuclear litigation); but there were also occasions on which NGOs have ensured that the Court has been unable to avoid delivering judgments of considerable social and political consequence (as evidenced by its approach to Stonewall's litigation to decriminalise homosexual activity). For the Court to engage with important social issues can only be a good thing.

The Court provides one platform upon which social debate can take place, and consequently provides a space for social developments to occur. As Sax notes in relation to the role of courts in environment litigation,

> the courtroom is an eminently suitable forum for the voicing of citizens concerns over the maintenance of environmental quality. The real virtues of environmental litigation have little to do with the common conception of niggling lawyers battling over the intricacies of some ambiguous words in an obscure statute. Rather, the availability of a judicial forum is a measure of the willingness of government to subject itself to challenge on the merits of decisions made by public officials, to accept the possibility that the ordinary citizen may have useful ideas to contribute to the effectuation of the public interest; and to submit to them if – in the rigorous process of fact gathering – those ideas are shown to have substantial. *Litigation is thus a means of access for the ordinary citizen to the process of governmental decision-making.* It is in many circumstances the only tool for genuine citizen participation in the operative process of government (emphasis added).[149]

When the Court takes decisions in relation to difficult social questions it does so through the lens of human rights, and is therefore in an inherent position of strength to voice concerns about government actions and policies, and it is consequently wholly unsurprising that pressure groups exploit the opportunity

---

[148] Jack Donnelly, *Universal Human Rights in Theory and Practice* 2nd edn (Ithaca, Cornell University Press, 2003) 227–8.

[149] Joseph Sax, *Defending the Environment: A Strategy for Citizen Action* (New York, Alfred A Knopf, 1971) 57.

that this presents to further their aims. In doing so, pressure groups also offer the Court the chance to ensure that the Convention maintains its relevance and is not unaffected by important social changes.

7

Conclusion

'The basic lesson of this study is that rights are not gifts: they are won through concerted collective action ...'[1]

I. Introduction

I N THIS STUDY, an attempt has been made to shed a different light on the ECtHR from that which is typically provided by legal analysis. The Court's litigation has been examined primarily as a process that is used by NGOs to bring about social and legal change. From this research what has emerged is that, although their role should not be overstated within the Convention system, NGOs nonetheless have a meaningful – and largely overlooked – impact on certain areas of the Court's litigation. In this chapter, the steps that have been taken during the progress of this research are re-traced, and the major conclusions that have been drawn from it are set out.

This book commenced with a critical examination of the robust individualistic liberalism that lies at the heart of the Convention's machinery for protecting human rights. That proved to be a daunting starting point. No one with an interest in human rights can fail to be impressed by the importance of the commitment that classical liberalism makes to individual freedom, which is referred to in the ECHR's preamble as a 'common heritage' of European countries. My intention was certainly not to undermine the values that are expressed in the Convention, nor to underestimate their importance to individuals. The very fact that these values had such a remarkable resurgence in twentieth-century Europe is an indication of their durability and strengths.

Nevertheless, in chapter two theories were examined which question both the ethical vision and the sociological relevance of liberal individualism. An emerging paradigm was identified, in which increasing importance is attached to civil society as a space for shaping and enforcing human rights. These ideas opened up

---

[1] Charles R Epp, *The Rights Revolution: Lawyers, Activists, and Supreme Courts in Comparative Perspective* (Chicago, University of Chicago Press, 1998) 197.

a particularly interesting, and largely untravelled, path from which to explore the ECtHR's litigation. In particular, they enabled me to move beyond viewing the Court's litigation either as a process of abstract metaphysical reasoning or as the resolution of microcosmic and discrete battles between individuals and States, and instead opened the door for me to examine it as a tangible socio-political process into which myriad actors are drawn. The writings of academics such as Jack Donnelly and Upendra Baxi, who have both highlighted the multitudinous and complex authorship of human rights, were of central importance to this research. Human rights, as they have been presented in this book, emerge from concrete social and political struggles and are the vocabulary of those seeking to alter engrained power structures.

In chapter two an extensive literature was referred to which recognises NGOs as essential actors in the global human rights movement. This literature establishes that NGOs have been central to the development and promotion of international human rights laws, in spite of the fact that they are still a long way from being formally recognised as subjects of international law. If human rights are the language of political claims, then it is clear that these claims have been most effectively articulated by NGOs.

One of the first hurdles to surmount when embarking upon this research was the dearth of literature on the chosen research subject. Although, as I mentioned above, a considerable literature exists that establishes the central role that NGOs have played in the development of international human rights laws, little had previously been written on the relationship between NGOs and the ECHR. This led me to adopt a mixture of quantitative and qualitative research techniques for the purposes of this research, which facilitated my desire to obtain both a de-centred perspective of the Court's functions and a systematic picture of the scale of NGO involvement in ECtHR litigation. Ultimately, the core of the research was primarily based on data obtained from a sample of 149 cases in which the Court had delivered judgment, and a plethora of associated materials, including extensive interviews with NGOs that were involved in those cases.

II. The Research Findings

In chapter three the results of quantitative analysis of the sample cases were outlined. NGO involvement was identified in a relatively modest number of the Court's cases. I concluded that NGOs are far from being the 'life-blood' of the ECtHR, which is a description that might aptly be applied to NGOs' relationship with other international and regional human rights tribunals. Nevertheless, in that chapter I suggested that although the dominant form of litigation before the Court is individualistic, this should not cloud the fact that the pursuit of individual justice is not the only model for understanding the Court's litigation. Nor, I argued, is it necessarily the most important. Although quantitative analysis highlights the fact that most ECtHR cases do not attract NGO involvement, it also highlights patterns that lead one to appreciate the meaningful impact that NGOs have on certain important sections of the Court's litigation. This realisation was to provide the basis of the case studies that formed the focus of chapters four to six.

That NGOs play a vital role in addressing gross and systematic violations of the Convention was one of the most important conclusions drawn from this research. Such situations were considered in detail in chapter four, which focused on the litigation of the Kurdish Human Rights Project and the European Roma Rights Centre as case studies. The litigation of these organisations brings into sharp focus the fact that certain States within the Council of Europe have 'massively defaulted on their normative commitments',[2] and that a considerable amount of blood has been shed on European soil since the Convention came into force. In that chapter I suggested that an individualistic model of litigation is particularly inadequate to deal with State-sponsored or State-tolerated violence that takes the form of systematic discrimination against minority groups. The individuals against whom such discrimination occurs are often not in a position to use the Strasbourg procedures to redress their rights: simple, yet crucial, factors can provide seemingly insurmountable obstacles to obtaining redress for the most serious human rights violations. Practical considerations that can inhibit potential applicants in these circumstances from submitting an application to the Court include not knowing of the Court's existence, language difficulties and financial difficulties. Problems in obtaining legal representation also arise when there is a general climate of prejudice against minorities. In any event, victims of the most serious and sustained human rights violations may place little faith in the ability of legal mechanisms to address the structural inequality that is at the heart of their experience. Furthermore, the Court's inter-State procedure has been of little assistance to oppressed minorities: States have proven themselves time-and-time-again to be inadequate defenders of gross and systematic violations of the Convention that have taken place outside their jurisdiction.

NGOs like the ERRC and KHRP use litigation strategies in order to alter the balance of power and in order to make human rights meaningful for oppressed groups. These organisations tend to take a large number of similar cases with the express purpose of highlighting the systematic nature of the violations that these groups experience. Their litigation strategies address deep-rooted problems of discrimination in a manner that individual applicants acting alone would be unable to. 'They are', in other words, 'part of a narrative of extending human rights to those who had been denied them that helped remove discriminatory

---

[2] Tim Dunne and NJ Wheeler, 'Introduction' in Dunne and Wheeler (eds), *Human Rights in Global Politics* (Cambridge, Cambridge University Press, 1999) 2.

barriers for many'.[3] These NGOs' cases consequently locate the individual applicants' stories within a wider context of deep-rooted and engrained injustice and discrimination, and in doing so they ask the Court to address issues of fundamental humanitarian and political importance.

Perhaps the least surprising finding of this study, given the data provided by previous researchers in this area, was the importance to ECtHR litigation of legally-oriented NGOs that work towards the general protection and promotion of human rights. The role of these 'pure human rights' organisations (as they have been termed in this book) were examined in chapter five. In that chapter I focused in particular on the legal activities of the AIRE Centre and Liberty, both of which have been involved in numerous ECtHR cases over several years. This book has clearly highlighted the efforts that these organisations make to be constructive, expert and professional litigators. In particular, it was noted that they have good relationships with the governments against whom they litigate most frequently, and the Registry of the Court appears to view the contribution that they make to the Court's proceedings as a positive one.

Experience shows, of course, that even in mature democracies with a long-standing commitment to the ECHR there will inevitably be times when that commitment conflicts with other imperatives. In these circumstances, governments' attempts to adopt repressive populist measures that gradually erode human rights tend to occur in the guise of sophisticated legislation that pushes at the boundaries of the margin of appreciation that the Court grants to States. Consequently, human rights cases that arise in this context tend to be concerned with creative legal interpretation, as the limits of States' obligations under the Convention are tested. In this research I have suggested that the legal experience and expertise of 'pure human rights' NGOs equips them to play an important part in the technocratic human rights debates that ensue, and enables them to act as watchdogs that guard against the encroachment of valued freedoms.

In chapter six, attention turned to the role of single-issue groups, or pressure groups, in the Court's litigation. In particular, I considered PESUE's litigation on behalf of parents whose children have been placed in care, Stonewall's on-going campaign for homosexual equality, and finally, Greenpeace's litigation, which touched on the nexus between environmental and human rights concerns. These NGOs were distinguished from those discussed in earlier chapters as overtly campaigning grass-roots organisations that are not primarily legally orientated. The involvement of pressure groups in the Court's litigation has previously received little attention from legal academics, primarily because it tends to be small-scale and infrequent. However, I have suggested that this is an unfortunate

---

[3] Gary Younge, 'Extreme Prejudice', *The Guardian*, 7 March 2005. Available at: www.guardian.co.uk/Columnists/Column/0,5673,1432039,00.html.

oversight. Single-issue groups, such as Greenpeace and Stonewall, reject a cautious approach to interpreting the Convention, and their involvement in litigation can consequently generate momentum towards new understandings of human rights. Their litigation offers a pertinent reminder that human rights are dynamic and that the Court's role in interpreting the Convention is potentially far-reaching, although in practice the Court tends to be mindful of the restraints that State sovereignty places on it. These organisations can consequently create an interesting tension between their own utopian struggles and the Court's rather more cautious interpretive conventions. These NGOs are frequently unsuccessful in their litigation (if success is judged in a narrow legalistic sense); but by infusing their litigation with comparatively radical politics, they can contribute to the Court's awareness of social changes. In doing so, the litigation campaigns of organisations like Stonewall have occasionally pointed a finger in the direction that our understanding of human rights has subsequently taken.

III.   The Limitations of NGOs as Litigators

The contribution that NGOs make to the Court's litigation has been presented in a positive light in this book, but this optimism has not been entirely unqualified. Although the primary aim of this research was to assess the extent and the nature of NGO involvement in ECtHR litigation, this research raised questions about the nature of NGOs that received critical reflection in the conclusions to chapters four to six. It might now be useful to draw together the central strands of those reflections and consider the limitations under which NGOs operate as litigators.

A.   A Lack of Democratic Accountability?

Julie Mertus has framed the 'dangers of NGOs' in terms of democracy and good governance. She notes that while considerable power is wielded by NGOs within the global human rights movement, in the exercise of that power they are democratically unaccountable.[4] The decisions of NGOs, she notes, are often taken in an opaque manner and without pluralist participation.[5] Certainly, none of the groups I discussed operates in a manner that could readily be termed democratic. Furthermore, they are typically marginal political actors who have little leverage in more democratic arenas. As Galanter has noted, '[t]hose who seek change through the courts tend to represent relatively isolated interests,

---

[4] Julie Mertus, 'From Legal Transplants to Transformative Justice: Human Rights and the Promise of Transnational Civil Society' (1998–99) 14 *American University International Law Review* 1335. See also Kenneth Anderson, 'The Ottawa Convention Banning Landmines, the Role of International Non-Governmental Organizations and the Idea of International Civil Society' (2000) 11(1) *European Journal of International Law* 91.

[5] *ibid*, 1372–4.

unable to carry the day in more political forums'.[6] In relation to this research, this raises the spectre of NGOs influencing the Court's agenda without popular support and without being answerable to others for their actions.

A related concern is that NGO involvement in litigation can unhelpfully reduce genuinely complex political disputes to simplistic rights-based arguments. Away from the consensus that tends to emerge in more democratic fora, NGOs in their litigation appear in principle to be free to pursue their ends without reference to the real concerns and dissent of others. This is likely to be of particular concern to those who understand human rights claims to be the unbending and limitless pursuit of power. Costas Douzinas argues that solutions to complex problems are unlikely to be forged through human rights arguments because 'it removes the fight from the terrain of warring interests into that of allegedly absolute truths and uncompromising entitlements'.[7] In other words, one could argue that the case studies outlined in this research represented baldly-stated claims to entitlement by NGOs, which were more likely to result in antagonism rather than conciliation.

The lack of democratic constraint under which NGOs operate raises the possibility that their claims might appear, at times, to represent positively unattractive views. In this book I have gone as far as to assert that human rights are political claims, the makers of which have only a loose connection to a pre-ordained ideology. No attempt has been made to judge the value of the claims that were made by NGOs in the sample cases. Nevertheless, it is worth noting that because making human rights claims requires only the barest of nods to liberal values, the role of NGOs in ECtHR litigation is not inevitably benign. Although it is not an issue that was of particular concern in the context of this research, this study implicitly acknowledges that reactionary and conservative organisations could attempt to influence the Court's agenda.[8]

How, then, can we respond to the questions raised by NGOs' lack of demo-cratic accountability? We might at least begin by acknowledging that these concerns reflect a tension within the human rights movement itself. Although human rights can assist in securing democratic participation, they are also fundamentally anti-democratic. During the drafting of the Convention, it will be recalled, the individual application procedure itself was criticised for being anti-democratic (ie anti-Statist). One need only refer to decisions such as *Tyrer v*

---

[6] Marc Galanter, 'Why the "Haves" Come out Ahead: Speculations on the Limits of Legal Change' (1974) 9 *Law and Society Review* 95, 135.

[7] Costas Douzinas, *The End of Human Rights: Critical Legal Thought at the Turn of the Century* (Oxford, Hart Publishing, 2000) 251.

[8] The Society for the Protection of Unborn Children, for example, was permitted to submit written comments in *Open Door and Dublin Well Woman v Ireland* Series A no 246-A (1993) 15 EHRR 244 and *D v Ireland* (admiss dec) (App no 26499/02) ECHR 28 June 2006, (2006) 43 EHRR SE16. The Catholic Bishops' Conference of England and Wales was permitted to submit written comments in *Pretty v United Kingdom* ECHR 2002-III, (2002) 35 EHRR 1.

UK,[9] in which the Court found the practice of judicial 'birching' – popularly-supported in the Isle of Man – to be a violation of the Convention, to see that human rights can conflict with beliefs held by the majority. And this, of course, is one of the acknowledged strengths of human rights: they provide a platform for those who would dissent from majoritarian views. The politics of the KHRP may not have received widespread support in Turkey, but they have nonetheless held a mirror up to the shameful treatment experienced by the minority Kurdish population. So it is at least questionable whether actors in human rights litigation should be judged solely on the extent to which they are accountable to a popular will: the argument that the views of human rights NGOs are not democratically representative rather misses this point.

If human rights litigation is a highly political space in which conflicting views of the good life are put forward, this does not mean that NGOs are free to wield power anarchically when they are involved in ECtHR litigation. The sociological realism adopted in this study demonstrated that although the NGOs discussed herein were not democratically accountable, they were nonetheless compelled to operate within the confines of the ECHR system. In practice, this served to considerably curb and modify their more radical claims. Rather than being major power-players in ECtHR litigation, NGOs are revealed as one voice in a system that accommodates many influences. It is therefore unhelpful to exaggerate the conditional and contingent power that NGOs have: rather, they should be acknowledged as making a significant contribution to the continuous political dialogue that takes place between various actors in the ECHR system. NGOs themselves are revealed in this research as pragmatists who are generally aware of the limitations under which they operate, and most treat litigation as a welcome opportunity to present their position as coherently and convincingly as possible. As the case studies in this book have demonstrated, they would be foolish and mistaken to believe that their views unquestioningly prevail in litigation.

There is, however, an ambiguity in the position that NGOs currently occupy within the global human rights movement. The real concern about their lack of democratic accountability probably lies in the fact that while NGOs have clearly gained considerable importance within that movement, they do not yet wield sufficient power to merit full recognition under international law and consequently lack the regulation and constraints upon their operation that that recognition would bring. In many respects, this is to their advantage: NGOs are relatively unencumbered activists who have considerable freedom to work towards the realisation of human rights. However, they are also left largely free of formal accountability in their pursuit of that work. We saw, for example, that NGOs play a role in the litigation of the ECtHR that is largely informal and unregulated. The obvious solution might appear to be to take steps towards formalising their position within the ECHR system (relaxing the rules of standing

---

[9]   *Tyrer v United Kingdom* Series A no 26 (1979–80) 2 EHRR 1.

to allow for greater NGO participation would be one obvious way of achieving this). This suggestion raises a plethora of potentially detailed policy questions that fall outside the scope of the present research. It is worth noting, however, that any attempts to move NGOs from the shadows to the centre-stage of the ECtHR system will strengthen their position within that system and consequently raise more intense questions about their accountability.

B. A Lack of Accountability to Applicants?

An associated question is the nature of the relationship between NGOs and those whose interests they seek to represent in ECtHR cases. In relation to the NGOs that represent oppressed minorities discussed in chapter four, I identified a vast chasm between those organisations and the applicants in whose name they litigate. In many of the cases discussed in that chapter, the NGOs that had considerable involvement in them had not been in contact with the applicants at all (sometimes, it might be added, not for want of trying). It might consequently be argued that these NGOs do not articulate the authentic voice of those on whose behalf they profess to litigate. Baxi's concern that '[i]njustice and human violation is headline news only as the pornography of power'[10] is of particular relevance to those who seek to use the suffering of others to further political campaigns. The inherent danger in NGO litigation strategies is that the individual's humanity is overlooked.

Without having close contact with applicants and making attempts to be sensitive to their multifaceted characters, human rights litigation is likely to caricature the applicants in whose name a case is brought. One legal activist that I spoke with who works for the furtherance of Roma rights contrasted, with evident frustration, the difficulties that his organisation faced when compared with the 'success' that gay rights campaigns have had. His comment appears to rather casually preclude the possibility that his organisations' constituency might include any gay Roma. It is also noteworthy that issues of gender discrimination had little troubled the ERRC and the KHRP when I conducted my research at those organisations. One might reach the conclusion that in NGO litigation, the applicant, and by implication her case, cannot be release from the constraints of the ambition that NGOs have for it.

Most NGOs that I spoke with during the course of this research recognised that they have a duty both to their own aims and to those of the person in whose name a case is brought, and most try and accommodate what they see as the best interests of the applicant within their litigation strategies. The victim-hood requirement ensures that NGOs are usually in some form of contact with the applicants upon whom they are dependent for cases to be brought before the Court, especially if they are acting as representatives. The AIRE Centre, in

---

[10] Upendra Baxi, *The Future of Human Rights* (New Delhi, Oxford University Press, 2002) 125.

particular, insists upon maintaining a close relationship with those on whose behalf they litigate. Nevertheless, all NGOs have their own interests to pursue in litigation, and it seems obvious that their aims are particularly prone to being prioritised in cases where they have little or no contact with the applicants concerned.

Although the NGOs discussed in this book may make no claims to democratic accountability, many do claim to represent the interests of the groups on whose behalf they litigate. Because ECHR cases are usually brought in the name of individual applicants, NGOs also have a real and direct impact on the lives people in whose name they litigate. It was acknowledged in chapter four that the disconnection of NGOs from those on whose behalf they litigate is particularly troublesome. I concluded somewhat pragmatically, however, that NGOs like the ERRC and the KHRP perform a valuable – albeit temporary – function in building a platform for excluded and marginalised minorities. In doing so, they help to ensure that the most serious and sustained violations of the Convention are brought to the Court's attention. This conclusion was also based on an ethical position which embraces the idea that human rights are rightfully a concern of the wider community.

There is clearly room, however, for many human rights NGOs to take the issue of accountability to their 'constituents' more seriously. Julie Mertus suggests that NGOs should concentrate on building close relationships with the communities they seek to represent. She argues that the closer an organisation is to the 'grass-roots', 'the greater its chances at promoting positive social change because it is more likely to represent a highly engaged constituency'.[11] Human rights, she goes on to suggest, are most effective when they are internalised, and they generally will not succeed if they represent 'forced impositions of outside ideas'.[12] The emphasis in this research on human rights as a space for dialogue between local and global actors, then, is important: it directs NGOs to build as many lines of communication as possible between themselves and the local actors they would seek to represent. As Mertus notes, this demands from NGOs a willingness to listen 'to their less powerful counterparts'.[13]

C.   The Ineffectiveness of NGO Litigation?

Perhaps most importantly from the perspective of NGOs themselves, there is a danger in being over-optimistic about the transformation that can be achieved through human rights litigation. Baxi has remarked upon the 'human rights

---

[11]   Mertus, 'From Legal Transplants' (1998–99) 1373.
[12]   *ibid*, 1345.
[13]   *ibid*, 1385–6.

romanticism', which 'leads NGOs to be over-optimistic about their achieve-ments',[14] and Dicklitch and Lwanga have cautioned against the 'danger of embracing [Human Rights Organisations] as panaceas for all regime limitations and transgressions'.[15] Certainly, human rights litigation strategies can seem far removed from the radical and de-stabilising potential that human rights dis-course sometimes hints at. The ECtHR is an institution in which transformation can happen, but it is a slow, incremental, and somewhat erratic process. Cases are often subject to several forces that are outside of the control of the NGOs driving them. At best, litigation strategies are piecemeal attempts at reform that cannot be a substitute for coherent policy-making.

Furthermore, Galanter has noted that there may be a good reason for exercis-ing caution when judging the potential effectiveness of targeted litigation strate-gies: even if courts can be induced to deliver judgments that challenge institutional power relations, they are not in a strong position to implement the changes they instigate. Because of this, Galanter concludes that litigation 'is unlikely to shape decisively the distribution of power in society'.[16] Stuart Schein-gold's analysis of what he refers to as 'the myth of rights' is even bleaker:

> The continued vitality of litigation may be read as a triumph of myth over reality – as a lesson in false consciousness. Or perhaps it is symptomatic of the willingness of middle class lawyers to settle for half a loaf – at least for their clients. Either way, litigation emerges as a strategy of desperation rather than hope.[17]

In the context of ECtHR litigation, respondent States are, almost by definition, going to be reluctant to embrace any change that results from the Court's judgments.

It is, then, reasonable to be cautious about the impact that NGO litigation can ultimately have. While this research establishes NGOs as important actors in cases brought under the ECHR, the litigation discussed herein is far from being a panacea for human rights violations. Despite the success of the litigation of the KHRP and the ERRC, their recent cases bear testimony to the continuing violence that occurs against the Kurdish and Roma populations of Europe. Despite Liberty's campaigns, the United Kingdom is in the process of instituting yet further unduly repressive legislation in the face of the on-going threat from terrorists. Furthermore, there has been little change in the marked inability of the Court to engage with the ecological perspective of litigators such as Greenpeace. However, given the numerous factors that are outside NGOs' control when taking a deliberately targeted test case, one might argue that it is something of an

---

[14]   Baxi, *The Future of Human Rights* (2002) 62.
[15]   Susan Dicklitch and Doreen Lwanga, 'The Politics of Being Non-Political: Human Rights Organizations and the Creation of a Positive Human Rights Culture in Uganda' (2003) 25(2) *Human Rights Quarterly* 482, 485.
[16]   Galanter, 'Why the "Haves" Come out Ahead' (1974) 151.
[17]   Stuart Scheingold, *'The Politics of Rights: Lawyers, Public Policy and Political Change*, (New Haven, Yale University Press, 1974) 95.

achievement that NGOs have had any impact on the ECtHR's litigation at all.[18] In fact, this research shows that, despite its drawbacks, ECtHR litigation is perceived by many NGOs to be a valuable campaigning tool.

This research points to a number of reasons why NGO litigation strategies before the ECtHR can be effective. First, the Court is the creation of the Council of Europe, which has the political authority to hold Member States to account. Secondly, international human rights standards have a moral authority that makes the finding of a violation particularly persuasive, and – although one should take care not to exaggerate this point – may generate international pressure for reform. When Galanter's analysis is applied to the ECtHR litigation, the Court's judgments look less isolated than described by that author and its potential for reform looks less doubtful. Thirdly, NGOs, as litigators, appear more likely to achieve social reform because of their ability to pursue implementation, through non-legal measures, of the transformation that has been indicated in legal judgments. Fourthly, NGOs as litigants are characterised by their single-minded focus on, and commitment to, principled causes.[19] Finally, the cases must be evaluated for the impact they have beyond the legal realm: the Court's judgments resonate more widely when viewed as disseminated messages rather than as authoritative statements of law.[20]

IV. Concluding Observations

Although an attempt has been made in this study to place the Convention in an alternative analytical framework, a radical liberal individualism remains so deeply embedded in our understanding of the Convention that it merits further exploration in future research. It was noted in chapter two that the foundations of the Convention rendered it a minimalist and compromised document, which was expected by its drafters to have little constitutional significance. As another author has noted, '[t]he post-war West European setting did not invite, neither did it require, unpredictable improvisation or heroic challenges to the expectations and desires of governing elites'.[21] Although the Convention has, of course,

---

[18]   Particularly given the length of time it takes for the Court to deliver a judgment, some rather obvious things can impede the utility of test cases are: the relevant law changing before a case is heard; the Court proceeding with the case in a manner that makes it irrelevant to the NGO's aims; and the Court disagreeing with the applicant's central argument.

[19]   Shamina Ahmed and David Potter, *NGOs in International Politics* (Bloomfield, Kumarian Press, 2006) 243.

[20]   The notion of judgments as the calculated projection of symbols is derived from Marc Galanter, 'The Radiating Effects of Court' in Keith O Boyum and Lynn Mather (eds), *Empirical Theories about Courts* (New York, Longman, 1983).

[21]   Tom Farer, 'The Rise of the Inter-American Human Rights Regime: No Longer a Unicorn, Not Yet an Ox' in David Harris and Stephen Livingstone (eds), *The Inter-American System of Human Rights* (Oxford, Clarendon Press, 1998) 31.

since been modified several times, and the Court's judgments have breathed life into its provisions, my view is that the Council of Europe's primary mechanism for human rights protection exhibits a conservatism which prevents it from fully meeting the expectations that can legitimately be placed upon it in the twenty-first century. One activist lawyer that I spoke with noted, with some regret, that the 'scope of the Convention is so narrow ... I can't get that excited about the ECHR'.[22] It is open to further exploration whether the root of this apparent conservatism lies to some extent in the Convention's radical individualism.

In addition, it is clear that the (liberal) ideal of providing judicial redress to individuals in respect of every violation of the ECHR – regardless of the potential jurisprudential significance of the case – is becoming increasing untenable in light of the workload problems that the Court is currently facing. The Council of Europe is yet unsure how to deal with the multiple and repetitive cases that a firm commitment to providing individual justice has placed at the Court's door. The current solution, in the form of Protocol 14, will not suffice and there is growing realisation within the Council of Europe that the Court cannot make good on its commitment to deliver individual judgments in respect of every violation of the Convention.[23] Judging from the rather compromised outcome of the Interlaken Conference in February 2010,[24] it is clear that there is urgent need for further critical reflection upon the theoretical foundations upon which the Convention rests.

In this research I established a clear connection between the law of the ECtHR and political movements, a connection that is too often overlooked by lawyerly analysis of the Convention. The Convention's rights arose out of the struggles of the past, and will be shaped and determined by the struggles of the future. Human rights norms, including those developed in the jurisprudence of the ECtHR, emerge in order to challenge conventional political structures. As Donnelly notes, the connection of these norms with any pre-ordained philosophical reasoning is, at best, abstract: human rights are a politically-driven process of social learning that reflects the countless struggles to defend human dignity.[25] This process of social learning is a continuous one and the development of human rights norms consequently has a constant momentum, much of which is generated by NGOs.

The conceptual concerns outlined in this research might suggest that human rights are arbitrary, merely to be applied at the whim of the most powerful

[22]   Interview, Lilla Farkas, Attorney with the Hungarian Helsinki Committee, 11 September 2002, London.
[23]   These ideas have been developed more fully by me in Loveday Hodson, 'The European Court of Human Rights: Which Way Next?' in Thomas Gross (ed), *Legal Scholarship in International and Comparative Law* (Frankfurt, Peter Lang, 2003) 173.
[24]   High Level Conference on the Future of the European Court of Human Rights, Interlaken, 18–19 February 2010.
[25]   Jack Donnelly, *Universal Human Rights in Theory and Practice* (Ithaca NY, Cornell University Press, 2003) 58.

groups in society. I would reject that analysis, and would instead embrace the idea of 'human rights dynamism'. Human rights are adaptable, and NGOs are the tangible embodiment of the social struggles that go to shaping them. Furthermore, I share Foucault's optimism about the benefits of this capacity for change:

> There's an optimism that consists in saying that things couldn't be better. My optimism would consist rather in saying that so many things can be changed, fragile as they are, bound up more with circumstances than necessities, more arbitrary than self-evident, more a matter of complex, but temporary, historical circumstances than with inevitable anthropological constraints.[26]

As it has been presented in this book, the litigation of the ECtHR is not inevitably bound to the idea of achieving individual justice: rather, it can generate, maintain and develop ethical norms for the community to which it applies. NGOs play an important part in creating a human rights ethic within Europe, in which human rights are enjoyed by individuals but are the concern of all. This Hegelian view of human rights – in which human rights are viewed as 'a battlefield with an ethical dimension'[27] – does not make human rights norms weak or arbitrary. Rather, they become 'deeply rooted social constructions that shape our lives'.[28] It is by understanding the politics of human rights, and understanding the importance of the political actors that struggle to achieve their realisation, that we come to appreciate the fragility of human rights norms. To acknowledge the fragility of the rights that are outlined in the Convention, and the fact that they are rooted in historic circumstances, is at once alarming and exhilarating; for so begins the battle for human dignity, the struggle for human rights.

---

[26] Michel Foucault, 'Practicing Criticism' in LD Kritzman (ed), *Michel Foucault: Politics, Philosophy, Culture* (1988) 156, quoted in Derek McGhee, *Homosexuality, Law and Resistance* (London, Routledge, 2001) 19.

[27] Douzinas, *The End of Human Rights* (2000) 288.

[28] Jack Donnelly, 'The Social Construction of International Human Rights' in Dunne and Wheeler (eds), *Human Rights* (1999) 85.

Appendix

A Detailed Description of the Adopted Methodology

I. Introduction

I PROVIDE HERE a detailed description of the methods adopted in this research in the belief that it might be of interest to some readers. In developing a research plan for exploring the role that NGOs play in ECtHR litigation it was clear that some difficult methodological questions and challenges would be faced. Yet this was never intended to be an abstract piece of theoretical research: the intention behind this project was to add realism in the form of socio-legal investigation to the conceptual concerns outlined in chapter two. As Michael Freeman notes, sociological methodology has much to offer those who understand human rights to emerge from political struggles:

> The concept of human rights is also political. The normative principles of human rights can motivate people to struggle for the entrenchment of human rights in law. The political sociology of law is therefore an important social science for understanding human-rights social action. The comparative study of social movements may help to explain variations on the making and implementation of human-rights law.[1]

There is thus much to be gained from meeting the challenges of applying a satisfactory methodological framework to human rights research.

In this appendix I outline and explain the adopted methodology that provided me with an effective and systematic means of exploring the broad theoretical concerns at the heart of this book. The methodological choices made are explained in some detail so that the analysis of the data can be better understood. In particular, I explain here why a multi-strategy approach – which combines

---

[1] Michael Freeman, *Human Rights: An Interdisciplinary Approach* (Cambridge, Polity Press, 2002) 77.

both quantitative and qualitative techniques – was found to be the most appropriate for the purposes of this research.[2]

II. The Aims and Scope of the Research Project

The aim of this study was to consider the nature and scope of the role played by NGOs in litigation before the ECtHR. Even before starting out on this exploratory journey, I realised I had created a conceptual difficulty for myself. 'Playing a role' is a somewhat imprecise notion, although it implies that some form of participation has taken place. For the purpose of this research, a decision had to be made about what types of participation in the Court's litigation would be encompassed. An obvious starting point was to consider NGO participation within the formal proceedings of the Court's litigation, but for various reasons I decided not to restrict this research in that way.

First, the literature discussed in chapter three shows that it is unduly restrictive to focus only upon formal participation. A significant amount of NGO activity is 'informal' in the sense that the NGO is not recognised as a participant in the proceedings before the Court. Furthermore, the 'informal' label does not necessarily indicate that a less important contribution has been made by an NGO to the litigation in question. For example, an NGO that actively seeks out an applicant to take a test case to the ECtHR and which subsequently funds the litigation entirely is clearly playing a more significant role in the litigation process that the third-party intervener who files a 10-page brief. The distinction between formal and informal participation is, moreover, somewhat deceptive, and does little to aid our understanding of the interests that influence the Court's litigation. For example, from both a theoretical and practical point of view there seems little point in differentiating between a situation in which an NGO submits third-party observations to the Court at the request of the applicant, and one in which an NGO draws up a report for the purposes of that litigation which the applicant files as an appendix to her memorial. Nevertheless, in the latter example the NGO in question would obviously not be a formal party to the litigation.

In sum, 'informal' participation has been encompassed within the scope of this research because, potentially, this can lead to richer and more pertinent findings. Nevertheless, the concept of an NGO having 'a role' in litigation is potentially almost limitless without some parameters being established. Consequently, in this research consideration is restricted to NGO participation in ECtHR litigation that is both direct and deliberate. Thus my approach to this issue was both clear

---

[2] In answering these questions, I am particularly indebted to the ideas of Derek Layder concerning multi-strategy approaches to social research. See Derek Layder, *New Strategies in Social Research: An Introduction and Guide* (Cambridge, Polity Press, 1993).

and flexible, and it allowed for an understanding of the roles that NGOs play in litigation to emerge organically, unhindered by any preconceptions about what those roles might be.

A.   The Need for Quantitative Research

The research presented in this book is based upon a two-stage research process. First, a sample of cases from applications made to the ECtHR was selected and analysed for the incidence and type of NGO participation (the quantitative stage). This was followed by qualitative research based on case studies of NGOs' litigation strategies that emerged from the quantitative findings (the qualitative stage).

The primary reason for including a quantitative research element was the exploratory nature of many of the questions posed by this research. Simple questions needed answering before considering why NGOs become involved in ECtHR litigation, such as: Which NGOs are involved in litigation? What kind of participation takes place? And what is the scale of NGO involvement in ECtHR litigation? In other words, the basic quantitative methods adopted allowed for more systematic analysis of the qualitative data. The aim of this first phase was, therefore, to establish the nature and frequency of formal and informal partici- pation by NGOs in ECtHR litigation. To the extent that statistical analysis of the sample cases (which is carried out in chapter three) revealed patterns of NGO participation, this stage of the process was also useful in enabling me to generate some theories about the research question. This tentative analysis was developed further once the qualitative research had been conducted.

The benefits of adopting the initial quantitative stage, which admittedly proved to be very time-consuming, were numerous. While the available literature pro- vides some idea of which NGOs are regularly involved in ECtHR cases – and many more of course regularly came to my attention through sources such as the internet and newspapers reports – to conduct case studies based solely on this information would have had significant limitations. In particular, I might thereby have been led to overstate the importance of high-profile human rights organisa- tions that appear regularly in the British media, such as Liberty and JUSTICE. Without quantitative research, there would be an inevitable bias towards British NGOs in this book, which, given that the Court is an international judicial organ, I was anxious to avoid as far as possible. Moreover, by starting with statistical analysis of a sample of cases, organisations not regularly involved in making applications to the ECtHR could be included within the scope of this research. In short, the aim of the quantitative research stage was to provide as comprehensive a picture as possible of NGO involvement in the Court's litigation at a given period of time.

Adopting a two-stage methodology also assisted with the qualitative research component. Using a sample of cases as the basis for this research meant that during interviews with NGO personnel I could retain the central focus of the research. I anticipated that for many NGOs their activities in relation to the ECHR might be a minor part of their work taken as a whole. Therefore, in order to be able to focus discussions with the relevant NGOs on this particular aspect of their work, it was useful to be able to present specific examples of ECtHR cases in which they had been involved. In this way it was hoped that accuracy and specificity would be obtained in the interviews. Instead of talking about what they believe they are doing in terms of the ECtHR, the interview could focus on the actual concrete experiences of NGOs in relation to specific cases.

III.   The Sample Analysed

It has clearly not been possible to analyse the entirety of the Court's case law in this study. The demise of the Commission as a filtering system and the growth in membership of the Council of Europe meant that this project was conceived at the start of what has continued to be a rapid increase in the Court's workload. The accelerating growth in the number of applications submitted to the Convention's organs since the 1980s is very well known and has been widely commented upon.[3] The vast majority of these applications are declared inadmissible. This research therefore concentrates on NGO involvement in cases in which the Court has delivered a judgment on the merits. Consequently, all applications that were discontinued, those that were declared inadmissible, those struck off the Court's list and those in which a friendly settlement was reached have not been considered.

There were a variety of reasons for this methodological choice. First, it preserves a sense of continuity with the small amount of research that already exists in the area, which has tended to focus on NGO involvement in cases in which the Court has delivered judgment on the merits. Secondly, cases in which a judgment has been delivered are, arguably, the most significant from a jurisprudential point of view. By focusing solely upon this body of cases, those that were either hopeless (in formal legal terms) or technically outside the Court's remit were eliminated from the sample. Given the enormous number of applications received by the Court each year, that was an important step. Finally, few, if any, third-party interventions have been overlooked as a result of this methodological choice, as it is usually only once a case has been declared admissible that third

---

[3] See Steven Greer, 'Reforming the European Convention on Human Rights: Towards Protocol 14' [2003] *Public Law* 663, Steven Greer, 'Protocol 14 and the Future of the European Court of Human Rights' [2005] *Public Law* 83, and Marie-Aude Beernaert, 'Protocol 14 and New Strasbourg Procedures: Towards Greater Efficiency? And at What Price?' (2004) 5 *European Human Rights Law Review* 544.

For details of the number of applications submitted each year, see the Court's annually published *Annual Reports* (and, for data prior to 2007, *Annual Survey of Activities*) which are available at: www.echr.coe.int/ECHR/EN/Header/Reports+and+Statistics/Reports/Annual+Reports/.

parties will seek to intervene.[4] Nevertheless, any conclusions drawn from this research are only valid in relation to admissible applications to the Court.

It was not possible to include all of the cases in which the Court delivered judgment within the sample, given the intention to conduct both quantitative analysis of the sample cases and qualitative analysis based on case studies drawn from that sample.[5] Therefore, the sample used for this research is drawn from cases in which the Court delivered a judgment on the merits in the year 2000. Although this may appear to be a considerable restriction of the data pool in quantitative terms, statistics provided by the Council of Europe show that the number of judgments delivered in that one year had risen dramatically from previous years and in fact represent 40 per cent of the total number of judgments delivered by the Court up to that date (see Figure 3).[6]

Basing the sample on cases in which judgment was delivered in 2000 was beneficial in a number of ways. First, the Court's rules relating to third party interventions became more accommodating in 1998: choosing a period after that change, therefore, meant that there was an emerging practice of NGO interventions to analyse. A further significant reason for this choice was to assist in the undertaking of effective qualitative research. Selecting a sample of cases in which judgment was delivered in the year 2000 gave the interviewees from NGOs sufficient time to reflect upon their experiences with the Court and to assess the outcome and impact of their involvement in the cases in question. The media interest in the case (if any) had usually subsided, and the legislative or administrative response to the judgment (if any) had normally taken place or had at least been indicated. Any appeals to the Grand Chamber had also taken place, which, as well as necessarily indicating the 'end of the Strasbourg journey', also meant that the case-files were available for research purposes. Of course, this necessarily means that this book is providing a snapshot of NGO activity before the Court at a certain period of time. More recent developments are commented upon in this book, but do not form the core of my data and analysis.

---

[4]   Rule 61(3) of the Rules of Court that were in force at the time the sample cases were before the Court (dated 4 November 1998), which relates to third party interventions, stated that 'leave for this purpose must be duly reasoned and submitted in one of the official languages, within a reasonable time *after the fixing of the written procedure*' (emphasis added).

The current Rules of Court, dated 1 July 2009, state that requests for leave to intervene must be received 'not later than twelve weeks after notice of the application has been given to the respondent Contracting Party'. See r 44(2)(b).

[5]   The Court's statistics show that by 2000 the Court had delivered 1,709 judgments. See *Survey of Activities: 2000* (Strasbourg, Council of Europe) 70. Available at: www.echr.coe.int/NR/rdonlyres/501D81E2-C4D9–4EAD-990E-AC27448F60E1/0/SurveyofActivities2000.pdf.

[6]   Overall, the trend in the number of judgments delivered by the Court has continued to show a rise in the years since 2000. For details of the number of judgment delivered since 2000, see the Court's *Annual Reports* and annual *Survey of Activities* available at available at: www.echr.coe.int/ECHR/EN/Header/Reports+and+Statistics/Reports/Annual+Reports/.

Figure 3: Judgments delivered by the Court, 1955–2000

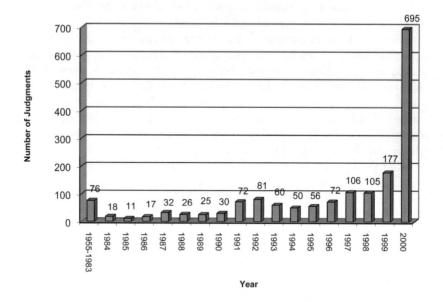

This graph was compiled using statistics provided by the Court in its *Survey of Activities: 2000*, 70. The number of judgments shown to be delivered by the Court in these statistics differs from mine, as they include cases before the Court that are struck out and those in which a friendly settlement was reached, as well as cases that are not examined on the merits and judgments for just satisfaction. For my purposes these have been excluded and I have focused solely on those cases in which a judgment on the merits was delivered. Consequently, whereas for my purposes there were 442 judgments delivered in 2000, the Court's statistics show there were 695. Nevertheless, the chart above is a valuable graphic representation of the considerable percentage of the Court's judgments that are considered in this research, even though it only considers judgments delivered in 2000.

The Court delivered a judgment on the merits in 442 cases in the year 2000. Closer inspection of these cases revealed something unusual about their pattern. Of the 442 cases in question, 235 had been brought against Italy alone.[7] It was apparent that the bulk of the Court's work in 2000 was taken up with one issue: of the 442 judgments on the merits delivered by the Court that year, 293 related to delay in domestic legal proceedings (including criminal, civil and administrative cases), most of which were brought against Italy.

---

[7] The next largest number of judgments delivered in cases brought against a single country in 2000 was 56 (against France).

The problem of 'delay' cases has been identified by the institutions of the Council of Europe for a number of years, and attempts made to distinguish cases on the basis of their importance. In 2001, the process that would lead to the adoption of Protocol 14 was already underway. Thus, in the *Report of the Evaluation Group to the Committee of Ministers on the European Court of Human Rights*[8] judgments delivered in 2000 are broken down into four categories based on their relative jurisprudential importance. The category descriptions and the numbers of judgments in each are as follows:

1. leading judgments selected for publication in the Reports of Judgments and Decisions [94 judgments];
2. judgments dealing with new questions but not considered of sufficient importance to justify publication [35 judgments];
3. judgments essentially applying standard case law [81 judgments]; and
4. straightforward cases concerning the alleged excessive length of domestic proceedings [485 judgments].

Although in 2000, 'delay cases' (category 4) were far more numerous than other categories of cases, they were also considered to be of least jurisprudential importance. In many ways, these cases can be seen as the catalyst of the recent reforms of the Court's procedures. Several authors expressed the opinion that the Court should not be devoting time to such unimportant cases. As long ago as 1992, John Andrews remarked in the *European Law Review* that the 'situation now is bordering on the farcical'[9] in relation to cases brought against Italy for delay in domestic trial proceedings. He asks the – still pertinent – question: 'What reason there can be for inundating a superior body with cases which raise no significant issue of law or principle?'[10] The Evaluation Group recommended that these repetitive cases should be 'frozen' while a lead case is dealt with.[11] They also proposed more radical suggestions for cases of 'minor or secondary importance',[12] which included giving the Court power to reject such applications.[13] Thus the seeds of Protocol 14 were sown.

---

[8]   Council of Europe, *Report of the Evaluation Group to the Committee of Ministers on the European Court of Human Rights*, EG Court(2001)1 27 September 2001, available at: www.coe.int/T/F/Droits_de_l'Homme/ECHRReform_process.asp.

[9]   John Andrews, 'Time Wasting in Italy and Strasbourg' (1992) 17(4) *European Law Review* 371, 371. See also 'Current Survey: Council of Europe' (1991) 16(4) *European Law Review* 359.

[10]   Andrews, 'Time Wasting' (1992) 371.

[11]   *Report of the Evaluation Group* (2001) para 51.
At the time, the Evaluation Group's recommendations were criticised by NGO staff for moving the Court away from a commitment to providing individual justice. See, for example, *NGOs' Response to the Report of the Evaluation Group* (2002, unpublished, copy on file with author), and John Wadham and Tazeen Said, 'What Price the Right of Individual Petition?: Report of the Evaluation Group to the Committee of Ministers on the European Court of Human Rights' (2002) 2 *European Human Rights Law Review* 169.

[12]   *Report of the Evaluation Group* (2001) para 92.

[13]   *Report of the Evaluation Group* (2001) paras 92–6.

From a research point of view, I was obviously concerned that a considerable amount of unfruitful time could be spent examining an extremely large number of repetitive cases, which held no interest for NGOs. Studying a sample of 35 of these repetitive cases showed that my concern was valid: the sample revealed no NGO participation. Consequently, 'delay' cases were not explored further in this research. Nevertheless, these early 'negative' research findings on delay cases helped to create some ideas about the role NGOs play in ECtHR litigation, and they also provided a critical point in the research that inevitably led to some re-evaluation of the theoretical foundations of the project. Within the context of my research, it was hard to see the Court's function as primarily constitutional, given the nature of these 'delay' cases. Equally, it was clear from this finding that the bulk of the Court's litigation would hold little or no interest for NGOs.

Once the choices outlined in this section had been made, a sample of 149 cases remained to be analysed in terms of the extent and form of NGO participation within them. These cases form the foundation of the subsequent quantitative and qualitative research.

IV.   The Quantitative Stage: Identifying NGO Participation

Once the sample had been selected, the next step was to identify NGO participation in those cases. Those who had conducted similar research before me offered a stark warning of the difficulties that might be encountered:

> Untangling puzzles of this sort is well nigh impossible. There is little continuity in the personnel of pressure groups. The groups do not keep accurate records, cannot always remember whether they were involved or, if they were running a test-case strategy, how many applications they made ... Groups may sometimes confuse telephone inquiries or informal conversations with legal advisers or other groups with more sustained participation. Sometimes they wish to lay claim to a successful case, sometimes they may prefer to hide their involvement, sometimes they are just unaware of it.[14]

In this section I explain the methods adopted in this research for 'untangling the puzzle' of identifying NGO involvement in the sample cases.

A.   The Court's Documentation

Much of the data presented in this study was obtained from the Court's judgments and the Commission's admissibility decisions and reports in respect of the sample cases, which are readily available from the Council of Europe's

---

[14]   Carol Harlow and Richard Rawlings, *Pressure Through Law* (London, Routledge, 1992) 256.

website.[15] These sources, of course, identify those NGOs that bring cases in their own name. It is also apparent from Lester's research that third-party interventions will usually be referred to in the Court's judgments, although he does cite one judgment in which a request to intervene that had been refused is not mentioned.[16] Although the judgments, decisions and reports did not provide sufficient information about *informal* NGO participation in the sample cases, they sometimes hinted at 'behind the scenes' NGO involvement that generated further enquiries. For example, a judgment might specifically mention that the applicant's lawyer was acting in collaboration with an NGO, or that evidence presented by the applicant was authored by an NGO.

The next source of information relied upon in this research was the Court's files, which contain invaluable information about the sample cases. According to Article 40(2) of the Convention,

> Documents deposited with the Registrar shall be accessible to the public unless the President of the Court decides otherwise.

While this provision seemed to suggest that getting access to the case files would be a simple matter, in practice some limitations were imposed on the use of these documents, which are outlined below. Notwithstanding the fact that these limitations were a frustration, examining the case-files proved to be an invaluable stage of the research process.

The practical aspects of arranging research trips to consult the Registry's files raised some difficulties. When the Registry was initially contacted it was clear that the scale of what was planned was out of the ordinary and would cause difficulties for the files' archivist. The Court could comfortably cater for those wanting to look at one or two files, but could not readily deal with requests to access large numbers of its files. Ultimately, it was agreed that a series of short visits would be undertaken and I would provide a list of files to be inspected a month in advance of each visit. There was also an expectation that at least three months would be left between each research visit.

Article 40(2), which is outlined above, is subject to certain provisos. First, and most importantly in this context, is the rule enshrined in Article 38(2), which states that all attempts by the Court to assist the parties in achieving a friendly settlement are to remain confidential. As Article 38(1) states that the Court *shall* put itself at the disposal of the parties for the purposes of reaching a friendly settlement, it seems fair to assume that there are at least some confidential documents in many, and perhaps even the majority, of the Court's files. Unfortunately, however, those documents were not kept separately from the rest of the file, and each time a file was requested the Court's lawyers read through it and

---

[15]   The HUDOC database is available via the Court's web-site: www.echr.coe.int.

[16]   Anthony Lester, 'Amici Curiae: Third-Party Interventions Before the European Court of Human Rights', in Franz Matscher and Herbert Petzold (eds), *Protecting Human Rights: The European Dimension* (Koln, Carl Heymanns Verlag KG, 1990) 348.

manually extracted confidential material. Apart from the time-consuming nature of this process, the fact that such correspondence could not be seen was not of grave concern: one can assume that such correspondence between the Registry and the applicant or the respondent State would not concern any otherwise unmentioned NGO participation.

Furthermore, Article 40(2) only applies to documents filed with the Court. All applications in the sample cases had originally been filed with the Commission, and, under the Commission's Rule 17(2), documents filed with that body are not accessible to the public. This means that documents in the sample cases that were filed before their transfer to the Court are not public. For the reasons outlined above, being unable to access the Commission's files did not adversely affect the findings relating to formal interventions in the sample cases; it did, however, limit the amount of information available about informal NGO participation in the sample cases.

The Court's Rules concerning the anonymity of applicants were also of relevance in this respect. Rule 33 states that documents deposited with the Registry are public. Rule 33(2), however, recognises exceptional circumstances in which documents will not be made public. The formulation of this Rule that was in operation for the sample cases read:

> [W]here the interests of juveniles or the protection of the private life of the parties so require, or to the extent strictly necessary in the opinion of the Chamber in special circumstances where publicity would prejudice the interests of justice.[17]

Any application for confidentiality must include reasons for the request and must specify whether it relates to all or only part of the documents in the case-file in question. In the sample cases, there was no occasion on which partial confidentiality was granted. I was, however, denied access to the Court's files in 18 cases on the basis of their confidentiality. A further 13 files relating to the sample cases were not accessed for other reasons, such as being in use by the Registry.

The language of the documentation in the Court's case-files also proved to be a consideration. The official languages of the Court are English and French,[18] both of which I can read. Under the Court's Rules in operation at the time when the sample cases were being heard, an applicant or her representative could communicate with the Court in an official language of any Contracting Party until an application was declared admissible.[19] Rule 34(3)(a), however, read:

> All communications with and pleadings by such applicants or their representatives in respect of a hearing, or after a case has been declared admissible, shall be in one of the

---

[17]   The formulation of r 33 in the current Rules of Court, dated 1 July 2009, is very similar.

[18]   Rule 34(1) of the Rules of Court. Under Rule 76(1), judgments are published in either English or French unless the Court decides that they shall be published in both. The earliest versions of the Rules of Court provided that all judgments were to be published in both languages.

[19]   Rule 34(2). This Rule has since been modified, and now provides that an applicant may communicate in any of the official languages of the Contracting Parties until notice of the application has been given to a Contracting Party.

Court's official languages, unless the President of the Chamber authorises the continued use of the official language of a Contracting Party.[20]

Despite this Rule, the communications in some of the files continued to be in a language other than French or English at the post-admissibility stage (this was particularly true of applications from Central and Eastern European countries).[21] Where case-files contained such correspondence, reading them in their entirety was obviously made difficult or impossible. Nevertheless, even in such circumstances requests to intervene from a third party were still readily identifiable. Beyond that, a small number of documents were translated at my request where there was good reason to believe that they contained information that was pertinent to this research.

B.   Other Sources Used for this Research

Although invaluable, the Court's documentation could provide only a starting point for identifying informal participation by NGOs in the sample cases. Consequently, for the purposes of this project it was necessary to undertake research beyond formal legalistic sources.

Baxi refers to 'cyber-space solidarity' as one of the techniques employed by NGOs to further human rights.[22] Many NGOs have of course recognised the internet's capacity to instantly communicate their message to a wide audience, and many have websites that provide large amounts of information about the organisations' aims and activities. Consequently, as part of the research process, numerous NGO websites were reviewed to see if they referred to an involvement in the sample cases. This proved to be a particularly important line of research in a project based upon transnational social enquiry. Inevitably, however, this source favoured the larger, more affluent NGOs that have regularly up-dated websites.

Where the Court's documentation hinted at the possibility of NGO participation in a sample case without providing any concrete evidence of this, the applicant's representative before the Court was contacted for information about the background to the case and asked about any NGO involvement. English language newspaper archives and academic articles were also searched for references to the sample cases. Human rights organisations and human rights lawyers in various European countries were also contacted directly (usually by e-mail) and asked about any involvement they might have had in the sample cases. From these sources it soon became clear that many of the NGOs that participate in

---

[20]   Rule 34(3)(a) currently provides that one of the Court's official languages must be used once notice of an application has been given to a Contracting Party.

[21]   There was very little correspondence on the files I consulted about this issue, and there were only a couple of instances where the applicants' representatives were reprimanded for corresponding in a non-official language at the post-admissibility stage. This happened, for example, in *Ciliz v Netherlands*, (App no 29192/95) ECHR 2000-VIII.

[22]   Upendra Baxi, *The Future of Human Rights* (New Delhi, Oxford University Press, 2002) 127.

Strasbourg cases have close links with one another, and these networks provided useful information about the operations of transnational human rights activists.

In light of the research steps outlined above, the statistical position concerning formal participation in the sample cases by NGOs can be confidently stated. However, for the reasons discussed above, the conclusions about the incidence of informal participation by NGOs in the sample cases are inevitably more tentative. Nevertheless, one can at least say that the researcher looked for evidence of informal NGO participation in the sample ECtHR cases to the extent that time and resources allowed. What this means is that the evidence presented in this book represents the *minimum* amount of NGO involvement in these cases. It is my firm view, however, that the amount of data discovered during this enquiry fully justifies the approach taken and that this research provides a revealing insight into a snapshot of cases heard before the Court.

V.   The Qualitative Stage: Understanding NGO Participation[23]

A.   Interviewing the NGOs Involved in the Sample Cases

The initial quantitative research stage outlined above was followed by more intense qualitative research, the aim of which was to examine both the attitudes and impact of the social actors who seek to influence the Court's litigation. This research took the form of semi-structured interviews conducted with personnel from the NGOs whose involvement in the sample cases had been identified.[24] Sue Jones succinctly identifies the value of such research:

> For to understand other persons' constructions of reality, we would do well to ask them ... and to ask them in such a way that they can tell us in their terms (rather than those imposed rigidly and *a priori* by ourselves) and in a depth which addresses the rich context that is the substance of their meanings.[25]

---

[23]   See, generally, Jane Ritchie and Jane Lewis (eds), *Qualitative Research Practice: A Guide to Social Science Students and Researchers* (London, Sage, 2003) and Norman Denzin and Yvonna Lincoln (eds), *The Landscape of Qualitative Research: Theories and Issues*, 2nd edn (London, Sage Publications, 2003).

[24]   For a discussion of the value of using mixed-method research techniques and, in particular, following quantitative with qualitative methods, see Jane Ritchie, 'The Application of Qualitative Methods to Social Research' in Ritchie and Lewis (eds), *Qualitative Research Practice* (2003) 42–3.

[25]   Sue Jones, 'Depth Interviewing' in Clive Seale (ed), *Social Research Methods: A Reader* (London, Routledge, 2004) 258.

This approach is particularly consistent with the theoretical perspectives outlined in chapter two, which 'challenge researchers to participate in a community's ongoing process of moral articulation'.[26]

Given that the working languages of the Court are English and French, it was unsurprising that the majority of the NGOs contacted for the purposes of this research were able to communicate well in one of those languages and, more often than not, in English. Interviews were semi-structured in nature, in order not to impose any pre-conceptions onto the interviewees about the significance of the organisation's participation in ECtHR litigation. NGO employees tend to change jobs frequently, and occasionally there was nobody working within an organisation who had been involved in the sample case(s) in question. In such situations, the interviewer unavoidably had to ask more generalised questions about the organisation's litigation strategy. In some cases former employees of the relevant organisations were contacted in order to discuss their involvement in the sample cases.

The international nature of this research meant that the NGOs with whom I wished to conduct interviews were spread throughout Europe and also, it transpired, the United States. This means that it was not practicable to visit them all in person, although I visited as many organisations as time and funding would allow. Where a face-to-face interview was not possible, a questionnaire was sent to the organisation. Replies to questionnaires were usually followed up with a telephone interview. No organisation that I contacted refused to assist with this research. However, in one instance, only a short telephone interview with the organisation's Director was agreed to. In another instance, no reply to my requests for information was received. In general, the NGOs contacted seemed very willing to assist with this research. The only hesitation expressed by some was based on their limited time and the issue of client confidentiality.

Consulting the relevant organisations' documentation is also a useful means of understanding the meaning that their litigation has to them. Where it was possible to visit an organisation's offices in person, I sought access to their files on the relevant ECtHR case(s) in which their involvement had been identified. The reason for this request was to fill in gaps in memory that the passage of time would inevitably have created. Many organisations were happy to agree to this request, although some did not allow access to their files for reasons of client confidentiality. The organisations' publications were also a particular useful source of information, and these were scrutinised both for references to the particular sample cases in question and for more general references to their involvement in litigation.

---

[26] Clifford Christians, 'Ethics and Politics in Qualitative Research' in Denzin and Lincoln (eds), *The Landscape of Qualitative Research* (2003) 232.

B.   Understanding the Historical, Sociological and Political Context out of which the Sample Cases Arose

During interviews conducted with NGO personnel it emerged that the interviewees took a lot of information about the background to their involvement in the sample cases for granted, information that it was clear would be useful for the interviewer to have an understanding of. Many interviewees attached great importance to the political and historical background to the cases under discussion, and this background seemed to provide the key to their motivation and rationale in participating in ECtHR litigation in a significant number of cases. Derek Layder provides useful research guidance on this point:

> [A] historical dimension will greatly enhance an appreciation of the way in which forms of power and domination have been incorporated into the structural features of settings and contexts, as a consequence of various forms of social development. A detailed and meticulous historical analysis is not a requirement here; we simply need a 'sense' of, or an 'approximate' indication of, the relevant historical factors. Such a 'blocking in' of historical material will add contextual depth to the analysis, and this will subserve and feed into the generation of theoretical ideas about the contemporary situation.[27]

Developing an understanding of, and sensitivity to, the wider context in which the NGOs operate became an essential part of this research. To this end, reference to historical, sociological and political science texts proved to be invaluable in analysing the responses that were received during the interviews.

VI.   Final Observations

Writing about his experiences of conducting ethnographic research, John van Maanen states that it is 'impossible to draw a clear distinction between data collection and analysis'.[28] It was apparent that as methodological choices were made during the course of this research, these were both shaped by my theoretical framework, as well as shaping it. Some methodological choices were largely beyond the researcher's control. Language constraints, for example, mean that this research may have a bias towards English-speaking organisations, although the methodological choices explained above attempt to mitigate this as far as

---

[27]   Layder, *New Strategies in Social Research* (1993) 118.
[28]   John van Maanen, 'Notes on the Production of Ethnographic Data in an American Police Agency' in Robin Luckham (ed), *Law and Social Enquiry: Case Studies of Research* (New York, Scandinavian Institute of African Studies, 1981) 221.

possible. Other, more deliberate, choices were, however, made by me. For example, I chose to focus on cases in which I believed the greatest preponderance of NGO activity would be found. Such choices best served the project's aims.

Bibliography

ANON, 'Current Survey: Council of Europe' (1991) 16(4) *European Law Review* 359

ANON, 'Nuclear Power Plant Licence – Neighbours' Right to Fair Trial Following Challenge to Grant of Licence' (1998) 1 *European Human Rights Law Review* 94

ANON, *Liberty Newsletter* (London, Liberty, Autumn 2000)

ANON, *NGOs' Response to the Report of the Evaluation Group* (2002, unpublished, copy on file with author)

ANON, 'Implementation of ECtHR Judgments in Chechen Cases' (2008) 10 *EHRAC Bulletin* 6

ACTON, Thomas, *Gypsy Politics and Social Change: The Development of Ethnic Ideology and Pressure Politics Among British Gypsies from Victorian Reformists to Romany Nationalism* (London, Routledge & Kegan Paul, 1974)

AHMED, Shamina and POTTER, David, *NGOs in International Politics* (Bloomfield, Kumarian Press, 2006)

AIRE CENTRE, *The AIRE Centre: A Decade of Rights, 1993–2003* (London, AIRE Centre, 2003)

AMNESTY INTERNATIONAL, *Bulgaria: Torture and Ill Treatment of Roma* (London, Amnesty International, 1993)

— *Turkey: A Policy of Denial* (London, Amnesty International, Feb 1995)

— *Turkey: No Security Without Human Rights* (London, Amnesty International, 1996)

— *Turkey: No Security Without Human Rights* (London, Amnesty International, 1996)

— *Bulgaria: Shootings, Deaths in Custody, Torture and Ill-Treatment* (London, Amnesty International, 1996)

— *Turkey: Lawyers Severely Ill-Treated Outside Buca Prison in Izmir* (London, Amnesty International, 1996)

— *Bulgaria: New Cases of Ill-Treatment of Roma* (London, Amnesty International, 1998)

— *Turkey: Still No Proper Investigation into 'Disappearances'* (London, Amnesty International, 1998)

— *Turkey: Creating a Silent Society* (London, Amnesty International, 1999)

— *Turkey: The Duty to Supervise, Investigate and Prosecute* (London, Amnesty International, 1999)

— *Turkey: Creating a Silent Society: The Turkish Government Prepares to Imprison Leading Human Rights Defender* (1 February 1999, AI Eur 44/05/99)

— *Turkey: Ocalan Lawyers at Risk* (26 February 1999, AI Eur 44/20/99)

— *Turkey: An End to Torture and Impunity is Overdue* (London, Amnesty International, 2001)

— *Turkey: Fear for Safety/Fear of Arrest of Human Rights Defenders* (16 January 2001, AI Eur 44/003/2001)

—— *Harassment of Human Rights Foundation, Diyarbakir, Turkey* (18 February 2002, AI Index: EUR 44/009/2002)

ANDERSON, Kenneth, 'The Ottawa Convention Banning Landmines, the Role of International Non-governmental Organizations and the Idea of International Civil Society' (2000) 11(1) *European Journal of International Law* 91

ANDREWS, John, 'Time Wasting in Italy and Strasbourg' (1992) 17(4) *European Law Review* 371

ANGELL, Ernest, 'The Amicus Curiae: American Development of English Institutions' (1967) 16 *International and Comparative Law Quarterly* 1017

APPIAGYEI-ATUA, Kwadi, 'Human Rights NGOs and their Role in the Promotion and Protection of Rights in Africa' (2002) 9 *International Journal on Minority and Group Rights* 265

ASHWORTH, Andrew, 'Human Rights: Adverse Inferences from Failure to Answer Police Questions' [2000] *Criminal Law Review* 679

BARANY, Zoltan, *The East European Gypsies: Regime Change, Marginality, and Ethnopolitics* (Cambridge, Cambridge University Press, 2002)

BARKER, Lucius J, 'Third Parties in Litigation: A Systematic View of the Judicial Function' (1967) 29 *The Journal of Politics* 41

BAXI, Upendra, 'Taking Suffering Seriously' in Rajeev Dhavan, R Sudarshan and Salman Khurshid (eds), *Judges and the Judicial Power* (London, Sweet & Maxwell, 1985)

—— 'Judicial Discourse: The Dialects of the Face and the Mask' (1993) 35 *Journal of the Indian Law Institute* 1

—— *The Future of Human Rights* (New Delhi, Oxford University Press, 2002)

BEERNAERT, Marie-Aude, 'Protocol 14 and New Strasbourg Procedures: Towards Greater Efficiency? And at What Price?' (2004) 5 *European Human Rights Law Review* 544

BELDEN FIELDS, A, 'Underlying Propositions for Grounding a Holistic Conception of Human Rights' in Andrew Chitty et al, *Papers in Social Theory: Rights, Movements, Recognition*, vol 6 (Brighton, Warwick Social Theory Centre and Sussex Centre for Critical Social Theory, 2001)

BELL, Stuart, *When Salem Came to the Boro* (London, Pan Books, 1988)

BENTLEY, Arthur F, *The Process of Government: A Study of Social Pressure* (Evanston, Principia Press, 1908)

BERHARDT, Rudolf, 'Human Rights and Judicial Review: The European Court of Human Rights' in David M BEATTY (ed), *Human Rights and Judicial Review: A Comparative Perspective* (Dordrecht, Kluwer, 1994)

BIRCH, Di, 'Suffering in Silence: A Cost-Benefit Analysis of Section 34 of the Criminal Justice and Public Order Act 1994' [1999] *Criminal Law Review* 769

BISSELL, Thomas St G, 'The International Committee of the Red Cross and the Protection of Human Rights' (1968) 1 *Revue des Droits de l'Homme* 255

BOB, Clifford, 'Introduction: Fighting for New Rights' in Bob (ed), *The International Struggle for New Human Rights* (Philadelphia PA, University of Pennsylvania Press, 2009)

—— (ed), *The International Struggle for New Human Rights* (Philadelphia PA, University of Pennsylvania Press, 2009).

BREEN, Claire, 'The Role of NGOs in the Formulation of and Compliance with the Optional Protocol to the Convention on the Rights of the Child on Involvement of Children in Armed Conflict' (2003) 25(2) *Human Rights Quarterly* 453

BRIAN SIMPSON, AW, *Human Rights and the End of Empire: Britain and the Genesis of the European Convention* (New York, Oxford University Press, 2001)

BROWN, Michael and MAY, John, *The Greenpeace Story* (London, Dorling Kindersley, Revised edn 1991)

BUCKLEY, Carla, *Turkey and the European Convention on Human Rights: A Report on the Litigation Programme of the Kurdish Human Rights Project* (London, KHRP, July 2000)

BURNS, Stewart (ed), *Daybreak of Freedom: The Montgomery Bus Boycott* (Chapel Hill NC, University of North Carolina Press, 1997)

BUTLER-SLOSS, Elizabeth, *Report of the Inquiry into child abuse in Cleveland 1987* (Cm 412, 1988) (London, HMSO, 1988)

CAHN, Claude, 'Justice and Empowerment' (2001) 1 *Roma Rights* editorial

CALDEIRA, Gregory A and WRIGHT, John R, 'Amici Curiae before the Supreme Court: Who Participates, When, and How Much?' (1990) 52 *The Journal of Politics* 782

ÇALI, Başak, 'The Logics of Supranational Human Rights Litigation, Official Acknowledgement, and Human Rights Reform: The Southeast Turkey Cases Before the European Court of Human Rights, 1996–2006' (2010) 35(2) *Law and Social Inquiry* 311

CAMERON, Iain, 'Turkey and Article 25 of the European Convention on Human Rights' (1988) 37 *International and Comparative Law Quarterly* 887

CAMPBELL, Beatrix, *Unofficial Secrets: Cleveland Sexual Abuse – The Cleveland Case* (London, Virago Press, 1988)

CASHMAN, Sean Dennis, *African-Americans and the Quest for Civil Rights: 1900–1990* (New York, New York University Press, 1991)

CASSESE, Antonio, 'How Could Nongovernmental Organizations Use U.N. Bodies More Effectively?' (1979) 1(4) *Universal Human Rights* 73

CHALIAND, Gerard, *The Kurdish Tragedy*, trans Philip BLACK (London, Zed Books, 1994)

— (ed), *A People Without a Country: The Kurds and Kurdistan*, trans Michael PALLIS (London, Zed Books, 1993)

CHAPPELL, Marisa, HUTCHINSON, Jenny and WARD, Brian, '"Dress modestly, neatly … as if you were going to church": Respectability, Class and Gender in the Montgomery Bus Boycott and the Early Civil Rights Movement' in Peter J LING and Sharon MONTEITH (eds), *Gender in the Civil Rights Movement* (New York, Garland Publishing, 1999)

CHARNOVITZ, Steve, 'Nongovernmental Organizations and International Law' (2006) 100 *American Journal of International Law* 348

CHRISTIAN, Louise et al, *The European Convention Under Attack: The Threat to Lawyers in Turkey and the Challenge to Strasbourg – A Report of Delegations to Turkey Between February and May 1995* (London, KHRP [etc], August 1995)

CHRISTIANS, Clifford, 'Ethics and Politics in Qualitative Research' in Norman DENZIN and Yvonna LINCOLN (eds), *The Landscape of Qualitative Research: Theories and Issues*, 2nd edn (London, Sage Publications, 2003)

CLAPHAM, Andrew, 'Creating the High Commissioner for Human Rights: The Outside Story' (1994) 5 *European Journal of International Law* 556

CLARK, Ann Marie, *Diplomacy of Conscience: Amnesty International and Changing Human Rights Norms* (Princeton NJ, Princeton University Press, 2001)

CLARK, Roger, 'The International League for Human Rights and South West Africa 1947–1957: The Human Rights NGO as Catalyst in the International Legal Process' (1981) 3(4) *Human Rights Quarterly* 101

COHEN, Barbara and STAUNTON, Marie, 'In Pursuit of a Legal Strategy: The National Council for Civil Liberties' in Jeremy COOPER and Rajeev DHAVAN (eds), *Public Interest Law* (Oxford, Basil Blackwell, 1986)

COHEN, Robin and RAI, Shirin (eds), *Global Social Movements* (London, The Althone Press, 2000)

COLEMAN, Christopher, NEE, Laurence D and RUBINOWITZ, Leonard S, 'Social Movements and Social-Change Litigation: Synergy in the Montgomery Bus Protest' (2005) 30 *Law and Social Inquiry* 663

COLLINS, Paul M Jr, 'Friends of the Court: Examining the Influence of Amicus Curiae Participation in U.S. Supreme Court Litigation' (2004) 38 *Law and Society Review* 807

— 'Lobbyists Before the U.S. Supreme Court: Investigating the Influence of Amicus Curiae Briefs' (2007) 60(1) *Political Research Quarterly* 55

COMMISSIONER FOR HUMAN RIGHTS, *Final Report on the Human Rights Situation of the Roma, Sinti and Travellers in Europe* (15 February 2009, CommDH(2006)

COOK, Helena, 'Amnesty International at the United Nations' in Peter WILLETTS (ed), '*The Conscience of the World': The Influence of Non-Governmental Organisation in the U.N. System* (London, Hurst & Co, 1996)

COUDENHOVE-KALEGRI, Richard, *The Totalitarian State against Man* (London, Paneuropa, 1938)

COUNCIL OF EUROPE, *Collected Edition of the 'Travaux Préparatoires' of the European Convention on Human Righ*ts (Dordrecht/Boston/Lancaster, Martinus Nijhoff, 1985)

— *Digest of Strasbourg Case-Law Relating to the European Convention on Human Rights*, vol 4 (Köln, Carl Heymanns Verlag KG, 1985)

— *The Rebirth of Democracy: Twelve Constitutions of Central and Eastern Europe* (Strasbourg, Council of Europe, 1996)

— *Survey: Forty Years of Activity 1959–1998* (Strasbourg, Council of Europe, 1998)

— *Survey of Activities, 2000* (Strasbourg, Council of Europe, 200?)

— *Report of the Evaluation Group to the Committee of Ministers on the European Court of Human Rights*, EG Court (2001)1, 27 September 2001

— *Protocol No. 14 to the Convention for the Protection of Human Rights and Fundamental Freedoms, amending the control system of the Convention: Explanatory Report*

— *50 Years of Activity: The European Court of Human Rights, Some Facts and Figures*

COX, Barry, *Civil Liberties in Britain* (Harmondsworth, Penguin, 1975)

COXALL, Bill, *Pressure Groups in British Politics* (New York, Longman, 2001)

CULLEN, Holly and MORROW, Karen, 'International Civil Society in International Law: The Growth of NGO Participation' (2001) 1 *Non-State Actors and International Law* 7

DASGUPTA, Modhurima, 'Social Action for Women? Public Interest Litigation in India's Supreme Court' (2002) *Law, Social Justice & Global Development Journal (LGD)* 1

DAVIES, Norman, *Europe: A History* (London, Pimlico, 1997)

DE MEYER, Jan, 'La Situation des "personnes physiques", "organisation non-gouvernementales" et "groupes de particuliers" dans la procédure devant la Cour Européenne des Droits de l'Homme' in *Annales de droit* (Louvain, Université Catholique de Louvain, 1974) 65

DENZIN, Norman and LINCOLN, Yvonna (eds), *The Landscape of Qualitative Research: Theories and Issues*, 2nd edn (London, Sage Publications, 2003)

DE SCHUTTER, Olivier, 'Sur l'émergence de la société civile en droit international: le role des associations devant la Cour européenne des droits de l'homme' (1996) 7 *European Journal of International Law* 372

DICKLITCH, Susan and LWANGA, Doreen, 'The Politics of Being Non-Political: Human Rights Organizations and the Creation of a Positive Human Rights Culture in Uganda' (2003) 25(2) *Human Rights Quarterly* 482

DICKSON, Brice, 'The Council of Europe and the European Convention' in DICKSON (ed), *Human Rights and the European Convention: The effects of the Convention on the United Kingdom and Ireland* (London, Sweet & Maxwell, 1997)

DINGWALL, Robert, EEKELAAR, John and MURRAY, Topsy, *The Protection of Children: State Intervention and Family Life* (Oxford, Basil Blackwell, 1983)

DI RATTALMA, Marco Frigessi, 'NGOs before the European Court of Human Rights: Beyond *Amicus Curiae* Participation?' in Tullio TREVES (ed), *Civil Society, International Courts and Compliance Bodies* (The Hague, TMC Asser Press, 2005)

DONN, Gari (ed), *Missiles, Reactors and Civil Liberties* (Glasgow, Scottish Council for Civil Liberties, 1982)

DONNELLY, Jack, *International Human Rights* (Boulder CO, Westview Press, 1998)

— 'The Social Construction of International Human Rights' in Tim DUNNE and Nicholas J WHEELER (eds), *Human Rights in Global Politics* (Cambridge, Cambridge University Press, 1999)

— *Universal Human Rights in Theory and Practice*, 2nd edn (Ithaca NY, Cornell University Press, 2003)

DOUGLAS, Davison M, 'The Limits of Law in Accomplishing Racial Change: School Segregation in the Pre-Brown North' (1997) 44 *UCLA Law Review* 677

DOUZINAS, Costas, *The End of Human Rights: Critical Legal Thought at the Turn of the Century* (Oxford, Hart Publishing, 2000)

DRZEMCZEWSKI, Andrew, 'The Role of NGOs in Human Rights Matters in the Council of Europe' (1987) 8 *Human Rights Law Journal* 273

DUNAY, Pal, 'Nationalism and Ethnic Conflicts in Eastern Europe: Imposed, Induced or (Simply) Re-emerged' in Istvan POGANY (ed), *Human Rights in Eastern Europe* (Aldershot, Edward Elgar Publishing, 1995)

DUNNE, Tim and WHEELER, NJ, 'Introduction' in DUNNE and WHEELER (eds), *Human Rights in Global Politics* (Cambridge, Cambridge University Press, 1999)

— (eds), *Human Rights in Global Politics* (Cambridge, Cambridge University Press, 1999)

DYSON, Brian, *Liberty in Britain 1934–1994: A Diamond Jubilee History of the National Council for Civil Liberties* (London, Civil Liberties Trust, 1994)

EHRAC, *Annual Report: 2006* (London, EHRAC, 2007)

ENGLE MERRY, Sally, ROSEN, Mihaela Şerban, LEVITT, Peggy and YOON, Diana H, 'Law from Below: Women's Human Rights and Social Movements in New York City' (2010) 44(1) *Law and Society Review* 101

EPP, Charles R, *The Rights Revolution: Lawyers, Activists, and Supreme Courts in Comparative Perspective* (Chicago IL, University of Chicago Press, 1998)

ERMACORA, Felix, 'Non-Governmental Organizations as Promoters of Human Rights' in Franz MATSCHER and Herbert PETZOLD (eds), *Protecting Human Rights: The European Dimension* (Koln, Carl Heymanns Verlag KG, 1988)

ESKRIDGE, William, 'Some Effects of Identity-Based Social Movements on Constitutional Law in the Twentieth Century' (2002) 100 *Michigan Law Review* 2062

EU-MIDIS, *European Union Minorities and Discrimination Survey: Data in Focus 1 – The Roma* (European Union Agency for Fundamental Rights, 2009)

EUROPEAN COMMISSION, *EU Support for Roma Communities in Central and Eastern Europe* (Brussels, European Commission Enlargement Information Unit, 2003)

— *2004 Regular Report on Turkey's Progress Towards Accession*, 6 October 2004 (2004) COM 656 final

EUROPEAN ROMA RIGHTS CENTRE, *Profession: Prisoner – Roma in Detention in Bulgaria* (Budapest, ERRC, December 1997)

— *Assenov & Others v Bulgaria: Written Comments of the European Roma Rights Centre* (29 April 1998, unpublished)

— *Biannual Report: 2001–2002* (Budapest, ERRC, 2002)

— *Memorandum Concerning The Implementation And State Of General Measures In The Judgment Of D.H. And Others v The Czech Republic (Application No. 57325/00)*

FARER, Tom, 'The Rise of the Inter-American Human Rights Regime: No Longer a Unicorn, Not Yet an Ox' in David HARRIS and Stephen LIVINGSTONE (eds), *The Inter-American System of Human Rights* (Oxford, Clarendon Press, 1998)

FOLEY, Conor, OUTRAGE and STONEWALL, *Sexuality and the State: Human Rights Violations Against Lesbians, Gays Bisexuals and Transgendered People* (London, Liberty, 1994)

FORSYTHE, David P, 'Human Rights and the International Committee of the Red Cross' (1990) 12 *Human Rights Quarterly* 265

FORTIN, Jane, 'Rights Brought Home for Children' (1999) 62 *Modern Law Review* 350

FREEMAN, Michael, *Human Rights: an Interdisciplinary Approach* (Cambridge, Polity Press, 2002)

GALANTER, Marc, 'Why the "Haves" Come out Ahead: Speculations on the Limits of Legal Change' (1974) 9 *Law and Society Review* 95

— 'The Radiating Effects of Courts' in Keith O BOYUM and Lynn MATHER (eds), *Empirical Theories about Courts* (New York, Longman, 1983)

GARROW, David J, *Bearing the Cross: Martin Luther King, Jr. and the Southern Christian Leadership Conference* (New York, William Morrow and Co, 1986)

GHEORGHE, Nicolae and ACTON, Thomas, 'Citizens of the World and Nowhere' in Will GUY (ed), *Between Past and Future: the Roma of Central and Eastern Europe* (Hatfield, University of Hertfordshire Press, 2001)

GHUGHINSKI, N, 'Roma Wins a Lawsuit Against the Ministry of Internal Affairs' (January–April 1996) 1(1) *Focus: The Newsletter of the HRP* 7

GOLDSTEIN, Joseph, FREUD, Anna and SOLNIT, Albert J, *Beyond the Best Interests of the Child* (London, Burnett Books, 1980)

GOLDSTON, James A and ADJANI, Mirna, 'The Opportunities and Challenges of Using Public Interest Litigation to Secure Access to Justice for Roma in Central and Eastern Europe' in Yash GHAI and Jill COTTRELL (eds), *Marginalized Communities and Access to Justice* (Abingdon, Routledge, 2010)

GOSTIN, Larry, *A Human Condition: The Law Relating to Mentally Abnormal Offenders: Observations, Analysis and Proposals for Reform* (London, MIND, 1977)

— 'Contemporary Social Historical Perspectives on Mental Health Reform' (1983) 10 *Journal of Law and Society* 47

GRAUBART, Jonathan, 'NGOs and the Security Council: authority all around but for whose benefit?' in Bruce CRONIN and Ian HURD (eds), *The UN Security Council and the Politics of International Authority* (London, Routledge, 2008)

GREEN, James, 'NGOs' in Abdul Aziz SAID (ed), *Human Rights and World Order* (New York, Praeger, 1978)

GREER, Steven, 'Reforming the European Convention on Human Rights: Towards Protocol 14' [2003] *Public Law* 663

—'Protocol 14 and the Future of the European Court of Human Rights' [2005] *Public Law* 83

— *The European Convention on Human Rights: Achievements, Problems and Prospects* (Cambridge, Cambridge University Press, 2006)

— 'What's Wrong with the European Convention on Human Rights?' (2008) 30 *Human Rights Quarterly* 680

GREY, Antony, *Quest for Justice: Towards Homosexual Emancipation* (London, Sinclair-Stevenson, 1992)

GLENDON, Mary Ann, *Rights Talk: The Impoverishment of Political Discourse* (New York, The Free Press, 1991)

GRIFFITH, John, 'The Democratic Process' in Peter WALLINGTON (ed), *Civil Liberties: 1984* (Oxford, Martin Robertson & Co, 1984)

GROSZ, Stephen and HULTON, Susan, 'Using the European Convention on Human Rights' in Jeremy COOPER and Rajeev DHAVAN (eds), *Public Interest Law* (Oxford, Basil Blackwell, 1986)

GUNTER, Michael M, 'Towards a Consultative Relationship Between the United Nations and Non-Governmental Organizations' (1977) 10 *Vanderbilt Journal of Transnational Law* 557

GUY, Will (ed), *Between Past and Future: the Roma of Central and Eastern Europe* (Hatfield, University of Hertfordshire Press, 2001)

HANNETT, Sarah, 'Third Party Intervention: In the Public Interest?' [2004] *Public Law* 128

HARBY, Catharina, 'The Experience of the AIRE Centre in Litigation Before the European Court of Human Rights' in Tullio TREVES et al (eds), *Civil Society, International Courts and Compliance Bodies* (The Hague, TMC Asser Press, 2005)

HARRIS, DJ, O'BOYLE, M and WARBRICK, Colin, *Law of the European Convention on Human Rights* (London, Butterworths, 1995)

HARRIS, DJ, O'BOYLE, M, WARBRICK, Colin, BATES, Ed and BUCKLEY, Carla, *Law of the European Convention on Human Rights*, 2nd edn (Oxford, Oxford University Press, 2009)

HARLOW, Carol, 'Public Law and Popular Justice' (2002) 65 *Modern Law Review* 1

HARLOW, Carol and RAWLINGS, Richard, *Pressure Through Law* (Abingdon, Routledge, 1992)

HAYEK, FA, *The Road to Serfdom* (London, Routledge & Kegan Paul, 1944)

HEINZE, Eric, 'Principles for a Meta-Discourse of Liberal Rights: the Example of the European Convention on Human Rights' (1999) 9 *Indiana International and Comparative Law Review* 319

— 'Even-handedness and the Politics of Human Rights' (2008) 21 *Harvard Human Rights Journal* 7

HELFER, Laurence R, 'Redesigning the European Court of Human Rights: Embeddedness as a Deep Structural Principle of the European Human Rights Regime' (2008) 19(1) *European Journal of International Law* 125

HERMAN, Didi, 'The Politics of Law Reform: Lesbian and Gay Rights Struggles into the 1990s' in Joseph BRISTOW and Angelina R WILSON (eds), *Activating Theory: Lesbian, Gay, Bisexual Politics* (London, Lawrence & Wishart, 1993)

HEWITT, Patricia, 'The NCCL Fifty Years on' in Peter WALLINGTON (ed), *Civil Liberties: 1984* (Oxford, Martin Robertson & Co, 1984)

HIGGINS, Rosalyn, 'Conceptual Thinking about the Individual in International Law' (1978) 4 *British Journal of International Studies* 1

HODSON, Loveday, 'The European Court of Human Rights: Which Way Next?' in Thomas GROSS (ed), *Legal Scholarship in International and Comparative Law* (Frankfurt, Peter Lang, 2003)

HOME OFFICE, *Setting the Boundaries: Reforming the Law on Sex Offences* vol 1 (London, Home Office Communication Directorate, July 2000)

HOWLAND, Todd, 'How El Rescate, a Small Nongovernmental Organization, Contributed to the Transformation of the Human Rights System in El Salvador' (2008) 30 *Human Rights Quarterly* 703

HUDSON, Manley, 'The Central American Court of Justice' (1932) 26 *American Journal of International Law* 759

HUMAN RIGHTS PROJECT, *Annual Report: 1994* (Sofia, HRP, 1995)

HUMAN RIGHTS WATCH, *Bulgaria: Police Violence Against Gypsies* (New York, Human Rights Watch, 1993)

— *Bulgaria: Increasing Violence Against Roma in Bulgaria* (New York, Human Rights Watch, 1994)

— *Violations of the Right of Petition to the European Commission of Human Rights* (New York, Human Rights Watch, April 1996)

— *Turkey: Violations of Free Expression in Turkey* (New York, Human Rights Watch, 1999)

HURRELL, Andrew, 'Power, Principles and Prudence: Protecting Human Rights in a Deeply Divided World' in DUNNE and WHEELER (eds), *Human Rights in Global Politics* (1999).

INSTITUTE FOR HUMAN RIGHTS AND DEVELOPMENT, *Compilation of Decisions on Communications of the African Commission on Human and Peoples' Rights Extracted from the Commission's Activity Reports 1994–1999* (Banjul, Institute for Human Rights and Development, 1999)

JANIS, Mark, KAY, Richard and BRADLEY, Anthony, *European Human Rights Law: Text and Materials*, 3rd edn (Oxford, Oxford University Press, 2008)

JARVIS, Francoise and SHERLOCK, Ann, 'The European Convention on Human Rights and the Environment' (1999) 24 *European Law Review Supp (Human Rights Survey)* 15

JEFFERY-POULTER, Stephen, *Peers, Queers and Commons: The Struggle for Gay Law Reform, from 1950 to the Present* (London, Routledge, 1991)

JENNINGS Anthony, 'Silence and Safety: The Impact of Human Rights Law' [2000] *Criminal Law Review* 879

JOACHIM, Jutta M, *Agenda Setting, the UN, and NGOs: Gender Violence and Reproductive Rights* (Washington DC, Georgetown University Press, 2007)

JONES, Sue, 'Depth Interviewing' in Clive SEALE (ed), *Social Research Methods: A Reader* (London, Routledge, 2004)

KALDOR, Mary, 'Transnational Civil Society' in Tim DUNNE and Nicholas WHEELER (eds), *Human Rights in Global Politics* (Cambridge, Cambridge University Press, 1999)

KAMMINGA, Menno, 'Is the European Convention on Human Rights Sufficiently equipped to Cope with Gross and Systematic Violations?' (1994) 12(2) *Netherlands Quarterly of Human Rights* 153

KEARNEY, Joseph D and MERRILL, Thomas W, 'The Influence of Amicus Curiae Briefs on the Supreme Court' (1999–2000) 148 *University of Pennsylvania Law Review* 743

KECK, Margaret E and SIKKINK, Kathryn, *Activists Beyond Borders: Advocacy Networks in International Politics* (Ithaca NY, Cornell University Press, 1998)

KENNEDY, David, 'The International Human Rights Movement: Part of the Problem?' (2002) 15 *Harvard Human Rights Journal* 101

KIDD, Ronald, *British Liberty in Danger: An Introduction to the Study of Civil Rights* (London, Lawrence & Wishart, 1940)

KING Jr, Martin Luther, *Stride Towards Freedom: The Montgomery Story* (New York, Ballentine Books, 1958)

KLUG, Francesca, *Values for a Godless Age: The Story of the United Kingdom's New Bill of Rights* (London, Penguin, 2000)

KOREY, William, *NGOs and the Universal Declaration of Human Rights: 'A Curious Grapevine'* (New York, St Martin's Press, 1998)

KRISLOV, Samuel, 'The Amicus Curiae Brief: From Friendship to Advocacy' (1963) 72 *The Yale Law Journal* 694

KURDISH HUMAN RIGHTS PROJECT, *Freedom of the Press in Turkey: The Case of Özgür Gündem* (London, KHRP and Article 19, undated)

— *State Before Freedom: Media Repression in Turkey* (London, KHRP and Article 19, July 1998)

— *Ertak v Turkey, Timurtas v Turkey; State Responsibility in 'Disappearances' – A Case Report* (London, KHRP, 2001)

LAUTERPACHT, Hersch, *An International Bill of the Rights of Man* (New York, Columbia University Press, 1945)

— *International Law and Human Rights* (London, Stevens & Sons, 1950)

LAYDER, Derek, *New Strategies in Social Research: An Introduction and Guide* (Cambridge, Polity Press, 1993)

LAW COMMISSION, *Criminal Law: Bail and the Human Rights Act 1998*, Law Commission Consultation Paper No 157

LEACH, Philip, 'Automatic Denial of Bail and the European Convention' [1999] *Criminal Law Review* 300

— 'The Chechen Conflict: Analysing the Oversight of the European Court of Human Rights' (2008) 6 *European Human Rights Law Review* 732

LEARY, Virginia, 'A New Role for Non-Governmental Organizations in Human Rights: A Case Study of Non-Governmental Participation in the Development of International Norms on Torture' in Antonio CASSESE (ed), *UN Law/Fundamental Rights* (Alphen aan den Rijn, Sijthoff & Noordhoof, 1979)

LENG, Roger, 'Losing Sight of the Defendant: The Government's Proposals in Pre-Trial Disclosure' [1995] *Criminal Law Review* 704

LESTER, Anthony, 'Amici Curiae: Third-Party Interventions Before the European Court of Human Rights' in Franz MATSCHER and Herbert PETZOLD (eds), *Protecting Human Rights: The European Dimension* (Koln, Carl Heymanns Verlag KG, 1990)

LIBERTY, *The Right to Silence: Liberty Parliamentary Briefing December 1993* (London, Liberty, 1993)

— *Liberty: Annual Report 1993* (London, Liberty/Civil Liberties Trust, 1993)

— *Liberty/The Civil Liberties Trust: Annual Review 2001* (London, Liberty/Civil Liberties Trust, 2001)

LILLY, Mark, *The National Council for Civil Liberties: the First Fifty Years* (London, Macmillan Press, 1984)

LINDBLOM, Anna-Karin, *Non-Governmental Organisations in International Law* (Cambridge, Cambridge University Press, 2005)

LONGFORD, Michael, 'NGOs and the Rights of the Child' in Peter WILLETTS (ed), *'The Conscience of the World': The Influence of Non-Governmental Organisation in the U.N. System* (London, Hurst & Co, 1996)

MacDONALD, Charles G and O'LEARY Carole A, *Kurdish Identity: Human Rights and Political Status* (Gainesville FL, University Press of Florida, 2007)

MACKLEM, Patrick and MORGAN, Ed, 'Indigenous Rights in the Inter-American System: The Amicus Brief of the Assembly of First Nations in *Awas Tingni v Republic of Nicaragua*' (2000) 22(2) *Human Rights Quarterly* 569

MAHONEY, Paul, 'Developments in the Procedure of the European Court of Human Rights: The Revised Rules of Court' (1983) 3 *Yearbook of European Law* 127

— 'Judicial Activism and Judicial Self-Restraint in the European Court of Human Rights: Two Sides of the Same Coin' (1990) 11 *Human Rights Law Journal* 57

MAIMAN, Richard J, '"We've had to Raise our Game": Liberty's Litigation Strategy under the Human Rights Act 1998' in Simon HALLIDAY and Patrick SCHMIDT (eds), *Human Rights Brought Home: Socio-Legal Perspectives on Human Rights in the National Context* (Oxford, Hart Publishing, 2004)

MARCUS, Aliza, 'Turkey's Kurds After the Gulf War: A Report from the Southeast' in Gerard CHALIAND (ed), *A People Without a Country: The Kurds and Kurdistan*, trans Michael PALLIS (London, Zed Books, 1993)

MARTENS, Kerstin, 'Mission Impossible? Defining Nongovernmental Organizations' (2002) 13 *Voluntas: International Journal of Voluntary and Nonprofit Organizations* 271

MARTIN, Ian, 'Combining Casework and Strategy: The Joint Council for the Welfare of Immigrants' in Jeremy COOPER and Rajeev DHAVAN (eds), *Public Interest Law* (Oxford, Basil Blackwell, 1986)

MARTIN RICHES, William T, *The Civil Rights Movement: Struggle and Resistance* (London, Macmillan Press Ltd, 1997)

MASSON, Judith, 'Human Rights in Child Protection: Emergency Action and its Impact' in Peter LØDRUP and Eva MODVAR (eds), *Family Life and Human Rights: Papers Presented at the 11th World Conference of the International Society of Family Law* (Oslo, Gyldendal, 2004).

MAZOWER, Mark, *Dark Continent: Europe's Twentieth Century* (London, Penguin Books, 1998)

McCANN, Michael, 'Reform Litigation on Trial' (1992) 17 *Law and Social Inquiry* 715

McCONVILLE, Mike, SANDERS, Andrew and LENG Roger, *The Case for the Prosecution* (London, Routledge, 1991)

McDOWALL, David, *The Kurds* (London, Minority Rights Group International Report 96/4, 1996)

— *A Modern History of the Kurds* (London, IB Tauris, 1997)

McGHEE, Derek, *Homosexuality, Law and Resistance* (London, Routledge, 2001)

MENDEZ, Juan E and VIVANCO, Jose Miguel, 'Disappearances and the Inter-American Court: Reflections on a Litigation Experience' (1990) 13 *Hamline Law Review* 507

MERTUS, Julie, 'Doing Democracy "Differently": The Transformative Potential of Human Rights NGOs in Transnational Civil Society' (1998–99) *Third World Legal Studies* 205

— 'From Legal Transplants to Transformative Justice: Human Rights and the Promise of Transnational Civil Society' (1998–99) 14 *American University International Law Review* 1335

— 'The Rejection of Human Rights Framings: The Case of LGBT Advocacy in the US' (2007) 29(4) *Human Rights Quarterly* 1036

MINOGUE, Kenneth, 'What is Wrong With Rights' in Carol HARLOW (ed), *Public Law and Politics* (London, Sweet & Maxwell, 1986)

MINOW, Martha, 'Rights for the Next Generation: A Feminist Approach to Children's Rights' (1986) 9 *Harvard Women's Law Journal* 1

MOHAMED, Abdelsam, 'Individual and NGO Participation in Human Rights Litigation before the African Court of Human and Peoples' Rights: Lessons from the European and Inter-American Courts of Human Rights' (1999) 43 *Journal of African Law* 201

MOORE, Michael, *Stupid White Men: . . . and Other Sorry Excuses for the State of the Nation!* (London, Penguin Books, 2001)

MOYER, Charles, 'The Role of Amicus Curiae in the Inter-American Court of Human Rights' in *La Corte Interamericana de Derechos Humanos: Estudios y Documentos* (San Jose, Instituto Interamericano de Derechos Humanos, 1985)

NADER, Lucia, 'The Role of NGOs in the Human Rights Council' (2007) 7 *SUR: International Journal on Human Rights* 7

NELKIN, Dorothy and POLLAK, Michael, *The Atom Besieged: Extra-parliamentary Dissent in France and Germany* (Cambridge MA, The MIT Press, 1981)

NØRGAARD, Carl Aage, *The Position of the Individual in International Law* (Copenhagen, Munksgaard, 1962)

NOWICKI, Marek, 'NGOs before the European Commission and Court of Human Rights' (1996) 14(3) *Netherlands Quarterly of Human Rights* 289

O'CONNOR, Karen, *Women's Organizations' Use of the Courts* (Lexington MA, Lexington Books, 1980)

ODINKALU, Chidi, 'Back to the Future: The Imperative of Prioritizing for the Protection of Human Rights in Africa' (2003) 47 *Journal of African Law* 1

ODINKALU, Chidi Anselm and CHRISTENSEN, Camilla, 'The African Commission on Human and Peoples' Rights: the Development of its Non-State Communication Procedures' (1998) 20 *Human Rights Quarterly* 235

OFFICE OF THE HIGH COMMISSIONER FOR HUMAN RIGHTS, *Working with the United Nations Human Rights Programme: A Handbook for Civil Society* (New York, OHCHR, 2008)

O'NIONS, Helen, *Minority Rights Protection in International Law: The Roma of Europe* (Aldershot, Ashgate, 2007)

OPPENHEIM, Lassa, *International Law: A Treatise* (London, Longmans & Green, 1905)

OPROMOLLA, Adriana, 'Children's Rights Under Article 3 and 8 of the European Convention: Recent Case Law' (2001) 26 *European Law Review Supp (Human Rights Survey)* 50

OTTO, Dianne, 'Nongovernmental Organizations in the United Nations System: The Emerging Role of International Civil Society' (1996) 18 *Human Rights Quarterly* 107, 135

OVEY, Clare and WHITE, Robin CA, *Jacobs and White, the European Convention on Human Rights*, 4th edn (Oxford, Oxford University Press, 2006)

PARKS, Rosa (with REED, Gregory J), *Quiet Strength: The Faith, the Hope and the Heart of a Woman who Changed a Nation* (Grand Rapid, Zondervan Publishing House, 1994)

PARKS, Rosa, '"Tired of Giving In": The Launching of the Montgomery Bus Boycott' in B COLLIER-THOMAS and VP FRANKLIN (eds), *Sisters in the Struggle: African American Women in the Civil Rights/Black Power Movement* (New York, New York University Press, 2001)

PARSON, Donald, 'The Individual Right of Petition: A Study of Methods used by International Organizations to Utilize the Individual as a Source of Information on the Violations of Human Rights' (1967) 13 *Wayne Law Review* 678

PARTON, Nigel, *The Politics of Child Abuse* (Basingstoke, Macmillan, 1985)

PEARSON, Zoe, 'Non-Governmental Organizations and the International Criminal Court: Changing Landscapes of International Law' (2006) 39 *Cornell International Law Journal* 243

PESUE, *Collection of Articles Concerning the Human Rights Situation in Finnish Child Welfare* (unpublished, on file with the author)

PETROVA, Dimitrina, *Violations of the Rights of Gypsies in Bulgaria* (Sofia, Human Rights Project, 1994)

— 'Political and Legal Limitations to the Development of Public Interest Law in Post-Communist Societies' (1996) 4–5 *Parker School. Journal of East European Law* 541

POGANY, Istvan, *The Roma Café: Human Rights and the Plight of the Romani People* (London, Pluto Press, 2004)

POPPER, Karl, *The Open Society and its Enemies* (London, Routledge, 1945–47)

PREBENSEN, Søren C, 'Inter-State Complaints under Treaty Provisions: The Experience under the European Convention on Human Rights' (1999) 20 *Human Rights Law Journal* 446

PRICE COHEN, Cynthia, 'The Role of Nongovernmental Organizations in the Drafting of the Convention on the Rights of the Child' (1990) 12(1) *Human Rights Quarterly* 137

PUBLIC LAW PROJECT, *Third Party Interventions in Judicial Review: An Action Research Study* (London, Public Law Project, 2001)

RECHEL, Bernd, 'Bulgaria: Minority Rights Light' in RECHEL (ed), *Minority Rights in Central and Eastern Europe* (London, Routledge, 2009)

REID, Karen, *A Practitioner's Guide to the European Convention on Human Rights* (London, Sweet & Maxwell, 1998)

REIDY, Aisling, HAMPSON, Francoise and BOYLE, Kevin, 'Gross Violations of Human Rights: Invoking the European Convention on Human Rights in the Case of Turkey' (1997) 15(2) *Netherlands Quarterly of Human Rights* 161

RICHARDSON, Jeremy (ed), *Pressure Groups* (Oxford, Oxford University Press, 1993)

RINGOLD, Dena, ORENSTEIN, Mitchell and WILKENS, Erika, *Roma in an Expanding Europe: Breaking the Poverty Cycle* (Washington DC, World Bank, 2005)

RITCHIE, Jane, 'The Application of Qualitative Methods to Social Research' in Jane RITCHIE and Jane LEWIS (eds), *Qualitative Research Practice: A Guide for Social Science Students and Researchers* (London, Sage, 2003)

RITCHIE, Jane and LEWIS, Jane (eds), *Qualitative Research Practice: A Guide to Social Science Students and Researchers* (London, Sage, 2003)

ROBERTSON, AH and MERRILLS, JG, *Human Rights in Europe: A Study of the European Convention on Human Rights*, 4th edn (Manchester, Manchester University Press, 2001)

RODLEY, Nigel, 'Monitoring Human Rights Violations in the 1980s' in Jorge DOMINGUEZ et al (eds), *Enhancing Global Human Rights* (New York, McGraw-Hill, 1979)

ROSENBERG, Gerald N, *The Hollow Hope: Can Courts Bring about Social Change?* (Chicago, University of Chicago Press, 1991)

ROWE, Nicola and SCHLETTE, Volker, 'The Protection of Human Rights in Europe after the Eleventh Protocol to the ECHR' (1998) 23 *European Law Review (Supp) Human Rights Survey)* 3

RYSSDAL, Rolv, 'On the Road to a European Constitutional Court' (1992) 12 *Collected Courses of the Academy of European Law* 1

SANDS, Philippe, 'Human Rights, Environment and the López Ostra Case: Context and Consequences' (1996) 6 *European Human Rights Law Review* 597

SATHE, SP, *Judicial Activism in India: Transgressing Borders and Enforcing Limits* (New Delhi, Oxford University Press, 2002)

SAX, Joseph, *Defending the Environment: A Strategy for Citizen Action* (New York, Alfred A Knopf, 1971)

SAYAPIN, Sergey, 'The International Committee of the Red Cross and International Human Rights Law' (2009) 9 *Human Rights Law Review* 95

SCAFFARDI, Sylvia, *Fire Under the Carpet: Working for Civil Liberties in the Thirties* (London, Lawrence and Wishart, 1986)

SCHEINGOLD, Stuart, *The Politics of Rights: Lawyers, Public Policy, and Political Change* (New Haven CT, Yale University Press, 1974)

SCHERMERS, Henry, 'The Eleventh Protocol to the European Convention on Human Rights' (1994) 19 *European Law Review* 367

SCHIFF, David, 'Reconstructing Liberty in the Nuclear Age' in Carol HARLOW (ed), *Public Law and Politics* (London, Sweet & Maxwell, 1986)

SCHOENER, Wendy, 'Non-Governmental Organizations and Global Activism: Legal and Informal Approaches' (1997) 4 *Indiana Journal of Global Legal Studies* 537

SEARY, Bill, 'The Early History: From the Congress of Vienna to the San Francisco Conference' in Peter WILLETTS (ed), '*The Conscience of the World': The Influence of Non-Governmental Organisation in the U.N. System* (London, Hurst & Co, 1996)

SELWYN, Julie and STURGESS, Wendy, *International Overview of Adoption: Policy and Practice* (Bristol, University of Bristol, 2000)

SHELTON, Dinah, 'The Participation of Non-governmental Organisations in International Judicial Proceedings' (1994) 88 *American Journal of International Law* 611

SMITH, Jackie, PAGNUCCO, Ron and LOPEZ, George A, 'Globalizing Human Rights: The Work of Transnational Human Rights NGOs in the 1990s' (1998) 20 *Human Rights Quarterly* 379

STAMMERS, Neil, 'Social Movements and the Social Construction of Human Rights' (1999) 21 *Human Rights Quarterly* 980

—— *Human Rights and Social Movements* (London, Pluto Press, 2009)

STEINER, Henry, *Diverse Partners: Non-Governmental Organizations in the Human Rights Movement* (Cambridge MA, Harvard Law School Human Rights Program, 1991)

STYCHIN, Carl, *A Nation by Rights: National Cultures, Sexual Identity Politics, and the Discourse of Rights* (Philadelphia PA, Temple University Press, 1998)

TREHAN, Nidhi, 'In the name of the Roma? The role of private foundations and NGOs' in Will GUY (ed), *Between Past and Future: the Roma of Central and Eastern Europe* (Hatfield, University of Hertfordshire Press, 2001)

TREVES, Tullio et al (eds), *Civil Society, International Courts and Compliance Bodies* (The Hague, TMC Asser Press, 2005)

TRINDADE, Antonio, 'The Operation of the Inter-American Court of Human Rights' in David HARRIS and Stephen LIVINGSTONE (eds), *The Inter-American System of Human Rights* (Oxford, Clarendon Press, 1998)

UNDP, *At Risk: Roma and the Displaced in Southeast Europe* (Bratislava, UNDP, 2006)

UNICEF, *Breaking the Cycle of Exclusion: Roma Children in South East Europe* (Belgrade, UNICEF Serbia, February 2007)

VAJIC, Nina, 'Some Concluding Remarks on NGOs and the European Court of Human Rights' in Tullio TREVES et al (eds), *Civil Society, International Courts and Compliance Bodies* (The Hague, TMC Asser Press, 2005)

VAN BOVEN, Theo, 'The Role of Non-Governmental Organizations in International Human Rights Standard-Setting: A Prerequisite for Democracy' (1990) 20 *Californian Western International Law Journal* 207

VAN DIJK, P and VAN HOOF, GJH, *Theory and Practice of the European Convention on Human Rights*, 3rd edn (The Hague, Kluwer Law International, 1998)

VAN DIJK, Pieter, VAN HOOF, Fried, VAN RIJN, Arjen and ZWAAK, Leo (eds), *Theory and Practice of the European Convention on Human Rights*, 4th edn (Antwerp, Intersentia, 2006)

VAN MAANEN, John, 'Notes on the Production of Ethnographic Data in an American Police Agency' in Robin LUCKHAM (ed), *Law and Social Enquiry: Case Studies of Research* (New York, Scandinavian Institute of African Studies, 1981)

VERMEERSCH, Peter, *The Romani Movement: Minority Politics and Ethnic Mobilization in Contemporary Central Europe* (New York, Berghahn Book, 2006)

VERMEERSCH, Peter and RAM, Melanie H, 'The Roma' in Bernd RECHEL (ed), *Minority Rights in Central and Eastern Europe* (London, Routledge, 2009)

VIVANCO, Jose Miguel and BHANSALI, Lisa, 'Procedural Shortcomings in the Defense of Human Rights: An Inequality of Arms' in David HARRIS and Stephen LIVINGSTONE (eds), *The Inter-American System of Human Rights* (Oxford, Clarendon Press, 1998)

VOSE, Clement, *Caucasians Only: The Supreme Court, the NAACP and the Restrictive Covenant Cases* (Berkeley CA, University of California Press, 1959)

WADHAM, John and SAID, Tazeen, 'What Price the Right of Individual Petition?: Report of the Evaluation Group to the Committee of Ministers on the European Court of Human Rights' (2002) 2 *European Human Rights Law Review* 169

WALD, Michael, 'State Intervention on Behalf of "Neglected Children": A Search for Realistic Standards' (1974–75) 27 *Stanford Law Review* 985

WALLINGTON, Peter (ed), *Civil Liberties: 1984* (Oxford, Martin Robertson & Co, 1984)

WALTZER, Michael, 'Welfare, Membership and Need' in Michael SANDEL (ed), *Liberalism and Its Critics* (Oxford, Blackwell Publishers, 1984)

WARBRICK, Colin, '"Federal" Aspects of the European Convention on Human Rights' (1989) 10 *Michigan Journal of International Law* 698

WEBER, Stefan, 'Environmental Information and the European Convention on Human Rights' (1991) 12 *Human Rights Law Journal* 177

WEISS, Thomas G and GORDENKER, Leon (eds), *NGOs, the UN and Global Governance* (London, Lynne Rienner Publishers, 1996)

WEISSBRODT, David, 'The Role of International Nongovernmental Organizations in the Implementation of Human Rights' (1977) 12 *Texas International Law Journal* 293

— The Contribution of International Nongovernmental Organizations to the Protection of Human Rights' in Theodor MERON (ed), *Human Rights in International Law: Legal and Policy Issues* (Oxford, Clarendon Press, 1984)

WELCH, Claude E, *NGOs and Human Rights: Promise and Performance* (Philadelphia PA, University of Pennsylvania Press, 2000)

— 'Defining Contemporary Forms of Slavery: Updating a Venerable NGO' (2009) 31 *Human Rights Quarterly* 70

WEYLER, Rex, *Greenpeace: An Insider's Account* (London, Rodale, 2004)

WHITE, Robin CA, 'Tackling Political Disputes Through Individual Applications' (1998) 1
European Human Rights Law Review 61

WICKS, Elizabeth, 'The United Kingdom Government's Perceptions of the European
Convention on Human Rights at the Time of Entry' [2000] *Public Law* 438

WILLETTS, Peter, 'From "Consultative Arrangements" to "Partnership": The Changing
Status of NGOs in Diplomacy at the UN' (2000) 6 *Global Governance* 191

— (ed), *Pressure Groups in the Global System: The Transnational Relations of Issue-
Orientated Non-Governmental Organizations* (London, Frances Pinter, 1982)

— *'The Conscience of the World': The Influence of Non-Governmental Organisation in the
U.N. System* (London, Hurst & Co, 1996)

WILSON, Graham, 'American Interest Groups' in Jeremy J RICHARDSON (ed), *Pressure
Groups* (Oxford, Oxford University Press, 1993)

WINTEMUTE, Robert and ANDENÆS, Mads, *Legal Recognition of Same-Sex Partnerships:
A Study of National, European and International Law* (Oxford, Hart Publishing, 2001)

WISEBERG, Laurie and SCOBLE, Harry, 'The International League for Human Rights:
The Strategy of a Human Rights NGO' (1977) 7 *Georgia Journal of International and
Comparative Law* 289

WOODLIFFE, JC 'Nuclear Power: Does it Threaten Civil Liberties?' [1983] *Public Law* 440

WOOLF, Mitchell, 'Coming of Age? The Principle of the "Best Interests of the Child"'
(2003) 2 *European Human Rights Law Review* 205

ZAGORAC, Dean, 'International Courts and Compliance Bodies: The Experience of
Amnesty International' in Tullio TREVES et al (eds), *Civil Society, International Courts
and Compliance Bodies* (The Hague, TMC Asser Press, 2005)

Index

Introductory Note

References such as '178–9' indicate (not necessarily continuous) discussion of a topic across a range of pages. Wherever possible in the case of topics with many references, these have either been divided into sub-topics or only the most significant discussions of the topic are listed. Because the entire work is about the 'European Convention on Human Rights' and 'NGOs', the use of these terms (and certain others which occur constantly throughout the book) as entry points has been minimized. Information will be found under the corresponding detailed topics.